MALEDICTA

THE INTERNATIONAL JOURNAL OF VERBAL AGGRESSION

Volume X   1988-1989

REINHOLD AMAN

EDITOR

MALEDICTA PRESS

COPYRIGHT © 1990 BY REINHOLD AMAN

All Rights Reserved. Except for brief quotations embodied in critical articles or reviews, no part of this publication may be reproduced, stored, transmitted, translated, or used in any form or by any means—graphic, electronic, or mechanical, now known or hereafter invented, and **including photocopying,** recording, taping, or any information storage & retrieval system—without the prior written permission of the Publisher.

Library of Congress Catalog
Card Number 77- 649633

ISSN 0363-3659

ISBN 0-916500-30-6

NIHIL + OBSTAT
R 24 December 1989 A

Printed in the United States of America

CONTENTS
VOL. X • 1988-1989

Dump on Vulgarity	Tabitha King	5
Everyone Uses Nasty Language	Reinhold Aman	14
Folk Criticism of Religiosity in the Graffiti of New York City	Allen Walker Read	15
Medical Maledicta from San Francisco	Richard O. Barton	31
Artistic Riddle	Paul Smith	35
More Milwaukee Medical Maledicta	*Sue Ture	36
Elementary Georgian Obscenity	*Boris Sukitch Razvratnikov	37
Telephonic Cryptograms	Frank Nuessel	43
Phone-Smut	Reinhold Aman	45
Understanding Computer Technology	Folklore	48
Terms of Abuse, Terms of Endearment, and Pet Names for Breasts and Other Naughty Body Parts	Reinhold Aman	49
Pejorative Nicknames of Baseball All-Stars	Merritt Clifton	78
Cohen's Religious Museum	Aaron Cohen	79
Offensive Rock Band Names: A Linguistic Taxonomy	Joe Salmons and Monica Macaulay	81
Results of Maledicta Poll 1988	Reinhold Aman	100
Tattling the Racist Laughter of Alabama Leaders, 1950-1967	Louie Crew	105
Beyond the Metaphor: Cursing and Swearing in Ulster	Alan Crozier	115
Offensive Words in Dictionaries: IV. Ethnic, Racial, Religious, and Sexual Slurs in an American and an Australian Dictionary	Reinhold Aman	126
Letter to a Pennsylvania Postmaster	Reinhold Aman	136
The Peckerwood Poets: A Tribute	Sanford H. Margalith	137
1990 Attorney-Hunting Season and Bag Limit	Folklore	144
Egyptian Arabic Abuse	Dilworth B. Parkinson	145
Instructional Graffiti	*Rosetta Stone	162
Linguistic Taboos, Code-words and Women's Use of Sexist Language: A Double Bind	Sol Saporta	163
Challenger Shuttle Jokes	Reinhold Aman	167
Legman Announcements		183

---

* Pseudonym

Slogans to Promote National Condom Week *Reinhold Aman*	184
Real Estate Riddle .... *Folklore*	188
Catullus XXXIII .... *Joseph S. Salemi*	189
Martial XI.99 .... *Robert Wind*	191
An Irishman's Letter to the DHSS in Response to Receiving the AIDS Leaflet .... *Folklore*	193
Ethnic Rebus .... *Folklore*	194
Whose Anus? *Uranus* .... *Dennis R. Preston*	195
Departmental Counseling Sheet .... *Folklore*	200
Talk Dirty to Me: Sassy Sayings on Buttons, Cards, T-shirts, and Rubber Stamps .... *Reinhold Aman*	203
Pit, Tit, Clit .... *Anon*	208
God Curse You, and the Curse Is That You Be What You Already Are!: Swahili Culture, Power, and Badtalk .... *Marc J. Swartz*	209
The *Portagee* in Speech and Joke .... *George Monteiro*	231
Cacademic Linguistics (Cartoon) .... *Jeffrey Weber*	237
Word Finder & Spelling Checker: Or, Some of My Best Friends are Knitters .... *Reinhold Aman*	238
English (Poem) .... *Peter Kunzke*	239
The Taxonomy of Benediction and Malediction *Rudi Schmid*	240
Santa's Slip-up (Cartoon) .... *Folklore*	242
British Anti-Smoking Poster .... *Folklore*	242
An Open Letter to Mike Royko .... *Reinhold Aman*	243
A First Look at Armenian Maledicta .... *Vladimir I. Želvys*	245
Kakologia: A Chronicle of Ribald Riddles and Wicked Wordplays .... *Reinhold Aman*	247
Notes on Contributors	317

Frequently Used Abbreviations	
MAL	*Maledicta*
MJ	*Milwaukee Journal*
WF	*Waukesha Freeman*

A Curse On All Cheapskates Who Photocopy *Maledicta* Illegally:

May Zamfir ram his pan flute up your rectal sphincter!

DUMP ON VULGARITY

Tabitha King

Each book I have written has brought a few letters and a certain percentage of reviews asking if it is really necessary for me to use so much "gutter" language. Quite often they assert that it is not necessary to be explicit; the great novelists (Jane Austen) never had to stoop to vulgarity, let alone obscenities.

> Sticks and stones may hurt my bones,
> but words will never hurt me...

So, in childhood, we sing, in the schoolyard and on the sidewalk. The singsong is mere whistling past the graveyard and we know it. Words can and do hurt, names (*Four-Eyes! Fatty! Kike! Pussy!*) most obviously, but so almost any combination of words said in the wrong tone by the wrong person—the admonitions of parents, accusations of a spouse, angry words from a child, flung in the course of an argument. No one who writes for a living can doubt the potential power of words. At this moment, I am only concerned with what are sometimes called "four-letter words." Typical of the irrationality associated with them, many are composed of fewer or more than four letters, and not all are what my children call "swears," a contemporary childish variation on the older "oaths."

In fact, only a few are true "swears": *God damn, damn,* and *go to hell,* which are these days rated among the milder forms of bad language. These are the words or phrases that the Third Commandment forbids: *Thou shalt not take the Name of the Lord Your God in vain.* What that really means is we are forbidden to swear false oaths—commit perjury, or otherwise swear in the name of the Lord that something we know to be false is true, or to condemn anyone in God's name. Under this rubric, it was made clear in my catechism classes, as a matter of reverence, one did not use the name of Jesus Christ except in prayer or sermon or theological discussion. The use of most of those words my children call swears, I was also taught, is almost always a venial sin, the Catholic version of a misdemeanor.

In my childhood, all those words were forbidden to children—I remember one Sister of Mercy warning us solemnly against the use of *gee* or *gosh*, as those seemingly innocent words trespassed too closely to *God*. Despite the loosening of censorship in books and movies (somewhat tighter now than in previous years), and considerable parental laxity, I have yet to meet a child over five who did not understand that certain words are distinctly improper. Children use such language among themselves to one degree or another, as did the boys and girls in schoolyards of twenty years ago.

To one part of the reading public, the issue of freedom of speech as expressed in the written word may be settled, but for much of this country's population the struggle over what is obscene and what is not and what's to be done about what goes on. All over the country, know-nothings continue to try to throw books they consider to be obscene out of the schools and public libraries. The mere presence of a "dirty" word in a novel renders a book obscene in the eyes of know-nothings, and they continue to try (and frequently succeed) to ban books without regard to context or meaning. As always, the self-appointed censors have rarely read what they are trying to ban, except for the occasional public reading of the individual accused words. This particular group of words, the Gang of Four-Letters, continues to be perceived as a terrible threat to public decency and morality.

In the course of reading a short story at the *Boston Globe* Book Fair several years ago, I observed some of my audience leaving, the expression on their faces informing me that the violence of the language in which the story was told offended them. I wanted to tell them to stay and hear it out; the naughty words were essential to the story in a way they would only grasp when they arrived at the end. I decided against breaking the forward movement of the story. So the people who left never did find out that the story was being narrated by what a friend of mine calls a "morally deficient" character, that it was a confession, and the language in which it was told reflected the moral poverty and despair of the characters. It was in fact a story that could not have been related in any other language and still been the same story. In an absolutely essential way, the language *was* the story. At the time I was mildly amused that I had succeeded in shocking Boston. Probably it made their day, that instant of moral indignation. And to some extent I still feel that way. When you set yourself up as too pure or too refined to endure a specific book, movie, play, short story, sculpture, whatever, you review yourself first, unfavorably and devastatingly, as close-minded. It must be nice to be utterly certain of one's righteousness, to say nothing of one's taste.

I am not writing pornography, nor am I overly concerned with the freedom to publish pornography. Where films and photographs depict nonconsensual sexual acts, there may be grounds for prosecutions of morals violations. But the pornographic novel, the *stroke book*, is a constitutionally protected form of free speech. It is impossible to suppress without endangering free speech. Free speech suppressed is free thinking suppressed. If you believe that freedom of speech means the freedom to publish pornography, then the rare blurring of the lines between literature and pornography doesn't really matter.

Having been fortunate enough to encounter Latin both in my religious education and as a Catholic high school student, I have been aware since childhood of the Latin root of the word *vulgar*. The Bible was referred to as the "Vulgate," a word that meant it had been translated into the language of the common people, the *vulgus*. Mob was not necessarily implied in the term *vulgus*; in the context of Church Latin, it was mostly a class designation. Whenever I encounter the word *vulgar*, I think of class, and ask myself who's using that word and what do they mean by it?

The words we call *vulgar* or "dirty" are nearly all Anglo-Saxon and nearly all terms either for parts of the body or bodily acts, and those either sexual or having to do with elimination. There are equivalent terms that are more acceptable, more *proper*, available to us—mostly Latin-derived medical terminology. In ordinary every-day life, people rarely use the proper terms, and a great many don't even know them. But everyone knows the vulgar, the dirty words.

Why are the Anglo-Saxon forms somehow dirty, and the Latinate forms not? Most likely because Anglo-Saxon became the language of the *vulgus*, the common people, when England fell to the Normans in 1066. Our dirty words are Anglo-Saxon, instead of Welsh or Eskimo, because of a historical accident, a long-ago political event. Part of the reason they are improper is because they are common, the language of Anglo-Saxon yeomen of centuries ago. And so we go on calling them "vulgar" and give away the class origins of their impropriety.

There's more to tell, isn't there? These words all refer to the body and its functions: parts of the body, sex, elimination, excretion. In degree, the terms for elimination are less offensive—*pee*, for instance, or *poop*, which is nothing more or less than the Dutch word for "shit." But that's why it's okay, it's Dutch, not Anglo-Saxon, and at another remove from us. Blood, tears, mucus, excrement, and so on are taboo once out of our bodies. Yet nearly all these fluids and substances are absolutely necessary to our continued existence—a whole industry exists to keep our bowels moving, we are regularly exhorted to give up quantities of blood for other people, etc. Howard Hughes—the pathological exception. Yet a hair in our soup, a wet sneeze, even the sounds of our bowels at work are objectionable. The sole exception to this list is tears, the substance with which Mary Magdalene washed the feet of Jesus.

The real nastiness is contained in our sex words. The infamous *f-word*, a designation which came into my consciousness several years ago from my children, now seems to have achieved a kind of respectability among adults discussing questions of obscenity. It would be a mischief to interrupt these solemn usages with a query as to which *f-word* is being cited. Many other words referring to sex acts that were once considered extremely offensive have undergone sex change and are sometimes entirely separated from their original meaning—*jazz*, for instance. The word *screw* is now a very mild form, suitable for Presidential lips. Then there are the words for the male sex organs, which are—and now we are getting to where the bear makes doo-doo behind the Bush—very much less offensive, less obscene, than the words for the female sexual organs. *Dork* has become mostly an expression of mild insult. *Pecker*, perhaps because it diminishes the sexual function of the organ, is another fairly inoffensive term. But the four-letter word for the female genitalia remains as powerfully taboo as the *f-word* itself.

Are the terms for the female parts more offensive because the primary female organs are more offensive than the male's? You bet—that's exactly the way a lot of people feel—I can almost hear the silent exhalation of assent. Ponder this: there are dozens of ugly words for women, nearly all reducing them to their sexual organs—and for various minorities, gays, ethnic groups, etc., that are insulting and offensive though not obscene—but there are *none* for white males of equal weight and ugliness. *Honky* is nothing but a mild ethnic slur against Scandinavians that has slopped over to cover white men in general, but it's about the whole list.

The combination term *motherfucker* doesn't refer exclusively to males. If in fact these terms of opprobrium are rooted in a power struggle between the sexes, it's almost too good to be true that *motherfucker* has its source among blacks, the least powerful of males next to the homosexual. If the majority of black males grow up with a female head of household, a single parental authority figure of the opposite sex, the common experience of adolescent rebellion must be against their mothers. Fathers, because they are absent from the family, appear to have been defeated in their relationships with the powerful mothers. It is either an accusation of incest with mom or of being some mother's lover. Who is a mother's lover, after all, but a father? *Motherfucker* is a knot of anger and fear about being male in a part of society in which males are sexual drones.

Even as a teenager, it seemed to me a matter of sexual privilege—perfectly respectable men were allowed, particularly among their own sex, a latitude of speech that women were not granted, period. Should a naughty word escape the lips of a man in the presence of a lady, the lady was supposed to purse her lips, a clear signal that her tongue was not to be soiled, and otherwise she would likely pretend not to have heard. The man was expected to apologize profusely and never do it again. Class at work as well: the wash-woman and the waitress heard words that no lady would endure, though if the wash-woman or the waitress was a "good" woman, she would make it clear she would not tolerate the language either, and depending upon her force of character, the man might be more careful around her. And naturally one could not expect to rise in the world, unless, like Eliza Doolittle, one put aside the language of the gutter, as well as its accent.

So tell me, why should men be allowed the privilege of those mostly Anglo-Saxonisms when ladies are not? Not because a lady's delicate ears might spontaneously combust, but because she might be corrupted by those strangely powerful words, an illustration of the Victorian notion that women are not only the physically weaker sex, but the morally weaker sex as well, so weak as to be compromised, if not ruined, by such language.

This charming presumption—once called the Double Standard, before the days of the Velcro *f-word*—is still with us, so far as I can see, stronger than ever. Victorian prudery is alive and well, ninety years after the old Queen's passing. Witness the dismissal of our female Ambassador to Austria a few years ago because she took a divorced Austrian for her fourth husband and, apparently, because she wore her gowns cut too low. Would the First Lady, emphasis on *Lady*, have arranged the dismissal of a male Ambassador who committed a more or less public adultery culminating in divorce and remarriage, and who, perhaps, wore his trousers too tight to suit Mrs. Reagan? Scandal didn't keep Frank Sinatra from Mrs. Reagan's salon, did it?

Ah, yes, we ladies have a standard to uphold. Is it possible that some of the reviews castigating me for the use of strong language in my books would not have mentioned the subject at all if I were a male writer? The reviewing of books, as you may know, is mostly poorly paid piece work. Unconscious sexual bias is not unknown in journalism. I would not be surprised to discover that some of the good ladies who have reviewed my books are ordinarily assigned novels by women and rarely those by men, so that their grounds of comparison are thin. And since sexual prejudice certainly works both ways, I would not be surprised if some lady reviewers preferred reading and reviewing the works of women as opposed to men. Men, after all, are crass hairy beasts who sweat a lot and never outgrow their boyish love of adventure and cheap thrills (if you have no sense of humor, I am writing sarcastically). Let me assert that any number of male writers have produced countless novels using the same explicit language and in no greater profusion. Don't take my word for it; read my books, then go read any two dozen contemporary novels by men. Then go read the reviews.

I don't feel singled out. While anyone might have reservations about the indelicacies of Erica Jong's novels, or whether the public strip-mining of her own life is particularly creative, or ethical, or in good taste, or whether good taste is the proper concern of the creative artist; in fact, she has written nothing more raunchy than dozens of male writers but has provoked disproportionately more disturbance. I suspect that Judy Blume's books for young adolescents have in part incensed so many censorious guardians of public morality because they were written by a woman, and young girls read them.

Let us examine our consciences for prudery, for elitism, for sexism, an ugly word for an ugly practice. Why does this particular batch of words, combinations of consonants and vowels, scratches on paper, so offend us, and why more so when they come from a woman? Do we have a problem dealing with the fact that human consciousness resides in the flesh of an animal, and that flesh copulates, excretes, eliminates, bleeds, and weeps? Why is our fleshly nature so frightening, so obscene that we must never refer to it directly, except in those medical terms that allow us to distance ourselves from it? Who among us never farts?

WE invest those words with their power. It is our fear and disgust, our rejection of our physical being, our prudery that makes those words dirty. So we make them a male preserve, for big tough hairy men take the world as it is, and women, who do not understand throw-weights, are too weak and corruptible to be allowed to do that. Or conversely, to suit the other set of prejudices, men are just big hairy boys who like wallowing in fantasies of heroism and whoring, and women are the reservoirs of morality and intellect in the desert of the world.

When I write naughty words, when I write about characters doing some of them, saying most of them, I am sometimes merely describing what ordinary people do and say. Sometimes the language is meant to reflect foul acts and fouled hearts. It's frankly your problem if you think only the lives of the privileged and the sensitive are worth imagining and recording. You've got a further problem if you think privileged and sensitive people don't think about or commit sexual acts, or have sexual problems, or go to the toilet, or blow their noses, or if they are female, have menstrual cycles, or if they do, that those aspects of human life are unfit to be mentioned in print. I can't say I'm sorry if some terribly nice, intelligent, well-meaning people take offense. I'm doing my job, which is telling stories, speaking and writing about the ways this peculiar species lives. I function as a kind of zoologist, studying and reporting the strange behavior of my own species. I'm not allowed to fudge the observations because they might offend someone. To do so would spoil the story, make it a lie, and that's a greater offense than being unladylike. You see, I'm not a lady. I'm a writer.

Copyright © 1990 by Tabitha King. All Rights Reserved.

EVERYONE USES NASTY LANGUAGE

Reinhold Aman

I have always maintained that *everyone* uses verbal aggression and offensive language of some kind: insults, slurs, curses, swearwords, blasphemies, vulgarities, damnations, and other verbal nasties. Even the sweetest, most peaceful persons (who'll swear that they never swear) will utter offensive language *if sufficiently angered*: hit Mother Teresa[1] on the head, and she'll call you a *Qen bir qeni!* in her native Albanian.[2] Bump into Monsignor Cazzocorto's new $60,000 Ferrari, and he'll goddamn you to bloody hell.

Recently, I've experienced two first-rate proofs of my contention. After I had pulled a dumb April-Fool trick on an apparently super-sweet, anti-abuse, shy Wisconsin lady of 27 who "really hates" name-calling, I tried to get her forgiveness by asking her to call me a "stupid asshole." She refused, saying that she *couldn't* call me that: "I just can't say it!" she protested. However, before I told her, "April fool!", she had hissed "Fuck you!" and had stormed off to her bathroom.[3]

Two weeks later, I made her even angrier with a mean hoax. When I telephoned to find out her reaction, she told me angrily, in a loud and firm voice, "You asshole!" Not just once but thrice.[4]

Quod erat demonstrandum.

---

[1] Née Agnes Gonxha Bojaxhiu.
[2] "Son-of-a-bitch!" Lit., "dog son of-dog." (Translation by Victor F.)
[3] Why do women always run into the bathroom to cry?
[4] Actually, the nature of my hoax did not call for the epithet *asshole*. The appropriate terms would have been *bastard*, *prick*, or *son-of-a-bitch*, but one cannot expect perfection from a novice in this discipline.

FOLK CRITICISM OF RELIGIOSITY IN THE GRAFFITI OF NEW YORK CITY

Allen Walker Read

For several years I have been disturbed by a certain aspect of folkloristic activity—that is, the collecting of superstitions. The very act of labeling superstitions seems to imply that the folk are gullible and naive.

And yet in my work with graffiti, I have uncovered material that implies just the opposite—that there is a considerable element of skepticism in folk attitudes. Probably both attitudes are present concurrently, and my urban material may well over-stress the skeptical.

The collections of graffiti that I wish to present in this article are strictly limited to those that I have copied down with my own pencil from the subways of New York City, mostly scribbled on advertising posters. They date from the last fifteen years, subsequent to the paper I presented on November 21, 1965, at the annual meeting of the American Folklore Society in Denver, Colorado.[1]

This subject matter concerns the area that I have labeled "criticism of religiosity." The middle 1960s were especially rich in such material, because several well-meaning religious organizations embarked on a campaign of producing advertising posters, and they aroused the hostility of a surprising number of people. One series was entitled "Religion in American Life," and another, by the New York Bible Society, printed selected verses from the Bible. The campaign may have been counter-productive, as shown by the bitterness of the comments scribbled on the posters, and the posters were withdrawn after about two years.

Some of the comments may turn you off because of their virulence and hostility; but I am not offended by them, because I believe that a healthy society requires a stratum of skepticism at the folk level. The "village atheist" is found also in the big city and performs an unshackling function against the clamping down of "respectable" attitudes. We can be glad that the heretic is always with us, and the writing of graffiti is a safety-valve for dissident attitudes.

Let us begin with some characterizations of "God" such as this:

> **God is a 6,000 foot tall red jellybean!**
> (Another writing:) ***No I'm not!***
> (Another:) **I'm blue**
>
> IRT, Downtown, 116th St. & Broadway, April 10, 1967

Or take this:

> **God is a 5th generation computer.**
>
> IRT, Downtown, 116th St. & Broadway, April 9, 1967

Then on a poster of the "Religion in American Life" series:

> **GOD IS A DREAMER**
>
> IRT, Downtown, 116th St. & Broadway, July 6, 1967

On another:

> **GOD IS <u>NOT</u> IRISH**
>
> IRT, Downtown, 116th St. & Broadway, August 11, 1967

Or this:

> **GOD IS OMNIVEROUS Chitlin's, bagels, pizza, even enchiladas**
>
> IRT, Uptown, 116th St. & Broadway, September 29, 1968

A more thoughtful graffito, perhaps even by a budding theologian, is the following:

<u>GOD OF DYNAMICS</u>
A PRIME MOVER UNMOVED
ESSENCE SO PURE HIS
SOLE JOB IS ONE OF
SELF CONTEMPLATION
HENCE WE HAVE THE
METAMORPHOSIS OF
PLATO'S GOD LIKE
ARISTOTLE'S PERFECT MALE
A SELF ERECTED MAN.

IRT, Downtown, 157th St. & Broadway, October 18, 1965

On an advertisement of the New York Bible Society that went, THE BIBLE SAYS MAN SHALL NOT LIVE BY BREAD ALONE, BUT BY EVERY WORD OF GOD, was written:

BUT BREAD COMES FIRST, AND
IF IT DOESN'T THE WORD OF GOD
IS NOT WORTH AN EMPTY SHELL.

IRT, Broadway line, 181st St., Downtown, October 18, 1965

Criticism of the effrontery of religious claims is sometimes made. On another Bible Society poster, saying, CALL UPON ME IN THE DAY OF TROUBLE; I WILL DELIVER THEE, AND THOU SHALT GLORIFY ME, was the comment:

What an ego!

IRT, Broadway line, 116th St., Downtown, June 14, 1970

In a similar spirit is this one:

SAINTHOOD
IS
ALL EGO
TRIP

IRT, Broadway line, 116th St., Downtown, November 29, 1968

Another religious poster saying THE GREATEST GIFT OF ALL was added to with the penciled question:

> **What's so great about it?**

Also, the word GIFT was crossed out to make way for the substitute:

> **BULL SHIT**

Then another person crossed that out.

IRT, Broadway line, 116th St.,
Downtown, December 4, 1962

In several places occurred the epigraph:

> **BY ORDER OF GOD**
> **TOMORROW IS CANCELLED!!**

A commentator added in other handwriting:

> ***GOODBY***

IRT, Broadway line, 79th St.,
Uptown, August 5, 1969

Outright disbelief is freely expressed. Someone set down in quotation marks: "RELIGION IS THE OPIUM OF THE MASSES"—K. MARX. To this was added in other handwriting:

> **Opiates are the religion**
> **of the masses. —T. Leary**

IRT, Broadway line, 116th St.,
Downtown, June 14, 1970

A variant was scribbled on a "Religion in American Life" poster:

> **OPIATE OF THE ASSES**

IRT, Broadway line, 66th St.,
Uptown, October 29, 1965

Here is another:

> **GOD IS THE**
> **RICH MAN'S**
> **BEST TOOL**
> **TO ENSLAVE YOU**

IRT, Broadway line, 110th St.,
Downtown, September 6, 1967

On another:

> **RELIGION**
> **THE CANCER**
> **IN AMERICAN**
> **LIFE**
>
> IRT, Broadway line, 168th St.,
> Downtown, December 10, 1967

Written on the side of a Bible Society poster was:

> **MAN Created God**
> **in his image**
>
> IRT, Broadway line, 66th St.,
> Uptown, April 12, 1963

The same sentiment, four years later, appeared in the inscription:

> **An honest God is the noblest work of man**
>
> IRT, Broadway line, 116th St.,
> Downtown, April 21, 1967

The graffiti were very responsive to the GOD IS DEAD movement that was so active in the mid-1960s. A favorite that appeared in many places was this:

> **GOD IS**
> **ALIVE IN**
> **ARGENTINA**
>
> IRT, Broadway line, 116th St.,
> Uptown, October 29, 1965

This was no praise of Argentina, but a parody of reports about escaped Nazis.

Another inscription read:

> **God, please come home—**
> **all is forgiven**
>
> IRT, Broadway line, 116th St.,
> Downtown, April 9, 1967

A closer place was pointed out in the following:

> GOD IS NOT DEAD!
> HE IS ALIVE AND
> IS AUTOGRAPHING BIBLES
> TODAY AT
> BRENTANO'S
>
> IRT, Broadway line, 110th St.,
Downtown, September 6, 1967

Other graffitists concern themselves with God's power. This invitation appeared in a station on the Broadway line:

> The Creator made the world—
> come and see it
>
> IRT, Broadway line, 116th St.,
Downtown, October 3, 1970

In a somewhat different spirit was the following one:

> GOD IN HIS WISDOM
> MADE THE FLY
> AND THEN FORGOT
> TO TELL US WHY
>
> IRT, Broadway line, 66th St.,
Uptown, February 2, 1970

A poster of "Religion in American Life" saying: GIVE THEM A FAITH TO LIVE BY inspired this outburst:

TO HATE BY, AND TO BE STUPID BY...
HOW ABOUT THE CATHOLICS AND BUDDHISTS
                              IN VIETNAM?
            AND THE ORTHODOX
            AND REFORMED JEWS
            IN ISRAEL?
AND THE HINDOOS AND MOSLEM PAKISTANIS?
GIVE AN ANSWER TO THAT ON YOUR NEXT POSTER

IRT, Broadway line, 181st St.,
Downtown, October 18, 1965

An interchange was penciled on a "Free Europe" poster that pictured barbed wire, as follows:

IS GOD ON YOUR SIDE OF THE BARBED WIRE?

In other handwriting this was answered:

No — but he's not on your side, either.
IRT, Broadway line, 116th St.,
Downtown, October 22, 1965

Another message was this:

NATIONALIZE
AT&T
IBM
GOD

IRT, Broadway line, 116th St.,
Downtown, April 17, 1965

Many of the graffiti express outright derision of religion. I find some wit in the following:

**Life is a yo-yo
And God ties the knots in the string.**
IRT, Broadway line, 50th St.,
Uptown, April 20, 1967

My favorite of this type was one that I presented in my paper of 1965, but I wish to repeat it here. Someone who carried a rubber stamp and a stamping pad had stamped CALL ON JESUS NOW. Below it in pencil another person added:

IF NO ONE ANSWERS
LEAVE A MESSAGE AT
THE CANDY STORE

IRT, Broadway line, 50th St.,
Downtown, February 14, 1962

The gentle sarcasm of this is very effective, I think. Others are in bludgeoning bad taste, as in this:

<u>CHRISTIANS</u>
have a
FAT head

IRT, Broadway line, 168th St.,
Downtown, August 15, 1966

Similar in spirit is this, on a poster of the New York Bible Society:

> Weaklings use
> Religion as a
> crutch
>
> IRT, Broadway line, 66th St.,
> Uptown, July 17, 1969

A printed verse that read, BLESS THE LORD, O MY SOUL: AND FORGET NOT ALL HIS BENEFITS, had a penciled inscription below it:

> BENEFITS LIKE THE FLOOD IN ITALY
> WHICH DESTROYED CHURCHES
>
> IRT, Broadway line, 168th St.,
> Downtown, November 17, 1968

Very frequent in expressing derision are single words and phrases that adorn the posters. One series of posters began, GIVE THEM A FAITH TO LIVE BY, and a graffitist supplied the one word:

> POT
>
> IRT, Broadway line, 66th St.,
> Downtown, October 29, 1965

The same beginning had the addition:

> EVEN IF IT'S A LIE
>
> IRT, Broadway line, 66th St.,
> Uptown, January 28, 1966

An "Easter Message" had the inserted phrase:

> For morons
>
> IRT, Broadway line, 59th St.,
> Downtown, March 22, 1964

Directly below the heading, "Religion in American Life," was the penciled insertion:

> IS A FARCE
>
> IRT, Broadway line, 66th St.,
> Downtown, October 29, 1965

ANTI-RELIGIOUS GRAFFITI IN NEW YORK CITY • 23

The advertisement for the film, *The Greatest Story Ever Told*, had the word *Story* crossed out and the substitute:

BLUFF

IRT, Broadway line, 110th St.,
Downtown, June 4, 1965

The New York Bible Society poster saying, I AM THY GOD... I WILL HELP THEE, I WILL UPHOLD THEE, had the addition by a graffitist:

IF YOU'RE WHITE AND MIDDLE CLASS

IRT, Broadway line, 50th St.,
Uptown, September 19, 1970

Let us turn now to graffiti dealing with the person of Jesus. There are many hostile characterizations. The inscription

JESUS CHRIST WAS A COMMIE

found on an advertisement for shrimp cocktail, is probably hostile, because even a pro-Communist would not use the colloquial form of *Commie*.

IRT, Broadway line, 18th St.,
Downtown, October 5, 1964

Another is as follows:

God rules
Jesus is a bum

I took this from a billboard at the corner of 49th Street and 6th Avenue, the only example I am presenting from above ground.

February 10, 1968

At the Columbia University subway station, on a movie advertisement, was written:

CHRIST WAS A HOMOSEXUAL

IRT, Broadway line, 116th St.,
Downtown, May 16, 1964

On a religious poster using the words CHRIST THE LORD, a graffitist inserted:

The First Antisemite
IRT, Broadway line, 66th St.,
Uptown, December 7, 1967

Another critic gave this characterization:

JESUS
WAS A
JUNKY, HENCE
HIS BEING ABLE
TO CON ALL THE
FARMERS WHOSE EARS
WERE WITHIN HIS
REACH
IRT, Broadway line, 116th St.,
Downtown, July 5, 1965

Further reference to Jesus occurs in an inscription that has appeared in several parts of town:

Jesus Christ has been delayed.
IRT, Broadway line, Christopher St.,
Uptown, September 13, 1964

For one such example that I copied, I discovered when I came back a few weeks later that someone had added in red ink:

DOO-DAH, DOO-DAH!
IRT, Broadway line, 116th St.,
Downtown, September 27, 1964

When the Bible Society announced on its poster, ...AND HE ROSE AGAIN ON THE THIRD DAY, a graffitist asked in the margin:

Why So Late?
IRT, Broadway line, 59th St.,
Downtown, April 20, 1962

On an advertisement of a whiskey company, showing a penny in a glass, an inscription was made:

> O GREAT WHITE JESUS
> PLAY GAMES WITH THIS
>> IRT, Broadway line, 116th St.,
>> Uptown, September 7, 1962

Even more enigmatic is the following:

> Jesus is always here!
> That's why it's so special when
> Kilroy shows up!
>> IRT, Broadway line, 168th St.,
>> Downtown, November 5, 1967

The satirical import is clear in this one:

> KING KONG DIED FOR OUR SINS
>> IRT, Broadway line, 116th St.,
>> Uptown, September 24, 1967

No doubt related to this is the following graffito:

> Cancel my subscription to
> the resurrection!

This was followed in other handwriting by:

> *OKAY TURN IN YOUR BODY*
>> IRT, Broadway line, 116th St.,
>> Downtown, April 14, 1968

The Virgin Mary has also attracted attention. It is difficult to interpret the following:

> Virgin
> Mary
> is a
> Jewess
>> IRT, Broadway line, 116th St.,
>> Downtown, September 26, 1965

Inasmuch as the word *Jewess* is often pejorative, this may be a hostile inscription, but perhaps not. The most popular inscription of all on this subject, reported from several parts of the country, is widespread folklore. I found examples at both 96th Street and 116th Street on the Broadway line. It goes as follows:

> God is dead, but
> don't worry, the Virgin Mary
> is pregnant again.
>
> IRT, Broadway line, 116th St.,
> Downtown, June 18, 1968
> Also *ibid.*, IRT, Broadway line, 96th St.,
> Uptown, March 24, 1969

A series of posters with the heading WORSHIP THIS WEEK elicited a variety of responses. One graffitist added in big capitals:

> **WORSHIP WHAT?**
>
> IRT, Broadway line, 125th St.,
> Uptown, October 2, 1964

Another prefixed the word DON'T, making it DON'T WORSHIP THIS WEEK.

> Independent, Dyckman St.,
> Downtown, August 12, 1963

Another emended the advertisement by adding:

> **IF YOU HAVE**
> **TIME TO WASTE**
>
> IRT, Broadway line, 157th St.,
> Downtown, October 3, 1964

Another graffitist inserted the words THE DEVIL, so that it read WORSHIP THE DEVIL THIS WEEK.

> IRT, Broadway line, 116th St.,
> Uptown, January 7, 1963

Such cleverness!

Religious rituals have been subject to attack. We make what we can of the inscription that goes:

> **H.M. Rips Blessed Sacrament**
>
> IRT, Broadway line, 86th St.,
> Downtown, October 1, 1964

A bias is evident in this one:

> **HOLEY**
> **WATER**
> **BIG FAKE**
>
> IRT, Broadway line, 125th St.,
> Downtown, October 2, 1964

An advertisement for Levy's "real Jewish Rye" caused a graffitist to think of circumcision, so he wrote:

> **A CUT PRICK IS GOOD FOR YOU**
>
> IRT, Broadway line, 215th St.,
> Uptown, October 2, 1964

The subject of prayer has not fared very well. A poster on "Religion in American Life" was given the inscription:

> **SAY YOUR**
> **PRAYERS**
> **IN BED**

And later below, in other handwriting, appeared:

> ***YOU'LL NEED THEM***
>
> IRT, Broadway line, 168th St.,
> Downtown, November 17, 1963

On a "Worship this Week" poster was added:

> **PRAY FOR**
> **BETTER SUBWAY**
> **SERVICE**

But then someone crossed out PRAY and substituted:

> **FIGHT**
>
> IRT, Broadway line, 50th St.,
> Uptown, September 24, 1963

A fairly witty satire on THE FAMILY THAT PRAYS TOGETHER STAYS TOGETHER was constructed by a graffitist who wrote:

> The family
> that shoots
> together, loots
> together
>
> IRT, Broadway line, 116th St.,
Downtown, December 10, 1962

Another type of attack on religiosity may more properly be called anti-clericalism. Certain religious leaders have suffered attack. On an advertisement for a service by Billy Graham, a graffitist wrote:

> [HE] IS <u>NOT</u>
> THE JESUS OF THIS TIME
> GET RID OF PSEUDO-PROPHETS LIKE HIM!
>
> IRT, Broadway line, 116th St.,
Downtown, June 24, 1969

On a poster of the New York Bible Society appeared:

> MOTHER DIVINE
> SAYS FATHER
> DIVINE IS
> A LAZY BASTARD
>
> IRT, Broadway line, 66th St.,
Uptown, January 23, 1964

The anti-papist attitude is frequently expressed, as in this example:

> POPE TO PURGATORY
>
> ONE WAY FARE
>
> IRT, Broadway line, 125th St.,
Downtown, October 2, 1964

On an advertisement of The Paulist Fathers, a "Solemn Mass" was listed, but someone crossed out the word *Solemn* and substituted:

> GAY
>
> IRT, Broadway line, 66th St.,
Downtown, August 17, 1967

Another religious leader was mentioned at the Columbia University station, as follows:

> C S LEWIS
> IS ALIVE
> IN AVALON
>
> IRT, Broadway line, 116th St.,
> Downtown, September 4, 1967

My last group is a set of enigmatic graffiti that I scarcely know how to classify. What do you make of this one?

> **I'm a sex maniac.**
> **Jesus never fails**
> [SIGNED:] **the Ludicrous**
> **Misfit**
>
> IRT, Broadway line, 96th St.,
> Uptown, January 11, 1966

A poster of "Religion in American Life" had this inscription, apropos of nothing I could see:

> TAKE
> CHRIST
> OFF
> THE
> DASH BOARD
>
> IRT, Broadway line, 116th St.,
> Downtown, November 5, 1963

On another "Religion in American Life," a graffitist wrote:

> **THERE IS BLOOD ON MY HANDS**
> **AND IT WILL NOT COME OFF**

In other handwriting, someone else then added:

> *USE SOAP*
>
> IRT, Broadway line, 168th St.,
> Downtown, November 17, 1963

In closing, may I mention that I am impressed by the statement of the Scottish collector, Hamish Henderson, who said that the folklorist is "helping to interpret man to man—his beliefs, glories, dreams, darknesses."[2] Among the beliefs and darknesses, the anti-religious kind must find their place. The graffiti that I have here presented to you are strong documentation for this type of material.

NOTES

1. "Graffiti as a Field of Folklore," *Maledicta* 2 (1978), 15-31.
2. In his Preface, p. x, to Kenneth Goldstein, *A Guide for Field Workers in Folklore* (Hatboro, PA, 1964).

An earlier version of this article was presented at the Conference on the Folklore of Urban Public Spaces, sponsored by the New York Chapter of the New York Folklore Society, et al., at New York University, April 19, 1980.

EDITOR'S NOTE

The graffito TAKE CHRIST OFF THE DASH BOARD mentioned by Dr. Read may refer to plastic statues of Jesus kept by religious folks on their cars' dashboards. I have seen such a statue in Iowa, some 20 years ago. It was approximately four inches high and had an inscription on its base that read:

> I DON'T CARE IF IT RAINS OR FREEZES,
> AS LONG AS I HAVE MY DASHBOARD JESUS

MEDICAL MALEDICTA FROM SAN FRANCISCO

Richard O. Barton

The medical ancillary professions undergo substantial turnovers and random migrations of personnel. Consequently, regional medical slang does not stay regional very long. SHPOS (*sub-human piece of shit*), an Eastern term described in *Maledicta* 2: 69, has cropped up in San Francisco within the last few years. Who knows what San Francisco has sent back East or down South? Following below is a list of medical terms enjoying current use in hospitals around the San Francisco Bay area.

acting out originally a psychiatric term describing a patient's giving physical dimensions to fantasies and delusions. In current general usage, it refers to aberrant, agitated, often physically aggressive behavior.
Bend over, brown eyes! or **Bend over and enjoy it!** said of a patient undergoing a digital rectal examination or other colo-rectal procedure. Also stated stoically at shift change, as the supervisor hands out assignments.
blue happiness oral morphine, an aquamarine liquid
bobbing for apples digital fecal disimpaction. (Dig it?)
code brown copious, foul-smelling bowel movement deposited in an inappropriate place (bed, floor, corridor). **Code browns** are often intentionally perpetrated by dis-*grunt*led patients, such as *gomers* (see *Maledicta* 7: 38). This term is modeled after the official codes *code red* (fire) and *code blue* (cardiac arrest). Less frequent is **code yellow** for urinary incontinence.
crump, to same as POOT

crunch a patient with multiple traumatic injuries, usually the result of a vehicular accident. Not to be confused with TRAINWRECK.

doll eyes or **doll's eyes, to have** turning the eyes upward, such that only the white sclerae remain visible. Suggests neurological deficits. "Now this crunch has doll's eyes."

Expensive Care Unit the Intensive Care Unit. Also called INSENSITIVE CARE UNIT.

flooger a chunk of mucus coughed forcibly from a patient's tracheostomy opening. Probably a contraction of *flying* + *booger*. Many patients, even those who are comatose, seem to take unerring aim at ancillary staff.

F.O.S. *full of shit*, used both literally and figuratively.

glob same as HAWKER

go poopoo, to same as POOT

God's waiting room a convalescent facility or any residence for *mature individuals*. See MATURE.

goober or **green goober** mucus that is not coughed into the air like a FLOOGER. Also known as OYSTER.

hawk (up), to to expectorate a HAWKER with incremental coughing

hawker a chunk of sputum coughed up and expectorated through the tracheal-oral route. Also known as GLOB, GOB, (GREEN) GOOBER, HONKER, and WAD.

hepatic rounds same as LIVER ROUNDS

heroics extraordinary life-support measures, such as mechanical ventilation or bedside hemodialysis. The term is most often used sarcastically, when such methods are ordered for irreversibly terminal patients. "This guy's got a flat EEG, and they *still* want heroics?!"

honker same as HAWKER

hype an intravenous drug abuser. From *hypodermic* needle. Older terms are *junkie* and *dopefiend*; the latter is now almost exclusively a self-directed term used by drug abusers in recovery.

Insensitive Care Unit same as EXPENSIVE CARE UNIT

lesionaires, the gallows-humor appellation by members of a San Francisco AIDS/Kaposi's sarcoma support group for themselves

lights are on, but nobody's home refers to a patient who superficially appears oriented but cannot carry on an appropriate conversation (with another individual)

liver rounds or **hepatic rounds** code name (which enables placement of announcements throughout the hospital) for spirited party to be held on the premises, often in the interns' quarters. Named after the liver's detoxification of alcohol or liver damage caused by alcohol. "Hot damn! Liver rounds in the interns' quarters at 4 P.M.!" Has been called *Fluids and Electrolytes Conference* in Ann Arbor, Michigan.

loony tunes same as OUT TO LUNCH

M.D.B. *mega dirt ball*, a patient, often from the streets, who practices negative personal hygiene. An **M.D.B.**'s personality often parallels his/her physical appearance.

Manila General derogatory name given by xenophobes to any hospital department or unit overstaffed (in their opinion) by Filipinos

Mary's Hell jocular name for Seton Hospital, formerly called Mary's Help, a Catholic hospital in Daly City, California, on Interstate 280. Also known as MARY'S HINDRANCE, OUR LADY OF TWO-EIGHTY, and SATAN'S.

Mary's Hindrance same as MARY'S HELL

mature current euphemism for *old*

not too tightly wrapped same as OUT TO LUNCH

not with the program same as OUT TO LUNCH

Our Lady of Two-Eighty same as MARY'S HELL

out of the woods to be out of imminent danger and past the severest phase of an illness. "He's out of Expensive Care, but he's not out of the woods yet."

out to lunch confused and disoriented. Also, LOONY TUNES, NOT TOO TIGHTLY WRAPPED, NOT WITH THE PROGRAM

oyster same as GOOBER

oysters aRe in season a productive cough. The capital *R* in *aRe* refers to the months containing the letter *r* when oysters are in season on the eastern seaboard.

Pill Hill a somewhat elevated area in Oakland, California, whereon three major hospitals are located

poot, to to take a turn for the worst quickly and often irreversibly (said of a patient). Also known as TO CRUMP and TO GO POOPOO.

roadmap multiple interconnecting lacerations (usually facial), the result of striking a windshield or other glass object hard enough to shatter it

Satan's same as MARY'S HELL

school's out it is all over; I'm calling it off. "This code has been going too long; we haven't accomplished a damn thing, so I guess school's out."

silver goose a proctoscope

slug hyper-unmotivated patient who thoroughly frustrates the hospital staff by refusing to participate in any aspect of therapy or self-care. The patient *can* participate; s/he just *won't*.

snake, to to suction or aspirate mucus from a patient's trachea by inserting a narrow, flexible, serpentine, well-lubricated red rubber catheter into the trachea via the nose, then applying suction. The procedure is profoundly unpleasant for both patient and ancillary. "This slug won't cough, and his temp's 38.9. You'll have to snake him."

S.O.B. *short of breath*, dyspneic. Also, *son of a bitch*, thus "Patient is dyspneic & S.O.B." is not necessarily redundant.

St. Frantic jocular name for St. Francis Hospital in San Francisco

St. Puke's jocular name for St. Luke's Hospital in San Francisco

sundowner a (geriatric) patient whose behavior seems appropriate by day but who becomes confused, agitated, boisterous, and frequently combative at night

T.B.F. *total body failure*, a severely morbid, usually terminal state in which multiple body systems (cardio-vascular, renal, pulmonary) shut down and cease effectively to function. Poor prognosis.

trainwreck a patient with multiple major ailments, all in a state of simultaneous excerbation. **Trainwrecks** have a high mortality rate.

vitamin H haloperidol, a major tranquilizer often used for hyperexcitability, especially in geriatric patients. "If this sundowner doesn't get some vitamin H pretty soon, he's gonna keep the whole damn floor up all night!"

vitamin P sex. From *pussy*. Used by medical personnel. "My brother's old lady split, and now he's got a bad vitamin P deficiency."

wad same as HAWKER.

WHAT IS THIS?

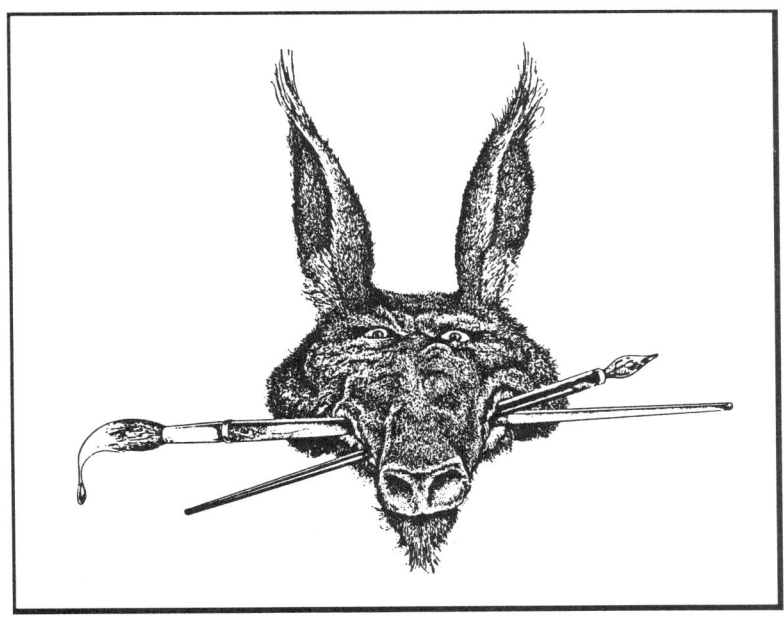

Copyright © 1989 by Paul Smith, The Waukesha Illustrator

See answer on page 143

MORE MILWAUKEE MEDICAL MALEDICTA

*Sue Ture

Except where otherwise noted, the following terms are used in Milwaukee (Wisconsin) area hospitals.

crispy critters severely burned patients. Named after the brand of toasted, animal-shaped cereal. Used by medical staff in a Midwest burn center.

drug holiday discontinuing all medications to a patient on multiple drugs (e.g., a Parkinson's patient), to differentiate between symptoms caused by illness or by medication. Used on official records.

G.M.O.F. a huge patient. From *great mass of flesh*. Used in Florida hospitals.

Goldfinger nickname of a Milwaukee proctologist

joint mouse a loose piece of cartilage in a joint (knee, elbow) causing it to squeak

oldtimer's disease Alzheimer's disease

Peter Rabbit ward pediatric ward. Like the preceding, often used by blacks attempting to pronounce unfamiliar medical jargon.

pill hill an area of a community where many physicians live

shortness of breast diagnosis seen in the admission record of a Milwaukee woman with breathing problems

space cadet a grossly overmedicated patient. From *spaced out*, "not in touch with reality, severely dazed."

stuffed owls attendants at a medical meeting who are there only to earn the credits

transferred to the big outpatient department in the sky died

ungrateful patient a patient who dies despite the best efforts by doctors and nurses.

ELEMENTARY GEORGIAN OBSCENITY

*Boris Sukitch Razvratnikov

This article is modeled on my "Elementary Russian Obscenity" (*Maledicta* 3: 197-204) and is the second in a series of articles on basic obscenity in a variety of languages. The principles of selection are those discussed in my previous article, namely the terms chosen are readily intelligible to the English-speaking student as obscene and at the same time form part of the idiomatic obscene lexicon of the target language—in this case, Georgian. I have included a few items which are merely vulgar or are not abusive but involve obscene words. I have also included a few items from the unwritten languages Laz, Mingrelian, and Svan, which are spoken mainly in Georgia and Turkey and which, together with Georgian, comprise the Kartvelian language family. The listing follows the order established in my previous article, and notes on sources, transliteration, and citation forms appear at the end.

I. BODY PARTS

qle ყლე *prick*

ķuţu კუტუ *wee-wee*. Also used in Mingrelian.

qveri (pl. *qverebi*) ყვერი (ყვერები) *ball(s)*

    šen qverebs venacvale შენ ყვერებს ვენაცვალე
    I adore your balls. Lit. "Let me be a substitute [in adversity] for your balls"; an expression of endearment from a parent to a son or, very rarely, of admiration addressed to a valiant man. Cf. Eng. "ballsy" or "gutsy."

muţeli მუტელი *cunt*

juju (pl. *jujuebi*) ძუძუ (ძუძუები) *tits*

ǰigari (pl. *ǰigrebi* or *ǰigani*) ჯიგარი (ჯიგრები, ჯი-განი) *tits*. Actually, the basic meaning of this word is "liver," and it is also used to mean "heart, lungs, viscera." According to a speaker from a village, this word can be used to mean "udder" and hence also as a very vulgar word for breasts. An urban speaker did not agree with this usage, but both cited the following expression:

genacvale ǰigrebši გენაცვალე ჯიგრებში

I love your guts/tits. This expression is addressed by a man to a woman. When whispered in private, it is an intimate endearment. When shouted in public, it is a gross insult, like our wolf whistle.

moǰigravs (1sg *miǰigravs*) მოჯიგრავს (მიჯი-გრავს) *feel up/French kiss.* Lit. "disembowel." The two meanings were cited by two different speakers. The speaker who cited "French kiss" was the one who did not accept the meaning "tits" for *ǰigrebi*. This speaker supplied another expression for "French kiss": *ķučis cveni amouǧo / amoǧeba* კუჭის ცვენი ამოუღო/ამოღება Lit. "[He] sucks out [her] stomach's juice."

ṭraķi ტრაკი *ass*

ṭraķši maķoce! ტრაკში მაკოცე *Kiss my ass!*

maztli gamičnda ṭraķze მაზთლი გამიჩნდა ტრაკზე *A callus appeared on my ass.* Used to mean "I worked my ass off. I busted my ass."

ra gaaṭraķa am ķacma რა გაატრაკა ამ კაცმა *What a pain in the ass that guy is.* The form **gaaṭraķa** is 3 sg. aor. derived from *ṭraķi*.

šen čemisa ra gaaṭraķe შენ ჩემისა რა გაა-ტრაკე *What a pain in the ass you are.*

meṭraķi მეტრაკი *gay male.* Lit. "ass-er", i.e. someone who goes after ass. Another expression is *bičebis moqvaruli* ბიჭების მოყვარული "lover of boys."

II. BODILY FUNCTIONS

1. Excretory

ṭqorin- ტყორინ- *fart.* This is Mingrelian and is related to Svan and Laz words meaning "to have diarrhea."

buzin- ბუზინ- *fart.* Another Mingrelian form; this one is related to the Georgian root *bzu-* "buzz"

gaaḳuebs გააკუებს *fart* (3 sg. fut.)

iǰvams (aor. *čaiǰva*) იჯვამს (ჩაიჯვა) *shit.* The Svan form is *sgēr-*.

    tavze dagaǰvi თავზე დაგაჯვი *I shat on your head.*
    ṗirši čagaǰvi პირში ჩაგაჯვი *I shat in your mouth.* This is more abusive than the previous expression.

mjǧneri მჯღნერი *shit* (noun)

    mjǧnero! მჯღნერო *(You) shit!* Cf. Eng. "Shithead!"

ṭraçi ტრაწი *the shits* (diarrhea)

    ṭraçi akvs / daemarta ტრაწი აქვს/დაემართა *He has the shits.* The words in this sentence are not vulgar in and of themselves, but their use to refer to diarrhea is vulgar.

psams ფსამს *piss*

    davapsi დავაფსი *I pissed on it.*
    dagapsi დაგაფსი *I pissed on you.*

gačirebuli გაჭირებული *can, crapper.* Lit. "need-place."

2. Sexual

daanjrevs დაანჯრევს *jack off.* This comes from a root meaning "shake," etc.

ṗirši aiğebs პირში აიღებს *blow job.* Lit. "[She] takes it in the mouth." Note: the specification of gender is not in the expression but was supplied by the informant.

moṭqnavs (aor. 1 sg. *movṭqani*, 3 sg. *moṭqna*) მოტყნავს (მოვტყანი, მოტყნა) *fuck*

    šeni deda movṭqan შენი დედა მოვტყან *I fucked your mother.*

deda mogiṭqan დედა მოგიტყან *I fucked your mother.*

mteli dġe moviṭqane მთელი დღე მოვიტყანე *I fucked all day.* Used to mean "I killed myself with work and nothing came of it."

ṭqnaurob mastan ტყნაურობ მასთან *You're fucking with him/her/it.*

ṭqnauri ტყნაური *fucking* (noun)

šeṗirmoṭqunulo შე პირმოტყუნულო
You fuckhead/fuckface! Lit. "You mouth-fucked!"

šecems შეცემს *fuck.* The basic meaning of the root *cem-* ცემ- is "give." It is used with a variety of prefixes to form different verbs, as in the expression *dageces mexi* დაგეცეს მეხი "May lightning strike you." The prefix *še-* შე- has the basic meaning "in, into."

ševcem mas შევცემ მას *I'll fuck him/her/it.*

imis dedas ševeci იმის დედას შევეცი
I fucked his mother.

šen dedas ševeci შენ დედას შევეცი *I fucked your mother.*

šen muṭelši šegeci შენ მუტელში შეგეცი
I fucked you in the cunt.

šegeci ṭrakši შეგეცი ტრაკში *I fucked you in the ass.*

ṗirši šegeci პირში შეგეცი *I fucked you in the mouth.*

txris (fut. with 2 sg. obj. *šegtxari*) თხრის (შეგთხარი) *buttfuck.* Actually, the verb means "dig, excavate," etc. and only becomes obscene contextually, or with the prefix *še-*.

šegtxare ṭrakši შეგთხარე ტრაკში *I fucked you in the ass.*

gtxridi ṭrakši გთხრიდი ტრაკში *I fucked your ass.*

daçers დაწერს *screw.* This verb actually means "write," but it can function as a slangy way of referring to sexual intercourse (the subject must be male) as in *davçere* დავწერე "I screwed her."

čoš- (passive pt. *na-čoš-*) ჩომ- (ნა-ჩომ-) *fuck*. This is the Svan verb with this meaning. It is cognate with Georgian *coli* ცოლი "wife."
aṭexili ატეხილი *horny*. Lit. "in heat" from *ṭexva* თეტხვა "unchained." Used only of women.
axurebuli ახურებული *horny*. Lit. "unleashed." Generally said of women, but possible for men.
mxurvale ṭani akvs მხურვალე ტანი აქვს
  He/She is horny. Lit. "He/She has a hot body."
udgas (aor. *edga*, fut. *audgeba*) უდგას (ედგა, აუდგება) *hard-on*. Based on the verb meaning "stand."
daamtavrebs დაამთავრებს *come*. This is based on the verb meaning "finish." Another variant based on the same root is *gaatavebs* გაათავებს.

III. SOCIAL INSTITUTIONS, AND OTHER EXPRESSIONS

bozi ბოზი *whore*. Also used to refer to a promiscuous woman, an adulterous wife, or a police informer of either sex.
  bozobs ბოზობს *she whores*
  gabozdeba გაბოზდება *She will become a whore.*
  bozikali ბოზიკალი *Loose woman.* This is a negative term.
  boziḳaci ბოზიკაცი *womanizer.* This is not a negative term. (So much for Georgian cultural attitudes.)
mruši მრუში *adulterer/adulteress*. According to one informant, this can be used to mean "whore" and is a very bad word.
  gamrušda გამრუშდა *Someone becomes a mruši.*
oğraši ოღრაში *pimp*. Vulgar, but not taboo.
jağlisšvilo! ძაღლისშვილო *Son of a dog!*
še virisšvilo შე ვირისშვილო *You son of an ass.*
še gorisšvilo შე გორისშვილო *You son of a pig.*

še sobeljaǧlo შე სობელდაღლო *Your parents are dogs.*

mamajaǧlo! მამადაღლო *Dogfather!* According to one informant, this word is the equivalent of the Russian *svoloč'* (see *Maledicta* 3: 203). It can be used as a term of abuse or when speaking of a clever child; cf. Yiddish *ganef*. According to another informant, this expression is only used affectionately, chiefly by a child's father, cf. English *rascal*.

daçqevlili დაწყევლილი *damned*
  ǧmertma daçqevlos ღმერთმა დაწყევლოს
  God damn you.

goyimi გოიმი *square/straight* (noun). Borrowed into Georgian slang from Hebrew.

SOURCES

I am deeply indebted to *Irma Kališvili who supplied me with most of the data in this article. I am also very grateful to two Georgian scholars who supplied me with most of the rest of the data. I also wish to thank Mixo the Flying Grape, wherever he may be, for his able assistance in the fieldwork. A few items are from G. A. Klimov's *Ètimologičeskij slovar' kartvel'skix jazykov* (Moscow, AN SSSr, 1964, pp. 51, 184, 210, 212, 230, 268). The transliteration and citation forms are based on Howard I. Aronson's *Georgian: A Reading Grammar* (Columbus, Ohio: Slavica, 1982; see *Maledicta* 8: 315).

A few notes will orient the reader familiar with Georgian from other sources. The letters j and ɉ are used for the voiced dental affricate [dz] and its palatal correspondent [dž], respectively. The letter ǧ represents the voiced uvular fricative, x is its voiceless correspondent, and q represents the glottalized uvular stop. Elsewhere, a dot under a letter (but over p for the sake of greater legibility) indicates glottalization. Nonglottalized voiceless stops and affricates are aspirated. Verbs are cited in the 3 sg. pres. or fut. unless otherwise stated. Due to the fact that Modern Georgian orthography does not distinguish lower and upper case, I have not done so in the transliteration.

EDITOR'S NOTE: The IPA symbols were graciously supplied by Ecological Linguistics (PO Box 15156, Washington, DC 20003), who also sell many "exotic" language fonts—from Mongolian to Mayan Hieroglyphics—for the Macintosh at reasonable prices. Include a SASE when writing to E.L.

TELEPHONIC CRYPTOGRAMS

Frank Nuessel

In a newspaper article,[1] Dan Carpenter described the cryptogrammic use of telephone numbers. Essentially, this phenomenon refers to the encoding of special messages into telephone numbers. A brief perusal of any rotary dial or push-button control mechanism discloses that the numbers 2 through 9 (eight digits) contain three letters of the alphabet in each position. Thus, twenty-four of the twenty-six letters of the English alphabet (excluding Q and Z) are found on standard U.S. telephones.

Two basic motives for cryptogrammic telephone numbers exist. First and foremost, such a significant combination facilitates recall. Second, this type of product or service identification constitutes an indirect form of commercial advertisement.

Linguistic, pragmatic, and sociolinguistic restrictions function in the conveyance of potential messages. First, the length of such a communication (word or phrase) may not exceed seven characters,[2] e.g., TICKETS[3] (= 842-5387, Chicago), and AIR-LINE (= 247-5463, Indianapolis). A union of digits and letters, of course, provides the opportunity for shorter messages, e.g., 63W-AYNE (= 639-2963, Indianapolis), and 588-POOL (= 588-7665, Louisville). The absence of the letters Q and Z compounds the linguistic restrictions. Furthermore, only a mathematically finite quantity of words and phrases may be generated by such a limited system. Thus far, certain syntagms remain unexploited (questions, commands, and declarative sentences). The encoding of lexical items from foreign languages also remains untapped. Practical constraints include the availability of certain telephone lines with an appropriate area prefix (for seven-character messages) which are not already in service. Likewise, cryptogrammic telephone numbers must not contain a 1 or a 0 since neither position has letters associated with it.

A sociolinguistic feature of such numeric sequences involves censorship. Telephone company bureaucrats will not confer special numbers to individuals if these concatenations are known to translate taboo lexical items. Nevertheless, such innovative use of language may escape official sanction if petitioners omit any reference to such proscribed verbiage.

This unexplored domain of maledictology offers unique possibilities to those nefarious individuals who may desire to convey either erotic, lecherous, licentious or profane and abusive messages. Seven-letter combinations may include questions such as WILL YOU (= 945-5968) or curses GOD DAMN (= 463-3266). The ubiquitous four-letter word is ideal for a combination of the three-digit exchange plus an appropriate blasphemy. It is even conceivable that a secret message already exists in your telephone number without your knowledge.

NOTES

1. Don Carpenter, "555-ZANY: Those ding-a-ling phone numbers!", *The Indianapolis Star*, May 21, 1984, pp. 1, 14.
2. U.S. Telephone numbers consist of a three-digit area prefix plus four additional numbers which distinguish individual lines.
3. All telephonic cryptograms will be written in upper case.

PHONE-SMUT

Reinhold Aman

In addition to Nuessel's "Telephonic Cryptograms" (preceding this article), there have been several news stories and articles on this topic. "Dial 686-2377 for NUMBERS" in *Time* (2 Febr. 1970: 36) lists among others HELP NOW, the Los Angeles Suicide Prevention Office, and GOD DAMN, which reaches the Hollywood First Methodist Church's recorded sermon (first reported in *The Realist*, ca. 1965). Producer-Director Alan Myerson's Los Angeles telephone number once was listed under HOLY PIG.

Word Ways had three discussions on this topic: Dave Silverman's "Telephomnemonics" (Aug. 1970: 170-171), showing SWINGER for the number of a jet-setter, and PYGMIES for the number of someone's diminutive friends. In the May 1981 issue, pp. 116-120, A. Ross Eckler delves deeply into "Telephomnemonics," and Richard Lederer reports some business numbers, such as 800 AIRLINE for TWA, in the May 1984 issue, p. 85.

In July 1986, the California Public Utilities Commission authorized Pacific Bell to offer vanity telephone numbers, allowing customers to individualize their numbers, such as 552-MARY, WEFIXIT, HAIRCUT, CALLSUE, BAD DUDE and COOL GUY. Letter numbers with sexual connotations or offensive to racial and ethnic groups are *verboten*. (WF, 16 July 1986: 6 and MJ, 17 July 1986: 6A)

During the past five years, more and more individuals and companies—from the staid to the sleezy—have been using customized telephone numbers. As heard on WLS

"If you're short you can make a pledge by calling toll-free 1-800-BUM-GIFT."
Copyright © 1986 by H. Matis

radio (Chicago) on 14 Jan. 1986, Illinois law firms specializing in defending drivers charged with "Driving Under the Influence" (of alcohol) have such numbers as DUI-LAWS and DIAL DUI. National Chatlines has 777-WET, 777-KISS, TALK-739, and USA-CHAT (*Penthouse*, Sept. 1989: 229). Sexual services have numbers advertising their specialties: 976-BODY (for "The Ultimate in Body Pleasures"), 976-HONY (Erotic Sexual Fantasy, "Put More Sting in Your Stinger"), and 970-CUNT, 976-COME, 976-FUCK, and 976-TITS, advertised in *Eidos* 4/3 (1989): 5.

While the use of easy-to-remember words for phone numbers continues to be employed by big corporations—a recent addition is 1-800-CHEER UP for the National Gift Liquor Company—it is not fully utilized in the private and professional sectors.* A plastic surgeon with the phone number 667-3562 would be easier remembered as NOSE JOB. 724-6825 could be almost any university administrator's number: SCHMUCK. A dumb relative's 346-4228 results in DINGBAT. The number of any cacademic creep who criticizes *Maledicta* ought to be 317-7448 = DIPSHIT. 227-8273 reaches a BASTARD. Useless and lazy folks with the numbers 522-5633 and 382-5633 are easily remembered as JACKOFF and FUCKOFF. Nasties ought to have any of these numbers: 382-5968 = FUCK YOU, 438-5678 = GET LOST, 746-8348 = SHOVE IT, 788-3348 = STUFF IT, or 879-6877 = UP

---

* If you like brain-games, cover the rest of this article with a sheet of paper, then uncover number by number, first trying to figure out what words the numbers stand for before looking at the "solution." On American telephones, 2=ABC, 3=DEF, 4=GHI, 5=JKL, 6=MNO, 7=PRS, 8=TUV, 9=WXY.

YOURS. I remember most editors and reporters at *The Milwaukee Journal (Urinal)* by the numbers 277-9473 = ASSWIPE, 427-2243 = GARBAGE, 668-4377 = MOTHERS, 744-8724 =SHITRAG, or 874-6257 = URINALS.

A Cadillac dealer's best number would be 966-6662 = YO MOMMA. Homosexual bordellos could sport 284-4377 = BUGGERS, 324-4687 = FAGGOTS, 429-4897 = GAY GUYS, 427-3667 = HARDONS, or 768-3837 = POUFTER. Lesbians could have 285-3953 = BULDYKE, 345-3637 = DILDOES or 537-2426 = LESBIAN. Naturally, the best phone numbers for fellators and fellatrices are 256-9562 = BLOWJOB and 448-4323 = GIV HEAD.

The phone numbers of professional men and women are easy to remember if they are associated with some stereotype or mnemonic device. Pediatricians should have the number 744-8279, reflecting the primary activities of their baby patients, SHIT CRY. Lawyers: 749-7837 = SHYSTER. Proctologists have five numbers to choose from: 277-4653 = ASSHOLE, 244-4327 = BIG HEAP, 244-7453 = BIG PILE, 727-7427 = PASS GAS, and 732-8867 = RECTUMS. Pharmacists can be reached under 266-3667 = CONDOMS, 342-3726 = DIAFRAM and 782-2377 = RUBBERS. Veterinarians have three choices: 228-7448 = CAT SHIT, 269-3864 = COW DUNG and 364-8873 = DOG TURD. Urologists can choose from six numbers: 342-5437 = DICKIES, 367-7546 = FORSKIN, 436-4825 = GENITAL, 742-5587 = PHALLUS, 727-6886 = SCROTUM, or 743-4547 = SIFILIS. Finally, gynecologists have ten choice phone numbers: 232-8377 = BEAVERS, 273-2787 = BREASTS, 286-8538 = CUNTLET, 626-4653 = MANHOLE, , 647-7537 = NIPPLES, 787-7437 = PUSSIES, 848-2662 = TIT BOOB 848-8437 = TITTIES, 848-7787 = TITS-R-US, and 824-4627 = VAGINAS.

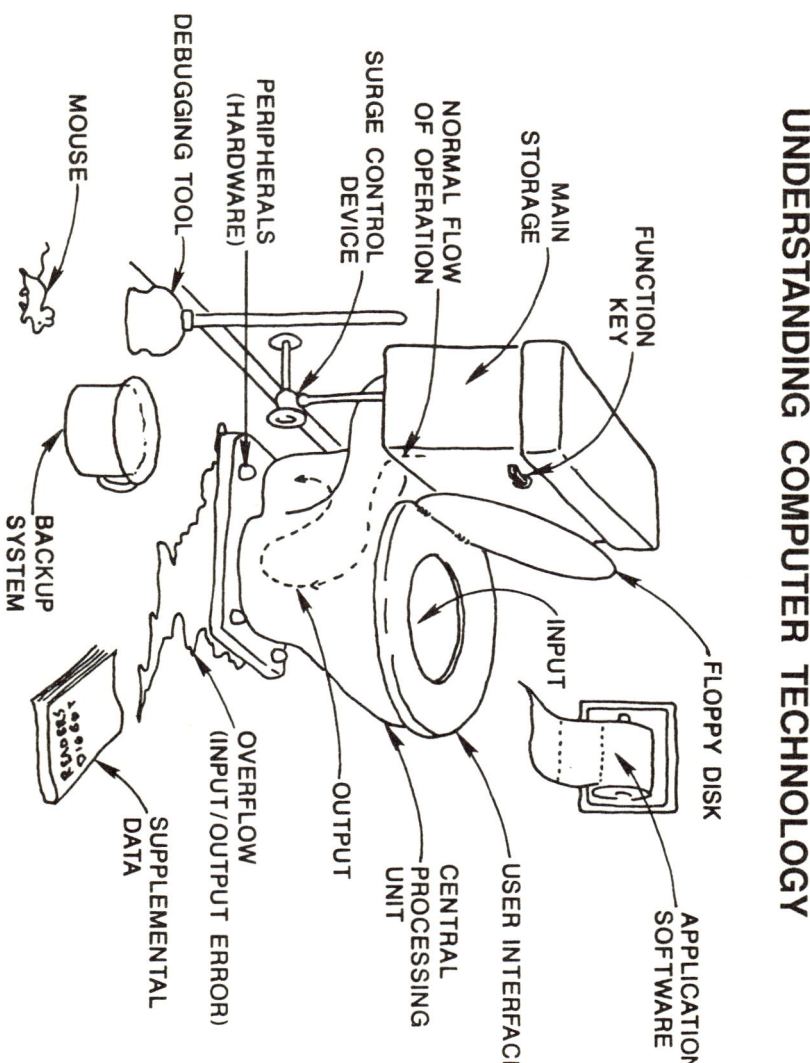

UNDERSTANDING COMPUTER TECHNOLOGY

Title varies, also "Understanding the Technology." Copies received in April 1989 from Emil D., Ohio, and David H., Kansas; in May from Jackie Y., Wisconsin; in Aug. from Len A., New York; in Sept. from Gordon S., Florida; in Oct. from Lon H., California; and in Nov. from Frank N., Kentucky.

TERMS OF ABUSE, TERMS OF ENDEARMENT, AND PET NAMES FOR BREASTS AND OTHER NAUGHTY BODY PARTS

Reinhold Aman

I. INTRODUCTION

The "nice" and "nasty" terms for breasts and genitals, as well as pet names for these organs presented here, are the first result of my *Maledicta Onomastic Questionnaire*. With this MOQ, I am collecting onomastic and semantic material deemed unfit for study by the cowardly and prudish establishment philologists and linguists. The acronym MOQ also mocks the University of Wisconsin's castrated and undaring DARE questionnaire and *Dictionary of American Regional English*.

My questionnaire consists of several hundred items organized by various categories. The number of items, about 500, seems to be the main reason why only 5% of the 6,000 recipients of the MOQ filled it out. Still, the terms collected so far in this ongoing project are overwhelming and will be presented in various articles like this one.

This article deals only with one short section from the MOQ, namely "Terms of Abuse and Endearment." There is a much longer, detailed section called "Body Parts" in the questionnaire that so far has yielded over 3,000 terms for *breasts*, *penis*, *vulva* and *vagina* alone and tens of thousands of terms for other topics—from excretions to angry utterances—familar to the most prudish professor but deemed too vulgar to investigate.

The terms are divided into various groups: in *general* and *descriptive* ones which, in the case of penis, show the designations for all kinds of such organs—whether they be big or small, thick or thin, long or short, soft or hard, straight or bent, wrinkled or smooth, and whatever else penes look like and are given names to characterize their appearance and functions. As to female breasts, the descriptive terms are designations for every conceivable type: big and small, hard and soft, pendulous, leathery, asymmetrical, and more. There are far too many terms to be included in this article; they will be presented later and, ultimately, in my **DRAT**, the *Dictionary of Regional Anatomical Terms*.

Another two groups, collected through Part 6 of the MOQ, are presented below. They cover *endearing* and *abusive* terms for sexual body parts, as well as *pet names* for bawdy body parts used by individuals and their spouses or friends.

The terms gathered for this study can be organized in many ways. Rather than boring you with too many statistics and tables, I will present some general comments on the findings and list the most commonly-cited endearing and offensive names, with a few remarks about my informants.

The personal information provided by participants in the ongoing MOQ survey includes their level of education, profession, and other matters. For this study, I have limited the personal data to geographic location, age, religion, race, and sex. The last item is very precise, thanks to the courage of my informants who indicated whether they are heterosexual, homosexual, or bisexual, which should make a difference in their vocabulary, especially in language dealing with sexuality.

The *sex* of the informants was the only significant factor as to whether they considered certain body-part terms "nice" or "nasty." The other characteristics did not, neither *age*, which ranges from 14 to 76 years, nor *race*, whether white, black, American Indian, Hispanic, Asian or mixed. *Religion* also shows no influence, ranging from Orthodox Jews and Roman Catholics to Greek Orthodox and Atheists. Finally, the *geographic background* of informants shows little difference in nice and nasty terms, whether they are from the United States, Canada, Great Britain, South Africa, Australia, or New Zealand. However, in the "Body Parts" section of the MOQ mentioned earlier, there are great differences in terms collected so far, especially those from Great Britain and Canada. Also, the foreign-language material received, in Dutch, French, German, Italian, Polish, Spanish, and Yiddish, provides interesting insights.

So that you get an idea of who my helpful informants are, a few numbers are necessary: as to *sex*, of the 318 total replies 86 are female and 232 are male; or, more specifically, 196 are heterosexual males, 22 homosexual males, and 14 bisexual males, as well as 78 heterosexual females, 2 lesbians, and 6 bisexual females. As to *race*, 308 are white, 8 are black, and 2 are of mixed background. By *religion*, 84 are Catholic, 35 Jewish, 35 Methodist, 108 practice no religion, and the remaining 56 are of various persuasions.

II. TERMS OF ENDEARMENT AND ABUSE

A. Breasts: "Nice" Terms

Regarding *terms of endearment and abuse for women's breasts*, of the 318 informants 291 provided nice terms, while 29 did not; 251 provided nasty terms, but 67 use no nasty terms. The most common nice terms for breasts are, by decreasing frequency: **breasts** (110, or about one-third of the respondents), **tits** (73), **boobs** (65), **titties** (30), and **boobies** (13). Other multiple entries are **bosom** or **bosoms** (8), knockers (8), jugs (6), 4 each chest and melons, tomatoes (3), and 2 each bazooms, bust, globes, hooters, mammaries, and teats.

The remaining nice terms were single occurrences, sometimes given with preceding adjectives: **beautiful chest, beautiful pair, blossoms, boobulars, borstjes** (Dutch, "breasts"), **bubbies, bumpers, cantaloupes, chichis** (Spanish, "tits"), **chichitas** (Spanish, "titties"), **cycuszki** (Polish, diminutive of **cycki,** cf. German *Zitze*, "teat"), **dairy farm, diddies, dugs, figure, frontage, groodies, headlights, juicy peaches, love-pillows, mazoomas, mounds, mountains, Möppchen** (German, diminutive, unknown meaning), **nay-nays, nice handful, nice puppies, nice set, norks, pair, peaches, pechitos** (Spanish, "breasties"), **pretty lungs, procelain spheres** (reported by a bisexual male), **rising beauties, set of jugs, soft cadaby** (unknown meaning), **sweat-glands, sweetest valley, tetinas** and **tetitas** (Spanish, "titties"), **the girls, tsitskelakh** (Yiddish, "titties"), and **the warmest valley.**

B. Breasts: "Nasty" Terms

While *tits* was commonly cited as a nice term (73 times), it was also considered a nasty term for breasts, 116 times, sometimes even by the same informants. Many qualified their responses in such cases by saying that it depends on the context, that is, who uses the term *tits* under what circumstances, with what tone of voice, facial expression, and the like. Also, they noted that the nice or nasty connotation is established by the preceding adjective. For example, in "You have great tits" or "What a lovely pair of tits!" the word is positive, nice, whereas in "ugly tits" or "Look at her sagging tits," the word *tits* has negative connotations. Still, in absolute terms, *tits* is considered by almost twice as many people nasty rather than nice.

Negatively-valued or nasty terms for breasts, in order of frequency, are: **tits** (116), **jugs** (23), **dugs** (20), **boobs** (18), **knockers** (13), **udders** (9), **bags** (7), 4 each **cans** and **melons**, 3 each **cow-tits, mosquito-bites, sagging tits,** and **titties**. Two responses each: **balloons, breasts, fried eggs, fuckin' tits, knobs, pancakes,** and **saggy tits**.

The following nasty terms were reported once each. In several cases, I have included the adjectives that were given with the nouns: "anything besides *breasts*," **bazooms, beaver-tails, bellys, body, boulders, chest, draggy udders, dried-up titties, droopers, dzwony** (Polish, "bells"), **Euter** (German, "udder"), **fat ugly wrinkled bottles, fat-sacks, fatty breasts, flab hangings, flabby melons, flapjacks, floppers, floppy tits, floppy whites, flops, globes, hairy stubs, hanging tits, Hänger** (German, "hangers," "hanging ones"), **honkers, lumps, lung-nuts, massive mammaries, milkers, milk-buckets, milk-glands, milk-sacks, molehills, no tits, old saggy tits, paps, peanuts, pimientos fritos** (Spanish, "fried green peppers"), **pimples, pimples on chest, pus glands, rocks, sagging summer squash, saggy pig tits, scar-crossed prunes, shitbags, skin, slugs, sweater-meat, teats, tieten** (Dutch, "teats"), **tired old tits, tube-socks with a golfball, ugly fat knockers, ugly jugs, waterbags,** and **wrinkled tits**.

Bosoms is used quite often, even though this plural is wrong, because *bosom* means both breasts. A woman can't have *bosoms*, unless she has a second set of breasts (preferably on her back, for dancing). The only woman I can think of who had *bosoms* was the Greco-Roman goddess Artemis or Diana of Ephesus who, as shown on a statue, sported at least 19 breasts—the ideal patron saint of the typical American mammophile.

Comparing *boobs* with *tits*, 65 informants think *boobs* is a nice term, while 18 think it is a nasty one. This 3:1 ratio shows that *boobs* is considered by most people to be a nice term. In the case of *tits*, and remembering the earlier comments about context, 73 respondents consider it a nice term, whereas 116 think it is a nasty word. As to the gender of informants, 14 females say that *boobs* is a nice term, but 10 think it is nasty. Eleven females think *tits* is a nice term, but twice as many, 22, consider it nasty. Eight homosexual and bisexual men think *boobs* is nice, while 2 say it is nasty. Seven gay males say that *tits* is nice, and 10 think it is nasty. As to lesbian and bisexual females, 2 think *boobs* is nice, but not one thinks it is nasty. Two of them say *tits* is nice, but 5 consider it nasty. See **Appendix** for details on region, sex, age, religion, and race of informants for this section.

C. Penis: "Nice" Terms

Of our informants, 252 provided nice terms for penis, 66 did not. The most frequently-cited nice name is **cock** (86), followed by **dick** (37), 17 each **pecker** and **penis**, **prick** (15), 8 each **love-muscle** and **peter**, **rod** (5), 4 each **pee-pee, sausage, tool, wang, weenie,** and **willy,** 3 each **dong, meat and, shlong** (Yiddish, "snake"), 2 each **dickie, dink, goober, little friend, love-stick, manhood, member, thing,** and **wanger.**

All others are cited only once: **baldheaded candidate, bat, best friend, big one, big piece of meat, big wand, cock of death, dinghy, dog, doohickey, dork, ducky-bird, dyduś** (Polish, no lit. meaning), **fat peter, friend, hacker, hampton, hampton wick, hard-on, horse's cock, hunky, jelly-bean, John Thomas, John Willie, johnson** (a black term, named after a large railroad brake lever), **joint, jolly roger, jongeheer** (Dutch, "young fellow"), **joystick, knob,** lingam (Sanskrit, from the *Kamasutra*), **little man, lollipop, love machine, love-gun, love-wand, mały** (Polish, "little one"), **member virile, muscle, nob, oak tree, one-eyed trouser-trout, organ, parts, penie, pet snake, pichita de oro** (Spanish, "golden cock"), **Piephahn** (German children's language, "dicky-bird," lit. "peeping cock"), **pink torpedo, pitonguita** (Spanish, "little python"), **privates, pud, puss, pussy, rig, Schniedelwutz** (German, unknown meaning, but dialectal *Wutz* means "pig" and "rolled object"), **Schniepel** (German children's language, lit. "tip, point"), **schwanger** (unknown meaning; perhaps from German, "pregnant"), **shmok** (Yiddish, lit. probably "snake"), **silky appendage, snatch pointer, soft, steel-rod, sugar-stick, third leg, throbbing member, throbbing muscle of pure love, tool of pleasure, trout, unit, wiener,** and **yang fella.**

D. Penis: "Nasty" Terms

Now we come to nasty names for the penis. Of the 318 total, 246 informants provided nasty terms, but 72 had none. As can be expected, about a dozen of the nasty terms for penis also show up in the nice column. Here are the nasty terms, again by decreasing frequency of citation: **prick** (81), **cock** (54), **dick** (21), **shlong** (8), **pecker** (6), 5 each **needle-dick, dong** and **dork,** and 3 times each **pencil-dick, penis, salami, shmok,** and **wee-wee.** There were 2 mentions each of **fuck-stick, thing, tool, weenie,** and **worm.**

The following terms appear once each as nasty terms for the penis, several times prefixed with *little*: **big clit, bitte** (French, "dick"), **blood-breaker, bug-fucker, capullito** (Spanish, "little [plant] bud"), **chuj** (Russian and Polish, "prick"), **cod, colostomy, crank, cunt-stabber, dangle-dong, dead worm, dimple-dick, dink, dipstick, dog, dribble-cock, dust cover for cunt, flaccid prick, fuckpole,**

God's revenge on a woman (submitted by a female), **gourd, green-colored dick, half a cob, joy-stick, lifeless, limp-dick, limp-prick, little dick, little peter, little pinkie, little sliver of flesh, little stick, little wiener, little worm, lul** (Dutch, "prick"), **man-meat, middle leg, millimeter-peter, minus a pinus, nothin' cock, old goat-peter, old warty cod, organ, pee-wee, penal dick, pichicorta** (Spanish, "short dick"), **piddler, pimple, pimple-prick, pine, piss-pipe, pisser, pissworm, poker, pots** (Yiddish), **puny prick, pus-rod, rod, rotten meat, scorz** (unknown meaning), **scrawny piece, shaft, shmendrik** (Yiddish, "little nobody, nincompoop"), **shorty, shriveller, shvants** (Yiddish, "tail"), **small, stupid dink, syphilitic prick, teeny, tossergash, ugly little dog-dick, unit, useless, verga** (Spanish, "dick"), **wet noodle, wet spaghetti, wimpy dick,** and **wrinkled dick.**

E. Vulva: "Nice" Terms

In this section I'll present names for vulva and vagina considered nice. Many informants, as also the general population, do not distinguish between *vulva* (the outer parts) and *vagina* (the channel, sheath).

As in the case of penis, many terms for vulva considered nasty also appear as nice terms in this collection. Of the 318 informants, 234 provided nice terms for vulva, while 84 had no nice name for it. Those who did not provide a nice name were of all sexual persuasions, by the way. Nasty terms were provided by 274 respondents, but 44 have no negative terms. By frequency, here is a list of nice names for vulva and vagina: the most frequent name was **pussy** (125), followed by **cunt** (20 times, including by 4 females), 9 each **snatch** and **vagina, twat** (8), **honey-pot** (6), 5 times each **beaver** and **muff,** 4 times each **love-tunnel** and **puss,** 3 times each **cunny, fanny, hole, love-box,** and quim, and twice each **cooze, furburger, love-nest,** and **rosebud.**

Other nice names mentioned once are: **baby-factory, belle chose** (French, "beautiful thing"), **box, bush, centric-part, chochito** (Spanish, "pussy"), **conchita** (Spanish, "little shell"), **dessert, Döschen** (German, "little box"), **fascinating furpiece, fount of femininity, fun-zone, fur-pie, fuzzy-muzzy, garden of love, Gizelle** (name), **hairy Mary, Holiday Inn, honeydew, inner self, inside, jelly-roll, joy-furrow, kitty, kitty-kat, kuciapka** (Polish, no literal meaning), **li'l pussy, lips, little kitten, love-cleft, love-organ, love-sheath, lovely flower, lunch, mick, Muschi** (German, "kitty-cat" and woman's name), **nookie, parts, peach-fish, play-pen, pocket, poo-poo, poontang, poozle, pud, slit, snackbar, sneetje** (Dutch, "little slit"), **soft furry mound of love, spread, sweet cunt, sweet pussy, tee-tee, thing, tight snatch, treasure-box, tunnel of love, vag, vertical smile, warm place, wazoo, wily,** and **yoni** (Sanskrit, from the *Kamasutra*).

F. Vulva: "Nasty" Terms

In his *1811 Dictionary of the Vulgar Tongue*, Captain Grose wrote that C**t is "a nasty name for a nasty thing." The most commonly-cited nasty word for the female organ of lust is still **cunt,** 179 times out of 318 responses, plus 14 instances where it is preceded by a specific adjective. Next in frequency is **gash** (20), **hole** (17), **twat** (14), **pussy** (13), 9 each **slit** and **snatch,** 3 each **canyon, smelly cunt,** and **stinkhole,** 2 each **box, crack, dirty cunt, fish,** and **stinky cunt.**

The remaining terms appear once each: "anything related to fish or smell," **ass, bayonet wound, bearded clam, beaver-trap, big cunt, big, cave, cheese factory, chocho gordo** (Spanish, "fat cunt"), **clit, cow-cunt, crater, dirty** hole, empty tunnel, envy-city, face, fanny, fat rabbit, fishbox, flabby cunt, foul-smelling cunt, fuck-hole, greedy pussy-lips, kut (Dutch, "cunt"), man-eater, man-entrapment, man-trap, Möse (German, "twat"), open well, open wound, panocha (Spanish, lit. "coarse brown sugar"), pee-hole, pestosa (Spanish, "diseased, stinky one"), piss-flaps, pizda (Polish, "cunt"), podrida (Spanish, "rotten, putrid one"), pox-ridden cunt, prat, rat-hole, rotten crotch, sardine can, scabby cunt, Schlabberfotze (German, "slobbery, watery cunt"), scum-twat, scumbag, siffed-up cunt-hole (from *syphilis*), slash, slime-hole, slippery slut, sloppy bot, smell-hole, smelly pussy, snapper, something crawled in and died, sperm-canal, split-tail, stink-pit, tuna, vag, vagina, Votze (German, "cunt"; also spelled Fotze), wet-mop, wound, wrinkled cunt, and yeast-mill.

III. GENITAL PET NAMES

After this litany of nasties, I'll present some comments on pet names for sexual organs. There were fewer than expected actual pet names, which was a surprise. Even many homosexuals, many of whom appear to be very much in touch with their genitals, as it were, have fewer pet names than expected. One should think that now as we are entering the Golden Age of Masturbation—no thanks to AIDS—people would be paying more attention to their only truly safe sex partner and have more appealing names than "my thing" or "the old fella."

Martha Cornog has published several articles on genital pet names, including "Tom, Dick and Hairy" in *Maledicta* 5 (1981), pp. 31-40 (followed by my "What Is This Thing Called, Love?" pp. 41-44) and "Names for Sexual Body Parts: Regularities in 'Personal' Naming Behavior" in the *Festschrift in Honor of Allen Walker Read*, DeKalb, Ill.,

1988, pp. 133-151. This topic also pops up in unexpected places, such as in the Sex & Health advice column in *Glamour*, "Why would a woman nickname her lover's penis?" (Sept. 1987, p. 412, sent by Bruce R.), where some dorky guy is "troubled by the fact that she's [his lover] given my penis a nickname." In *Maledicta* we also feature from time to time updates on new genital pet names. Doris L., Chicago, informed me that Henry Miller called his penis "John Thursday" in *Opus Pistorum*.

There are also jokes about penis pet names. Ingrid B. told me a German joke about what European women call a penis: German women call it "Curtain" (comes down after every act); English women call it "Gentleman" (rises in front of a lady); French women name it "Chanson" (goes from mouth to mouth); and Russian women call it "Guerrilla" (you never know if it's coming from the front or the rear).

There were some surprises in the genital pet name section of the MOQ. Informants not only have pet names for their own and their friends' sexual organs, but also for other body parts and related equipment. For example, one woman calls her left breast "Alice" and her right breast "Phyllis." Another woman names her breasts "Judo" and "Jello." An 18-year-old calls hers *Tasty* and *Delicious*. Several years ago, when I was introduced to the wife of a New York friend and sex researcher, I was tempted to ask her whether she calls her breasts "Schleswig" and "Holstein," respectively, as her ancestors came from the German state called Schleswig-Holstein. Considering the importance of breasts in many cultures, mammaries ought to produce playful mammonyms, such as *Tutti Frutti*, *Lo & Behold*, *Frick & Frack*, or *Sweet & Low*.

Two males have pet names for their **hands**: one calls his right hand "Rosy Palm," after the well-known "Rosy Palm and her five daughters," and another calls it "Little Jo-Jo," after his girlfriend's name. One lady wrote me that she calls her right hand "Little Reinhold." Speaking of which, a lawyer in Seattle is such a fan of *Maledicta* that he and his girlfriend have pet-named his penis after me, calling it "Rey." Such honor!

Testicles also have pet names. One professor of biology calls his testes "John Henry." Bill A.'s 24-year-old wife calls his penis "Little Buddy" and his testicles "Little Buddy's buddies."

Interestingly, **vibrators** also have pet names. In their article in this volume, Salmons & Macaulay reported "Steely Dan" (in William Burroughs's *Naked Lunch*). One of our New York informants calls her vibrator "Charlie," and a Wisconsin musician calls hers "B-flat," after the sound it emits at low speed. She also has a second pet name for it, the German "Wunderorgasmusmaschine."

To stimulate readers into pet-naming their privates, I have suggested several pet names in *Maledicta* 5, such as *Sumer* (it's *icumen in*), or *My Prince* (someday he'll come) or *The South* (it will rise again), as well as *Trouble* (many men like to get into it), but my efforts seem to have been largely wasted. Still, in personal correspondence, some confide in me what they call their own or their partner's organ. For example, a London educator calls the penis of her husband, an actor, "Yorick" (from *Hamlet*'s "Alas, poor Yorick, he is dead"). And a lady in Chicago suggested that I call my appendage *Bavarian Bratwurst*.

A. Penis Pet Names

Of the 204 pet names for penis collected so far, 117 are used by heterosexual men for their own organ, and 49 by their wives or girlfriends. Pet names used by homosexuals are discussed later.

Many of the penis pet names used by males are common terms, such as **dick** (15), **cock** (13), **pecker** (6), **prick** (5), **willie** (4), and twice **boy**, but there are very specific ones, of which the cleverest is by an Ohio physician who calls his penis "His Royal Highness, Prince Everhard of the Netherlands." Other pet names are often prefixed with *my* or *my little*. Here is the list of penis pet names gathered so far: **ace** (as in "ace in the hole"), **ascent, baby's arm, banger, big fella, big log, blue-steel, boy** (as in "You hungry, boy?"), **chachiporra** (Spanish, "big stick"), **Charlie, chinchin** (Japanese childrens' language), **o-chinchin** (the same, with the honorific prefix *o-*), **crank, dong, Elmer Pudd, flip** (from Philip), **Fred, friend, godgiven groover, Harvey** (after the giant rabbit in the movie), **husky, il mio amico** (Italian, "my friend"), **it, John, John Henry Longfellow** (*John* and *Henry* are pet names for his testicles), **John Thomas, joy-stick, junior, knob, leather cigar, little boy blue** (as in "come blow my horn"), **little buddy, little dickie, little guy with the German helmet** (from *German helmet*, a term for glans), **little guy, little John, love-muscle, love pump, love scepter, ma bitte** (French, "my dick"), **mack, mate, Milton, Mr. Happy, Mr. Johnson, Mr. Penis, my friend, my little friend, my thang, oak tree, old baldy, Opie, oral tube** (as in "Talk to me through this tube"), **Oscar, Ozymandias** ("...and despair," from Shelley's sonnet), **Pedro, pee-dee, pee-pee, penis, Percy, Pete, Peter, Pogo, purple throbber, rhythm and blues, rod, Roger, Roscoe** (twice), **Rufus, Schniepel** (German, 'dicky,' lit. "point, tip"), **simba, spunky, tally-whacker, tarzoon, teenager, the ever-famous, thing, Thomas Jefferson** (as in "all men are created equal"), **Throckmorton, tiddelly pod, Tom, tool of pleasure, toy, unit, Vivitar** (after the enlarging camera lens), **Walter, wang, war-head, weapon, wee-wee, Pwicked Willie, Winston** (as in "tastes good, like a cigarette should"), and **Yogi** (after the cartoon character).

Women use pet names for the penis of their husbands

or male friends, too, sometimes the same names as their male partners use. **Dick** was most frequent, with 4 listings, followed by 2 each **cock, Fred, him, John Thomas, little friend, tool, weenie,** and **whang.** The remaining occur once each: **ace, bat, big hard hot throbbing dick, cutums, deck, Freddie** (after her husband), **goober, good buddy, himself, his highness, junior, little dickie, little Elvis, little one, lollipop, Lou** (husband's name), **love-wand, Matthew** (husband's name), **moby** (from *Moby Dick*), **mouse, Mr. Happy, Mr. Microphone** (as in "I'll be back to pick it up"), **Mr. Wang, my fella, my friend, panchito** (Spanish, "little belly" and man's name), **pecker-mine, pee-pee, peeper, Pete, rod, Russell the love muscle, sausage & eggs** (for penis and testes), **special friend, super-dong, tally-whacker, the indicator, toy, Walter, Willie, Willy, winger,** and **woofer.**

B. Vulva and Vagina Pet Names

Out of the 86 women participating in the MOQ survey, 34 have pet names for their own vulva, and 101 males use pet names for their wives' or female friends' genitals.

The women's most frequent pet name is **pussy** (13), but terms considered nasty by others also appear in this listing, often preceded by *my*: twice each **box, pussy,** and **vulva,** and once each **coochy, cunny, cunt, friend, furry bits, good pussy, herself, hot wet pussy, junioress, Little Debbie, Little kitty, Matthilda, mouse's hole, my burger, peach-fish, precious pudenda, Priscilla, pussy galore, pussy, sex, snatch, tesorito** (Spanish, "little treasure"), **Virginia,** and **womanhood.**

The most frequent pet name for vulva by males also is **pussy** (41 times), followed by **cunt** (7), **vagina** (4), **twat** (3), and 2 each **bush, honey-pot, lips, muffy, peach-fish, rosebud, snatch,** and **sweet cunt.** Other pet names mentioned are: **belle chose** (French, "beautiful thing"), **box, buggy, cave, chatte** (French, "cat"), **chochito mío** (Spanish, "my little pussy"), **cock, coño** (Spanish, "cunt"), **coral, cunnie, cunny, Delores, Döschen** (German, "little box"), **fanny, flaps, furburger, fuzzy-bunny, Gizelle, hair-pie, home sweet home, honey-pie, jelly cave, jelly-roll, junioress, Kathy's pink surprise** (after a dish named thus, and his wife's name), **kitty, lei** (Italian, "she, her"), **li'l pussy, liesje** (Dutch, Lizzie and *lies*, "groin"), **Louis, love-box, love-nest, lunch, Magdalena** (after a very religious girlfriend), **Mary, Maxine, mick, money-pot, mouse, Ms. Mary, muff, Muschi** (German, "kitty-cat" and woman's name), **nether lips, pencil-sharpener, poussé** (fake French), **pretty little thing, princess, pussy cat, pussy-lips, Sally, Satchmo, satin doll, snutchie, squeeky, sugarbush, the Beave** (from *beaver*), **the Deep** ("she doesn't like it," he added), **thing, tukso** (Tagalog, "temptation"), **tunnel of love, tush, warm fuzzy, ying-yang**, and **zouzoune** (his wife is French).

C. Genital Pet Names Used by Homosexuals and Bisexuals

The remaining pet names are those provided by male and female homosexuals and bisexuals. Of 36 informants, 21 *homosexual and bisexual men* have pet names for their *own penis*, namely: **Baby Huey, best friend, Chester, big dick, cock** (2), **cunt-leg, dick** (2), **John Henry** ("the steel-driving man"), **John Thomas, Junior, little thing, my ten inches, Omar, pee-pee** (2), **Peter, piece, pinky weenie, prick, Schwanz** (German, "tail") and **willy**.

Pet names by *homosexual males* for their *friends' penis*: **cock, dick, handsome, little** (plus man's name), **love tool, Omar Junior, pee-pee, Peter, piece, pretty-dick, pussy, Schwanz, shlong, tally-whacker**, and **tiny tot**.

Pet names by *bisexual men* for their *friends' penis*: **cock** (2), **cute little pee-pee, dingus, joy-stick,** and **junior**.

One *lesbian* reported a pet name for her *own vulva*: **Penelope** (she's of Greek origin).

Pet names by *bisexual women* for their *own vulva* are: **clit, my pussy-cat, pussy** (2), **tee-tee,** and **vagina**.

Pet names by *lesbians* for their *friends' vulva*: **Fifi, little baby,** and **Monique**.

Finally, pet names by *bisexual females* for their *friends' vulva*: **clit, flower, fur-patch, love-nest, pussy, tee-tee,** and **vagina**.

IV. CONCLUDING REMARKS

So much for a first look at abusive, endearing, and pet names for body parts that *all* people have, including hypocritical scholars, journalists, book reviewers, and popular word gurus.

As is the case with human beings who are attacked with derogatory names if they deviate from the norm—fat, skinny, short, tall, ugly, smelly, useless ones—body parts, too, are given deprecatory names if they deviate from the norm of a society or an individual.

Also, as in the case of people, there are many more negatively-valued (nasty) than positively-valued (nice) terms for body parts. From these large collections of negatively-valued data one can establish what the ideal, "normal" person and body parts look like. From the nasty terms for penis and breasts, for instance, one can see what the ideal body parts should look like. As the nasty terms for penis predominantly deal with shortness, smallness, softness, uselessness, and illness, one knows that a so-called normal penis should be long, thick, hard, useful, and healthy. Similarly, the negatively-valued term for breasts tell us that "normal" breasts should not be small, flat, dried up, fat, wrinkled, floppy or saggy.

The norms for people and body parts vary from culture to culture, from epoch to epoch, but some characteristics are probably universal. I say "probably" because nobody has studied or even collected negative terms from most languages. This is where *Maledicta* comes in, to some degree continuing the frank work of late 19th-century and early 20th-century European researchers of folklore and offensive language whose work was also discredited by the hypocritical, brainless, repressed, prudish, intellectually dull establishment. Many of those earlier researchers who published their findings in *Am Ur-Quell*, *Kryptádia* and *Anthropophyteia* happened to be Jewish, which did not help much in anti-Semitic Europe. They were physically abused, driven out of the countries, or worse. I won't be driven out of the country, but I certainly "don't get no respect"— from the mousebrains, that is, whether they are cacademics or the general public. Luckily, enough intelligent people see the deeper significance of what I am doing, helping me carry on my lonely but cheerful uphill struggle. The easiest way to help me continue is to fill out questionnaires. Thus, when the revised MOQ appears in a future *Maledicta*, please don't give me excuses for failing to complete the questionnaire and don't be so bloody lethargic. Unlike certain shameless cacademics, I am not asking you for money, just for your time.

A much shorter version of this material was presented at the annual meeting of the American Name Society in Chicago, 16 October 1988.

V. APPENDIX

Nasty Terms for Women's Breasts
(MOQ Nr. T- 06)
by Geographic Distribution

It would take many pages of this publication to print out the results of MOQ information gathered so far. All of that material will appear, one day, in my *Dictionary of Regional Anatomical Terms*. The following list is just a sample of what can be done. The data can be extracted, sorted and arranged in any way needed, by age, sex, religion, race, profession, geographic location, and any combination thereof. For this list, I arranged the information by geography: first the USA, alphabetically by state (not all states are represented because of the lethargy of our readers), and within each state by postal ZIP code. Then follow English-speaking foreign countries, then other foreign countries.

The informant's confidential code shows the *region* where the terms are in use. It consists of abbreviated names of states or countries, postal codes, and initials.

The next column lists the *terms*. Missing terms (-) indicate that the informant did not supply any.

The next column shows the *sex* of the informant:
m = male heterosexual; **f** = female heterosexual; **g** = gay male; **l** = lesbian female; **x** = bisexual female; **z** = bisexual male.

The *age* is indicated by year of birth (new method) or by the actual age or by a letter indicating the age group:
t = 11-20 years; **y** = 21-35; **m** = 36-50; **e** = 51-65; **o** = over 65 years.

The informant's *religion* shows the current affiliation; where two are given (separated by a hyphen), the first is the religion in which the informant was brought up, the second is the current affiliation, if any.

Race: **b** = Black, **i** = American Indian, **w** = White

ABUSIVE, ENDEARING AND PET NAMES FOR GENITALS • 67

ABBREVIATIONS FOR RELIGIONS

agnos	= agnostic	mo.syn	= Missouri Synod
amer	= American	ortho	= orthodox
bapt	= Baptist	pract	= practicing
cath	= Catholic	presb	= Presbyterian
ch	= church	prot	= Protestant
congr	= Congregationalist	ref	= reform(ed)
cons	= conservative	sev.day	= 7th-Day Adventist
denom	= denominational	south	= southern
episc	= Episcopalian	unit	= Unitarian
meth	= Methodist	witch	= witchcraft

Region / Code	Term	Sex	Age	Religion	Race
Alabama					
AL36106JT	tits	m	m	south bapt - atheist	w
Arizona					
AZ85201LT	-	f	e	cath - none	w
AZ85741DL	-	m	o	bapt - none	w
California					
CA90000LF	jugs	m	y	atheist - agnos	w
CA90006DV	-	g	y	presb - christian	w
CA90024LL	knockers	f	y	jewish ref - agnos/atheist	w
CA90025PK	boobs	f	y	jewish ref - atheist	w
CA90028RS	tits	l	m	jewish -none	w
CA90036JS	jugs	z	e	bapt - none	b
CA90039AN	tits	x	m	bapt - taoist	b
CA90046RD	tits	g	m	meth - none	w
CA90057RM	boobs	m	o	prot	w
CA90069AN	tits	z	y	cath - none	w
CA90069AR	breasts	g	e	ch of england - atheist	w
CA90069MM	lumps	m	y	atheist	w
CA90210JK	saggy tits, knockers	m	y	cath - non-pract	w
CA90210RR	-	g	y	disciples of christ - none	w
CA90403RW	jugs	m	y	jewish cons - jewish	w
CA90405BR	-	m	m	jewish ref	w
CA91214GT	fatty breasts	f	y	mormon - agnos	w
CA91326SF	boobs	f	m	agnos	w
CA91403ET	dried-up titties	m	y	cath - none	w
CA91423RC	-	m	e	meth - unit	w
CA91604GL	bazooms	m	e	prot - atheist	w

Region / Code	Term	Sex	Age	Religion	Race
CA91605MG	slugs	m	m	jewish cons - jewish ref	w
CA91701CR	tits	f	m	agnos	w
CA91786DM	tits	m	y	episc	w
CA91786KM	knockers	f	y	episc	w
CA92083GR	boobs	f	1961	none - pagan	w
CA92109DF	tits	l	y	greek ortho - none	w
CA92120RD	-	m	e	presb - atheist	w
CA92277PS	breasts	z	1936	cath - atheist	w
CA92624NL	bags, tits	m	m	south bapt - prot	w
CA92703MA	knockers	f	y	lutheran - cath	w
CA92705EC	boobs	f	o	prot - deist/agnos	w
CA92706PK	shit-bags	m	y	agnos - pantheist	w
CA92715LH	jugs	m	m	meth/presb - none	w
CA93639FS	cans	m	y	cath	w
CA93726GK	tits	m	e	jewish - atheist	w
CA94025DW	dugs, udders	g	m	south meth - agnos	w
CA94101AN	tits	z	1959	none	w
CA94115MP	floppers	m	y	cath - none	w
CA94115MT	-	g	y	episc - agnos	w
CA94117SB	knockers	z	e	agnos	w
CA94702MZ	-	m	1950	jewish - none	w
CA94703BB	dugs	g	1947	meth - agnos	w
CA94704RS	dugs	m	m	jewish ref	w
CA94705MJ	tits	m	y	agnos	w
CA94707RS	tits	m	m	prot - none	w
CA94903DW	dugs	m	m	atheist	w
CA95008LT	anything besides breasts	f	1954	jewish atheist - none	w
CA95050JJ	cow-tits	g	e	cath	w
CA95128LC	boobs	f	y	none	w
CA95628RR	jugs	f	1948	meth/presb - neo-paggan /witch	w
CA95671JG	udders	m	y	cath	w
CA95671JL	jugs	m	1957	atheist	w
CA95696DC	body	z	1957	cath - none	w
CA95719RM	tits	m	e	prot - agnos	w
CA95827JA	knobs, tits	m	m	presb - none	w

Colorado

CO80207DB	-	m	e	bapt - none	b
CO81612MS	tits	m	o	none	w

Connecticut

CT06071JS	bellys	m	m	cath - christian	w
CT06239RG	mosquito bites	m	y	none	i
CT06430AN	sagging	m	e	jewish ref - agnos	w

Region / Code	Term	Sex	Age	Religion	Race
District of Columbia					
DC20002KC	hairy stubs	f	y	meth - none	w
DC20007SG	tits	m	t	jewish ref - agnos	w
DC20024KP	-	m	m	meth - atheist	w
DC20560CS	boobs	m	m	quaker - atheist	w
Florida					
FL32347JG	udders	m	m	bapt - atheist	w
FL32804AP	tits	m	y	lutheran	w
FL33040KJ	tits	m	y	prot - agnos	w
Georgia					
GA30067MO	tits	m	e	jewish	w
GA30318CW	jugs	f	t	bapt - holiness	b
Hawaii					
HI96813BB	-	m	m	episc	w
Illinois					
IL60047DW	tits	f	e	presbterian	w
IL60047WW	bags	m	e	cath	w
IL60060MM	jugs	m	y	lutheran	w
IL60201EW	(all but *breasts* are nasty)	m	1935	jewish	w
IL60202RF	milkers, udders	m	1945	lutheran - agnos	w
IL60302LM	-	f	y	atheist - theist	w
IL60304MF	titties	m	y	cath - agnos	w
IL60426SW	flab hangings	m	t	satanist	b
IL60542LS	tits	m	m	presb - lutheran	w
IL60600FF	tits	m	m	meth - atheist	w
IL60610GF	dugs	g	1951	dutch ref - presb	w
IL60613ER	floppy whites	m	y	jewish	w
IL60613SW	tits	g	y	cath - none	w
IL60614ER	tits, jugs	f	m	jewish	w
IL60614MH	lung-nuts	m	e	sev.day - none	w
IL60615AN	knockers	f	1962	cath	b
IL60626CW	dugs	f	1953	cath - agnos	w
IL60626SI	-	m	y	cath - christian	w
IL60643DM	dugs	m	1931	presbterian	w
IL60656DM	sagging tits	m	m	cath - none	w
IL60657CH	tits	f	y	jewish cons - agnos	w
IL60657FP	droopers, sweater-meat	m	1942	cath	w
IIL60658RS	tits	m	y	cath	w

Region / Code	Term	Sex	Age	Religion	Race
IL60660AS	tits	m	e	cath - meth	w
IL60660GS	tits	m	y	agnos - atheist	w
IL60660RZ	-	f	y	meth - none	w
IL61277DW	tits	m	y	meth	w
IL62704TS	jugs	m	m	lutheran - agnos	w

Indiana

IN46220EK	bags	f	y	agnos	w
IN46802LC	tits	f	20	prot - none	w
IN47150DC	dugs	z	e	presb - agnos	w
IN47401JB	tired old tits	g	1942	disciples of christ	w
IN47905TG	boobs	f	1957	atheist	w
IN47907ANON	sagging tits	f	1950	cath	w
IN47907MA	boobs	f	1934	christian (non-denom)	w

Kansas

KS64131TW	jugs	x	m	bapt	w

Kentucky

KY40031MA	tits	x	y	cath - none	w
KY40031WW	titties	m	y	bapt	b
KY40205TH	tits	m	m	presbterian	w
KY41101RB	-	m	m	meth - agnos	w

Louisiana

LA70360NL	-	m	e	cath	w
LA70502JH	bags	m	1955	cath	w
LA71058EA	saggin' tits	m	m	south bapt - none	w

Maine

ME04064DP	balloons	g	e	jewish ortho - jewish refo	w
ME04401TK	honkers	f	1949	cath - not practicing	w

Maryland

MD20740DH	sagging tits	m	y	meth - none	w
MD20741WK	tits	m	y	cath	w
MD20782KL	knockers	f	1970	cath - witch	w
MD20783AN	boobs	f	y	meth - episc	w
MD20815KM	tits	m	m	ch of christ - none	w
MD20912EB	peanuts,bags	z	1952	meth - agnos	w
MD20912GP	cow-tits	m	y	greek ortho	w
MD21157PS	tits	m	y	cath	w
MD21204MF	tits, jugs	f	y	cath - none	w
MD21204RS	tits	m	m	cath - not practicing	w
MD21206GD	tits	f	y	cath - presb	w
MD21212GB	-	m	e	bapt- none	w
MD21214MK	pimples	m	m	cath - atheist	w

ABUSIVE, ENDEARING AND PET NAMES FOR GENITALS • 71

Region / Code	Term	Sex	Age	Religion	Race
MD21214TB	jugs, udders, pancakes	x	25	bapt/mormon/cath - agnos	w
MD21225WW	scar-crossed prunes	m	m	meth - agnos	w
MD21228WS	-	m	e	episc (low) - none	w

Massachusetts

Region / Code	Term	Sex	Age	Religion	Race
MA02172MA	tits	m	y	jewish - neo-pagan, hindu	w
MA01570BF	tits	m	t	cath - none	w
MA01588DC	bags, tits	m	t	none	w
MA01614DB	tits	m	y	cath - atheist	w
MA01821SM	-	f	1957	cath - agnos	w
MA02115CP	-	f	m	prot - atheist	w
MA02129AL	-	m	y	jewish agnos - atheist	w
MA02129CP	-	x	y	meth - none	w
MA02144MT	tits	m	1958	episc - none	w
MA02155EA	-	m	y	jewish/agnos - agnos	w
MA02155PP	-	f	y	presb - none	w
MA02766MB	tits	f	1968	jewish cons - atheist	w

Michigan

Region / Code	Term	Sex	Age	Religion	Race
MI48043DD	udders	m	y	christian	w
MI48047LL	-	m	e	prot	w
MI48047ML	-	f	m	meth - none	w
MI48072MK	tits	f	e	presb - belief in force	w
MI48103JM	-	m	y	agnos - atheist	w
MI48152GF	tits	f	y	universalist unit	w
MI49204WF	-	m	y	prot - none	w

Minnesota

Region / Code	Term	Sex	Age	Religion	Race
MN55407JC	-	m	y	presb - atheist	w
MN55409	tits	m	y	prot (congregat) - none	w
MN55414DL	-	m	y	cath	w

Mississippi

Region / Code	Term	Sex	Age	Religion	Race
MS39531PR	-	m	1962	lutheran (mo.syn) - none	w

Missouri

Region / Code	Term	Sex	Age	Religion	Race
MO63100TS	tits	m	1954	prot - undecided	w

Nebraska

Region / Code	Term	Sex	Age	Religion	Race
NE68377HG	milk buckets	m	e	lutheran	w

Nevada

Region / Code	Term	Sex	Age	Religion	Race
NV89102RT	jugs	m	e	meth - unit/inactive	w

Region / Code	Term	Sex	Age	Religion	Race
New Jersey					
NJ07011MC	saggy pig tits	m	m	cath - russian ortho	w
NJ07424WL	flapjacks, mosquito bites	z	y	cath - atheist	w
NJ07885OB	no tits	m	o	congr - none	w
NJ08553WB	tits	m	m	presb - none	w
NJ08628DS	-	m	y	cath - none	w
NJ08854TS	knockers	g	y	south bapt - none	w
NJ08903AM	-	m	m	atheist - none	w
New Mexico					
NM87119RW	tits	m	m	meth	w
New York					
NY10000AN	-	m	e	meth - agnos	w
NY10000BN (NL)	-	g	m	jewish - zen-buddhist	w
NY10000JS	tits	m	e	jewish ref	w
NY10011MB	jugs	m	m	episc - none	w
NY10012RB	boobs	g	e	jewish - none	w
NY10014AN	boobs	g	m	cath - none	w
NY10019AS	udders	f	m	cath - none	w
NY10023GR	pus glands	f	y	greek ortho - none	w
NY10025JF	tits	z	o	cath - atheist	w
NY10032LT	boobs	m	m	jewish ortho - jewish	w
NY10128RM	tits	m	e	south bapt - unit	w
NY10475WR	tits, boobs	m	m	cath - agnos	w
NY10583RL	knockers	m	o	jewish ref	w
NY10591JW	bags	m	t	cath	w
NY10707JM	tits	m	41	cath	w
NY10952RK	tits	m	e	presb	w
NY11200HL	-	m	e	jewish - none/buddhist	w
NY11230RC	boobs	f	y	jewish ref - jews for jesus	w
NY11377JS	tits	m	m	cath	w
NY12123JC	tits	m	m	meth - none	w
NY13681JB	tits	m	o	cath - none	w
NY14063EL	tits	m	e	jewish - none	w
NY14075WK	udder	m	o	cath	w
NY14301EL	tits	m	e	cath - agnos	w
NY14411LT	paps	f	y	prot - atheist	w
NY14411TT	-	m	m	episc - agnos	w
NY14845JH	dugs	m	y	cath - atheist	w
NY14847AW	-	f	e	cath - episc	w

ABUSIVE, ENDEARING AND PET NAMES FOR GENITALS • 73

Region / Code	Term	Sex	Age	Religion	Race
North Dakota					
ND58368BE	boobs	f	y	united meth - none	w
ND58368JE	-	m	y	assembly of god - none	w
Ohio					
OH44113DR	-	m	e	ch of england - atheist	w
OH44504MH	tits	m	t	lutheran	w
OH44511CH	knobs	m	e	lutheran - unit	w
OH45324MR	tits	f	t	presb - none	w
OH45341LH	tits	m	1955	pentecostal	w
OH45371DH	massive mammaries	m	o	meth	w
OH45387RF	-	m	m	jewish atheist - jewish agnos	w
OH45701MM	tube-socks w. a golfball	m	m	meth - agnos	w
Oklahoma					
OK73115TR	-	m	e	meth - none	w
Oregon					
OR97202CR	tits	m	t	swiss ref prot - agnos	w
OR97310JW	fuckin' tits	m	y	cath - none	w
OR97331IP	dugs	m	1950	presb- christian (non-spec)	w
Pennsylvania					
PA15206SM	tits, boobs	f	1962	episc - uncertain	w
PA15226JM	tits, jugs	m	1960	cath - none	w
PA15537DN	dugs	m	m	prot - atheist	w
PA15857JS	saggy tits, draggy udders	m	m	cath - none	w
PA16602KD	globes	m	m	cath - none	w
PA16803DK	-	m	m	cath - none	w
PA17201SS	hanging tits	m	e	jewish cons	w
PA17601SG	-	m	1959	lutheran - none	w
PA18062RW	dugs	m	e	jewish - agnos	w
PA19087JT	-	m	e	meth - agnos	w
PA19144DD	tits	m	y	jewish - agnos	w
Tennessee					
TN37204JK	dugs	m	o	presb - unit	w
TN38343JQ	tits	f	y	bapt	w
Texas					
TX77349PR	-	z	y	lutheran - pentecostal	w
TX78217JF	jugs	f	y	presb - zen	w
TX78703AN	tits	f	m	south bapt - secular	w
TX78723AC	tits	f	1954	cath - none	w

Region / Code	Term	Sex	Age	Religion	Race
TX78758DA	tits	m	m	presb - none	w
TX78765AN	tits	g	y	fundamentalist - agnos	i
TX78765BM	boobs	f	1959	ch of christ - buddhist	w
TX78840RW	beaver-tails	f	y	meth	w

Virginia

Region / Code	Term	Sex	Age	Religion	Race
VA22012TS	summer sqash, sagging	f	1960	cath	w
VA22075EC	tits	f	y	cath - agnos	w
VA22180HC	tits	g	y	disciples of christ - none	w
VA22203BK	tits	g	y	meth - none	w
VA22203RT	tits	m	m	episc - atheist	w
VA22205AK	molehills	f	m	cath - none	w
VA22310EG	-	f	y	christian - pagan/taoist	w
VA23464AN	fuckin' tits	m	y	united meth	w
VA23868DR	chest	g	1962	bapt	b

Washington

Region / Code	Term	Sex	Age	Religion	Race
WA98133RH	-	m	m	jewish	w
WA98272LB	fat-sacks	m	y	christian - satanism	w
WA99205BS	milk-sacks	m	t	none	w
WA99208VB	tits	m	m	agnos - ch of god	w

Wisconsin

Region / Code	Term	Sex	Age	Religion	Race
WI53005JY	cans, jugs	f	1936	prot	w
WI53151DR	-	f	m	cath - none	w
WI53186RA	udders	m	1936	cath - agnos	w
WI53211CP	dugs, teats	f	y	atheist	w
WI53211GP	tits, jugs	m	y	cath - none	w
WI53211RP	boobs	m	e	prot	w
WI53211RR	tits	m	m	cath - none	w
WI53703DG	flaps	m	1946	atheist	w
WI53703LP	milk-glands	f	1948	presb - none	w
WI53703TM	-	m	1956	cath lapsed	w
WI53704GV	jugs	m	y	none - atheist	w
WI53704JM	titties	f	1963	united ch of christ - none	w
WI53704MS	knockers, melons, mosquito-bites	f	1961	prot - none	w
WI53711RO	cow-tits, water-bags, fried eggs	m	o	lutheran - none	w
WI53713EL	tits	f	y	amer bapt - don't go to ch	w
WI53713SC	dugs	m	y	agnos	w
WI54157JM	tits	m	y	cath	w
WI54912DT	fat ugly wrinkled bottles	z	1948	bapt - atheist	w

ABUSIVE, ENDEARING AND PET NAMES FOR GENITALS • 75

Region / Code	Term	Sex	Age	Religion	Race
Australia					
AUS 2086DM	-	m	y	ch of england - none	w
AUS 2601DL	tits	m	1936	ch of england - none	w
AUS 5081AR	tits, dugs	m	o	atheist/agnos	w
AUS SW	dugs	g	1947	cath - aquarian	w
AUS VT	-	m	1943	congr - non-religious	w
Canada					
CAN A1B1P1FW	-	m	e	anglican	w
CAN B0J3J0PC	jugs	m	m	anglican - atheist	w
CAN BC AN	tits	x	m	prot, united - atheist	w
CAN H2W1B7DP	boobs	m	27	agnos - atheist	w
CAN H3B4P1DM	dugs	f	30	united presb - atheist	w
CAN J0E1J0MC	-	m	y	cath/unit/sev.day - none	w
CAN J0E1J0PK	dugs	f	y	prot	w
CAN J8V1N2WD	rocks, flops, skin, melons, fried eggs	m	m	prot - agnos	w
CAN J8X1C7DC	cans	m	y	none	w
CAN K1R7T2RG	ugly fat knockers	m	e	episc	w
CAN K2B5R8BD	tits	m	e	united ch - atheist	w
CAN L2T1J5LB	tits	m	y	prot - none	w
CAN L3K1Y6PL	tits	m	y	cath - none	w
CAN L3K2M2PB	udders	m	y	bapt	w
CAN L3P3K2MJ	tits	m	m	anglican	w
CAN L5J4J9PD	wrinkled tits	m	y	greek ortho - atheist	w
CAN L6T2Y1JB	cans	f	y	cath - none	w
CAN M1T1R8SA	-	m	e	meth - atheist	w
CAN M4M3E8JA	jugs, old saggy tits, balloons	m	76	meth	w
CAN M5M2J2AU	tits	m	1950	jewish cons - none	w
CAN M5R2M5GR	tits	f	1956	cath - lapsed	w
CAN M9B4Z5GW	tits	m	y	anglican - atheist	w
CAN M9R3T5RJ	-	g	e	prot	w
CAN R8N1W1MC	-	m	t	cath	w
CAN R8N1W1PC	tits	m	m	anglican - none	w
CAN T0J0Y0JC	pancakes	f	m	presb - united ch of canada	w
CAN V5V2H2AB	knockers	f	m	atheist - none	w
CAN V6R2R5JD	-	z	e	prot - none	w
CAN V9R1W6JH	ugly jugs	f	m	none - agnos pantheist	w
England					
UK M68BTRW	dugs	m	y	ch of england - none	w
UK OXFORD JL	tits	m	1965	ch of england - agnos	w

Region / Code	Term	Sex	Age	Religion	Race
Ireland					
IR DUBLIN FM	flabby melons	m	1962	cath - atheist	w
IR DUBLIN GG	tits	m	1966	cath lapsed	w
IR DUBLIN JA	tits	f	1966	cath - atheist	w
IR DUBLIN MO	tits, melons, boulders	f	1964	cath	w
IR DUBLIN MP	-	f	1966	cath	w
IR DUBLIN NC	tits	f	1961	moslem - atheist	w
IR DUBLIN NM	-	f	1963	cath - atheist	w
IR DUBLIN RE	-	f	1966	cath	w
IR DUBLIN RM	tits	z	y	cath - atheist	w
IR DUBLIN SC	melons	f	1962	cath	w
IR-N	tits	m	1951	cath	w
IRE-SR	-	f	y	cath - none	w
New Zealand					
NZ GM	-	m	1935	bapt - none	w
NZ IRM	pimples on chest	m	1965	none	w
NZ JG	knockers	m	1953	anglican - agnos	w
NZ JR	-	f	1937	presb agnos - buddhist	w
NZ PB	floppy tits	m	65	none - anglican	w
NZ SG	tits	f	1923	none - cath	w
South Africa					
SA 1460JE	dugs	m	1935	anglican - meth	w
SA 1500 CVDB	tits	m	1970	meth - agnos	w
France					
FR 75665JB	-	m	1955	atheist - agnos	w
Germany					
GERM 5300RS	Euter	m	y	lutheran - none	w
GERM 6203PS	Hänger	m	1964	cath - none	w
GERM (USA))ET	-	m	m	meth - atheist	w
GERM (USA) KT	-	f	m	prot - pagan	w
GERM (USA) RK	tits	m	y	episc - south u.s. charism	w
Mexico					
MEX (IL) TS	-	m	m	lutheran - agnos	w
Netherlands					
NL LV	tieten	m	1922	netherlands ref - anglican	w

ABUSIVE, ENDEARING AND PET NAMES FOR GENITALS • 77

Region / Code	Term	Sex	Age	Religion	Race
Poland					
POL 61689WS	dzwony	m	y	atheist	w
Spain					
SP 41700RR	pimientos fritos	m	1941	ch of england - atheist	w

Copyright © 1986 by Neil Crawford

PEJORATIVE NICKNAMES OF BASEBALL ALL-STARS

Merritt Clifton

Catchers: *Nig* Clarke*, *Choo-Choo* Coleman (named for his childlike behavior)
First base: *Boner* Merkle (made most famous baserunning error ever)
Second base: *Spook* Jacobs*
Shortstop: *Pee Wee* Reese
Third base: *Heinie* Groh (German descent, played in World War I era)
Left field: *Ox* Eckhardt
Center field: *Dummy* Hoy (deaf-mute)
Right field: *Turkey* Donlin (a Hall-of-famer, once he outgrew youthful clumsiness)
Pitcher: *Dizzy* Dean
Infielders: *Boob* McNair, *Puddin'head* Jones, *Butts* Wagner (had the biggest buttocks ever stuffed into a uniform).

---

* Among first black big-leaguers. Clarke officially was white, according to most authorities, but he may have been "passing" during the first decade of this century, when baseball was segregated.

EDITOR'S NOTE

Paul Dickson recently published *The Dickson Dictionary of Baseball* (New York: Facts on File, 1989) containing many negatively-valued words and expressions, of which I'll publish excerpts in a future volume.

COHEN'S RELIGIOUS MUSEUM
Aaron Cohen, Honorable Curator

FEATURED EXHIBITS

- Three sheets of toilet paper used by Jesus himself
- A herpes scab from Buddha's left buttock
- A handkerchief with three boogers from Confucius
- A pillow containing Zoroaster's dandruff
- A bib stained with Mohammed's baby puke
- Candida scrapings from Teresa of Avila's twat
- A vial containing Gandhi's fasting farts
- Pubic hair from between Martin Luther King's teeth
- Lice from Moses's beard
- Gay pornographic drawings done by Abraham as a child
- Baha' Ullāh's unwashed truss
- Mary Magdalene's bra with Simon Paul's fingerprints
- Cardinal Spellman's ruler with cum spots from teen-aged male prostitutes
- Fungal scrapings from St. Augustine's crotch
- Cowflop from between Ramachandra's toes
- Contents of the boils in St. Thomas Aquinas's armpits
- Milk from Kuan Yin's right tit
- The muddy towel on which God wiped his hands after creating the heavens and the earth
- Pus from the Baal Shem Tov's adolescent acne
- Mother Teresa's earliest menstrual rags
- Suspiciously clouded urine specimens from the Johns: Calvin, Knox, and Wesley
- The bloody hammer from when Martin Luther missed the nail
- Granulation from the eye infection Eve got when staring at Adam's prick
- A mucus-soaked rag from John the Baptist's lifelong head cold before its miraculous cure

- Two hemorrhoids belonging to Joseph the Carpenter
- A tape recording of Mary Baker Eddy's dying belch
- Birdshit combed from the hair of Francis of Assisi
- Sun Myung Moon's extra GET-OUT-OF-JAIL-FREE card
- Barabbas's sweaty loincloth
- A diaphragm found inside Joseph Smith's fifth wife
- The unbroken hymens of 12 Vestal Virgins
- Ignatius Loyola's monogrammed flintstone
- The original oversized smelly sneakers of the first Hare Krishna mendicant
- An afterbirth from the Virgin Mary
- A Kirlian photo of Joan of Arc talking to her saints
- Lord Krishna's childhood patent-leather dancing pumps
- The toenails of Torquemada's one-thousandth victim
- Nail parings with chipped blue polish from 479 ancient Druidic priestesses
- St. Matthew's foreskin
- The rubber band that prevented two centuries of popes from pissing their cassocks in public

---

OUT, OUT, DAMNED N**D!

Aaron Cohen

One stubborn turd would not be flushed.
Thrice it swirled while water gushed
Around the bowl, then down the drain.
Its message clear is grimly plain:
Filth's persistent, won't submit—
In human form or as pure shit.

Copyright © 1989 by Aaron Cohen. All Rights Reserved.

OFFENSIVE ROCK BAND NAMES
A LINGUISTIC TAXONOMY[1]

Joe Salmons *and* Monica Macaulay

INTRODUCTION

Rock music has always been a form of rebellion, and as such has always been intended to shock those who do not count themselves among its followers. The outward manifestations of such rebellion have become more outrageous with each succeeding generation. Appearance and behavior have always played a part, although the *Beatles'* "long" hair seems mild next to the day-glo mohawks, funereal makeup and safety pin earrings of more recent youth fashion. Elvis's hips have given way to slam dancing and spewing green vomit from stage. Screamin' Jay Hawkins climbing out of a coffin to open his shows in the 1960s may sound strange even today, but it is mild next to Ozzy Osbourne biting the heads off bats on stage or the use of chainsaws during live performances.

Lyrics have also played a part—witness the increase in explicitness from *Tommy James and the Shondells'* "(My Baby Does the) Hanky-Panky" (recorded in 1963-1964 and a number one hit in 1966) by way of the *Beatles'* "Why Don't We Do It in the Road" (November 1968) to the *Dead Kennedys'* "Too Drunk to Fuck" (1981).

Only in the last ten years or so, however, have many bands given themselves *names* that participate in this development. To be sure, trends in band names have always been observable. Among the more notable:

a) **insect names** in the early 1960s, beginning with Buddy Holly's *Crickets* and the takeoff on that by the *Beatles*;

b) **psychedelic names** of the 1960s, such as *The Strawberry Alarm Clock*, *Jefferson Airplane* and **light/heavy oxymorons**, for instance, *Iron Butterfly* and *Led Zeppelin*;

c) **literary names**, which have long been popular, such as *The Droogs* (from *Clockwork Orange*) and Hesse's *Steppenwolf*.

However, offensive band names remained very rare until the late 1970s. The most famous early example is, of course, the British band the *Sex Pistols*, formed in 1976 by promoter Malcolm McLaren, whose explicit goal was to offend the public (cf. Hebdige 1979 and Robbins 1983). Since then, offensive band names have proliferated on both sides of the Atlantic.

A look at well over 150 such band names from the alternative rock scene in the 1980s—gathered from alternative/college radio play lists, *fanzines*[2], and personal experience in the alternative rock scene—shows clear patterns of preference for particular types of offensive, shocking, and/or insensitive names over others. This article gives an annotated taxonomy of a corpus of such names.

We can touch on only a fraction of the possible topics, but a few other areas deserve mention. First, the explosion in the number of small, independent record companies (*indies*) has given us offensive, often humorous record company names, e.g., *Toxic Shock*, *Psycho*, *Self Immolation*, *Braineater*, *Slash*, *Doo Doo Productions*, *Roadkill Records*, *Stiff*[3] and *Rabid Cat*. Second, rock pseudonyms play an important role, such as *Sid Vicious* and *Johnny Rotten* (both *Sex Pistols*), *Richard Hell* (*Voidoids*), *Jello Biafra* (*Dead Kennedys*) and *Venus Penis Crusher* (*Cycle Sluts from Hell*).

Finally, we have concentrated only on the British and American scenes, reflecting our experience and knowledge. These phenomena are, however, international. From the German-speaking countries, for instance, come bands such as West Germany's *Geile Tiere* ("horny animals")[4] and *Schleimkeim* ("slime-seed") from the German Democratic Republic, as well as the West German record labels *Totenkopf* ("skull, death head") and *Giftplatten* ("poison records").

THE TAXONOMY

In the taxonomy which follows (and in the alphabetical list of the entire corpus found in the appendix), we have tried to exclude bands not part of the alternative rock scene, e.g., metal (be it heavy metal, speed metal, etc.) and rap/hip-hop.[5] The lines between genres are notoriously difficult to draw, however, especially since many alternative musicians consciously seek to break down such distinctions, and since bands evolve over time—e.g., *The Cult*, which began as an alternative band, *Southern Death Cult*, but which has gained a more metal-oriented audience. As a result of the fuzziness of some boundaries, we realize that some readers may well disagree with our inclusion or exclusion of particular items.

"Alternative music" is extremely difficult (if not impossible) to define, but some characteristics should be noted. It has been defined simply as "any kind of rock music not found on commercial radio."[6] Alternative certainly includes the various genres and subgenres of punk (from the late 1970s: *Sex Pistols*, *Ramones*, etc.) and thrash (generally, a later development: *Angry Samoans*, *Black Flag*), both of which are often classed under the broader heading of "hardcore." Closer to the mainstream but still clearly alternative are the "garage rock" bands of the early 1980s (*Green on Red*, *Vandals*, *Cramps*), which emphasized rawer production and sound than "new wave," although much of the latter is also widely considered alternative. Numerous hybrids have also grown up in the alternative scene:

surf-punk, cow-punk, metal-core and speed metal (the last two existing on the boundary between alternative and heavy metal), etc.

Musically, key features often include simple instrumentation (of the genres mentioned, only new wave regularly included keyboards), simple song structure (often two or three chords), high volume and a very fast beat. In general, one finds a "raw" sound, in conscious opposition to the highly produced sounds of commercial bands.

The corpus is broken down into four major categories: **Sex**, **The Body**, **Death**, and **Society**, with subdivisions as appropriate. As might be expected, many items fit into more than one category, and in such cases, we have included bands under both or all headings.

I. SEX

Sexual allusions, ranging from euphemistic to explicit, figure prominently throughout the language of alternative rock. For example, "cover bands" (bands that play popular songs rather than original music) are known within the alternative scene as *cover whores*, referring to the fact that cover bands can earn far more money than original bands, who often play for free even in established clubs. That is, they are motivated by money and not simply by the desire to play. *To jerk off* or *to masturbate* means to play long and unstructured solos, i.e., to indulge oneself at the expense of other musicians and the audience. Musicians who are particularly eager to play (often working with several bands at once, plus jamming with others on the side) are called *sluts*. *Jazz fags* are players who show too much musical sophistication and are seen as lacking aggression and regarded as soft.[7]

We have divided this category into four subgroups:

Genitalia; *Acts, Positions, etc.*; *Homosexuality*; and *General and Other*.

A. Genitalia

Both male and female genitalia are among the most popular sources for taboo band names.

HIS

Big Balls and the Great White Idiot
Buzzcocks[8]
Cocks in Stained Satin
Dicks
Hard-ons
Man-Sized Action
Penetrators
Raw Meat. This Indianapolis band uses as its logo a spurting penis, removing any potential ambiguity about the meaning of its name. Meat references are generally common in band names, for instance *Meatpuppets* and *Meatmen*.
Revolting Cocks
Sex Pistols
Throbbing Gristle

HERS

Several of these bands are entirely or predominantly female.

Clit Boys
C*nts
Killer Pussy
Les Blank's Amazing Pink Holes
Pussy Galore. Named after the character in the James Bond movie *Goldfinger*.
Slits

B. Acts, Positions, etc.

Bob on This
Circle Jerks
Doggy Style
Lubricated Goat. We may have miscategorized this, but we doubt it.
Meat Beat Manifesto

Strangulated Beatoffs
Tupelo Chain Sex
Vibrators. A far subtler but parallel name was the 1970s band *Steely Dan*, named after a vibrator in William Burroughs's novel *Naked Lunch*.

C. Homosexuality

1,000 Homo DJs
Art Phag
Fudge-packers
Gay Cowboys in Bondage
Gaye Bykers on Acid
Homo Picnic
Homosexuals. This is not overtly offensive, but is striking for its choice of the most general, least marked name for an often stigmatized group, and for its clinical tone.
Lesbian Dopeheads on Mopeds
Pink Fairies
Violent Femmes. *Femme* meant "queer, fag" in Wisconsin—where the *Violent Femmes* come from—when one of the authors was growing up there. It is reported to be archaic or obsolete within the gay community itself, except in classified ads.

D. General and Other

Alien Sex Fiend
Crucifucks. This name manages to combine more offensive references than virtually any other: *Sex* (general/other), *Society* (religion), and *Society* (profanity).
Cycle Sluts from Hell
Deviants
Gigolo Aunts
Necropolis of Love
Root Boy Slim & the Sex Change Band
Sex Boys
Sex Gang Children
Sic F*cks
Soviet Sex

II. OTHER PHYSICAL

A. The Body

Note that all non-genital body parts and related topics taken together are far less common than genitalia-based band names alone.

> 4-skins
> Afterbirth
> **Bollock Brothers.** This band was started by Johnny Rotten of the *Sex Pistols*. Note the allusion to the *Sex Pistols'* first album "Never Mind the Bollocks," a title considered offensive by many in the United Kingdom. U.K. *bollocks* = U.S. *balls*.
> **Butthole Surfers**
> **Cancerous Growth**
> **Carnivorous Buttock Flies**
> **Cramps**
> **Contractions**
> **Lost Cherees**
> **Mighty Sphincter**
> **Neurotic Arseholes.** This may be a social rather than a physical reference.
> **Sarcastic Orgasm**
> **Severed Heads**
> **Stretch Marks**

B. Bodily Fluids and Excretions[9]

Excretion and various other bodily fluids (and related topics) also appear. It is perhaps surprising, however, how few references there are to feces and how many there are to vomit.

> **Bloody Mess and the Skabs**
> **Bulimia Banquet**
> **Discharge**
> **Fartz**
> **Johnny Vomit**
> **New Roger Diarrhea**
> **Seemen**

Smegma
Specimen
Spermbirds
Spit
Stains
Strangulated Beatoffs
Technicolor Yawns. This is a euphemism for throwing up.
Thrownups
Vomit and the Zits
Vomit Launch
Vomitorium
Yeastie Girls. Rap fans will instantly recognize the takeoff on the *Beastie Boys*.

C. Abortion, Fetuses, etc.

Aborted at Line 6. This is actually a computer reference, i.e., a program that failed to run past line 6.
Dayglo Abortions
Fetus Productions
Foetus Interruptus
Freddy Fetus & the Abortions
Fried Abortions
Scraping Foetus Off the Wheel. This band has also released records under other names: *You've got Foetus on your Breath, Foetus über Frisco*, etc.
Screaming Fetus
Sharon Tate's Baby

III. DEATH[10]

There is a genre of alternative rock known as "death rock," but the names of its best-known purveyors (e.g., *Bauhaus* and *Joy Division*[11]) surprisingly do not include references to death. This category is so well-represented among non-death rock band names that we can present only a very incomplete list here.

Bone Orchard
Capital Punishment
Christian Death

Condemned to Death
Corpse Grinders
Dead Can Dance
Dead Hippies
Dead Kennedys
Dead Milkmen. This name incorporates reference both to the *Dead Kennedys* and the well-known "Monty Python" sketch.
Death of Samantha. This band appeared after Samantha Smith, child goodwill ambassador to Russia, was killed in an airplane crash.
Death Piggy
Heads on Sticks
Hollywood Autopsy
Killing Joke
MDC. These initials have been glossed as *Multideath Corporation*, *Millions of Dead Cops*, and *Millions of Dead Children*.
My Dad is Dead
My Life with the Thrill Kill Kult
Napalm Death
Necropolis of Love
Necros
Rotting Corpses
Screaming Dead
Severed Heads
Southern Death Cult. This band is now known simply as *The Cult*, after a transitional stage as *Death Cult*.

IV. SOCIETY

Note how often these names are topical, usually focussing on death or other misfortune covered in the news media, e.g., *Death of Samantha, Jerry's Kids, Boat People, Battered Wives*.

A. Ethnicity

In diverse musical circles, references to African-American culture play a complex role. For example, common insults about musicianship (even among white musicians) include "to play white," "they're too white," "white boys," etc. This is motivated, at least in part, by an attempt to identify with African-American musical culture. Furthermore, punks (and many others in the alternative scene) see themselves as marginalized by the rest of society and thus attempt to identify with other marginalized groups. Note, in this context, Richard Hell's famous quote "Punks are niggers" (Hebdige 1979: 62). For more information, the reader is referred to Hebdige's 1979 study, much of which is devoted to tracing the complex relationship between British punk rock and West Indian culture in Great Britain.

17 Pygmies
Beat Nigs. This band makes clear on its album cover that *nig* is a positive word for them, a general term for all oppressed groups, consistent with the discussion above.
Boat People
Clive Pig & the Hopeful Chinamen
Closet Negros
Coolies
Drunk Injuns
Inca Babies
Tar Babies
Tragic Mulatto

B. Politics

Note how many of the bands in this category refer directly to the Kennedy assassination, largely no doubt as a result of the influential band, *Dead Kennedys*.

Baby Jesus Hitler
Bhopal Stiffs
Capital Punishment
Dead Kennedys
Dead Oswalds. This is probably a direct takeoff on the *Dead Kennedys*.
Elvis Hitler
Fearless Iranians from Hell. According to Robbins (1989), this band actually has an Iranian member.

Flaming Mussolinis
Jack Rubies. Reference to Kennedy assassination.
Naked Raygun. Cf. *Ray & the Guns* as another reference to Ronald Reagan.
Peace Corpse
Single Bullet Theory. Reference to Kennedy assassination.
Trotsky Icepick

C. Religion

Agnostic Front
Baby Jesus Hitler
Bad Religion
Blind Idiot God
Blessed Virgins
Catholic School Boys from Hell
Christian Death
Crippled Pilgrims
Crucifucks
False Prophets
Jesus and Mary Chain
Jesus Chrysler
Part-time Christians
Pope Paul Pot. This name represents a blend of two rather unlikely characters: *Pope Paul* and *Pol Pot*.
Vatican Commandos

D. Profanity

In order to avoid even more censorship than they would already encounter, several bands have used asterisks for vowels in particularly taboo words (*C*nts, Sic F*cks*). Similarly, some taboo words occur with non-standard orthography (*Scumfucs*) and a few other groups have chosen euphemistic forms (*FU's, F-word*). Notice the predominance of *fuck* over all other vulgarities, and the complete absence, throughout the corpus, of *shit*.

Bitch Magnet. In contemporary youth culture, this refers to males who are considered particularly attractive by females. The figure of speech finds full expression in the description of how to pick up women: Tie a rope around the leg of a *bitch magnet* and throw him out a car window while cruising slowly through a crowded area. Pull him back in and pick the women off.
Cheetah Chrome Motherfuckers
Crucifucks
C*nts
F-word
FU's
Flaming Fuckheads
GG Allin and the Scumfucs
Reverb Motherfuckers
Richard Hell & the Voidoids
Sic F*cks

E. Violence

Battered Wives
Chainsaw Dawg
Deep Wound
Impulse Manslaughter
My Bloody Valentine
Nurse with Wound
Rapeman[12]
Stranglers
Suicidal Tendencies
Tex and the Horseheads. This "cow-punk" band's name combines cowboy imagery and the violent imagery typical of punks. This probably explains the use of the word *horseheads*, as a subtle reference to the movie *The Godfather*.
Verbal Abuse
Violent Apathy
Violent Children
Violent Femmes

F. The Handicapped

Autistics
Crippled Pilgrims
House of Freaks

Th' Inbred. The fact that this band comes from West Virginia lends its name particular significance, given stereotypes about Appalachian culture.
Jerry's Kids
Phantom Limbs
Poster Children
Retarded Elf
Slow Children

G. Children

Black Market Babies
Catholic School Boys from Hell
Death of Samantha
Inca Babies
Jerry's Kids
Peter and the Test Tube Babies
Poster Children
Sex Boys
Sex Gang Children
Slow Children
Tar Babies
Violent Children

NAMING PATTERNS

There are a few patterns that deserve comment here. First, there is the consciously derivative name: *Celibate Rifles (Sex Pistols), Lesbian Dopeheads on Mopeds (Gaye Bykers on Acid), Yeastie Girls (Beastie Boys)*. Oxymorons are also popular: *Violent Femmes, Violent Apathy*, etc., as are puns: *Jesus Chrysler* (also, naturally, a euphemistic form of the exclamation *Jesus Christ*), the *Thrownups, Peace Corpse, Slow Children*.

One of the most time-honored traditions in rock music is the formula *[Proper Name] and the -s*. Among offensive names, many are distinguished by the choice of last name and/or the plural noun phrase: *Richard Hell and the Voidoids, Clive Pig & the Hopeful Chinamen, GG Allin and the Scumfucs*. A recently popular twist on this is to have an initial noun phrase that is not a name replace the proper name: *Bloody Mess & the Skabs, Vomit & the Zits, Big Balls & the Great White Idiot* (in this item, note also the inversion of singular and plural from the usual pattern). Also, [*NP*(plural)] *from Hell* occurs frequently: *Catholic School Boys from Hell, Cycle Sluts from Hell, Fearless Iranians from Hell*.

[*Proper Name*] + [*Proper Name*], often with clashing images, is another recent naming strategy: *Elvis Hitler, Baby Jesus Hitler, Jesus Chrysler, Pope Paul Pot*, etc.

Finally, one syntactic trend that has intensified in the last decade is that of sentences as names—cf. *The Teardrop Explodes, They Might be Giants, Frankie Goes to Hollywood, Gene Loves Jezebel*, etc. This goes back at least to the early 1970s band, *It's a Beautiful Day*. So far, however, only a few offensive sentence-names have surfaced: *Bob on This, My Dad is Dead, Dead Can Dance*.

CONCLUSION

Why this pattern of offensive names, extending beyond the bands to record labels, pseudonyms, etc.? The answer lies no doubt in the fact that the aesthetic of the alternative scene has, in no small part, evolved out of the punk movement. That working aesthetic and its rhetoric were "steeped in irony" according to Hebdige (1979: 63), who describes the scene in terms of "darkly comic signifiers" and "gutter-snipe rhetoric." What one finds today in the alternative scene is a dual motivation to offend. On the one hand, the overtly political bands consciously exploit offensive material politically. This is particularly common for much early English punk and hardcore in general; from bands in our list, take for example the following titles: *Dead Kennedys* "Nazi Punks Fuck Off," *MDC* "John Wayne Was a Nazi," *Dicks* "Bourgeois Fascist Pig," *Crucifucks* "Hinkley

Had a Vision." On the other hand, some bands such as *Dead Milkmen* are not as clearly political, aiming more for humor or general shock value. Usually, however, in practice this line cannot be clearly drawn—both politics and humor play significant roles.

As a result of their efforts to shock and offend, members of the alternative scene have been the target of much censorship. For example, the *Dead Kennedys'* 1985 album "Frankenchrist" contained a poster by H.R. Giger (*Landscape #20*, featuring numerous rather abstract genitalia) that was deemed obscene by the state of California (cf. Wishnia 1987 for details). This happened despite a warning on the album that "the inside foldout to this record cover is a work of art by H.R. Giger that some people may find shocking, repulsive, or offensive. Life can be that way sometimes." Lead singer Jello Biafra was arrested in 1986 on charges of "distribution of harmful matter to minors," after a 14-year-old San Fernando Valley girl gave her younger brother a copy of the album. Biafra and the *Dead Kennedys'* record label, "Alternative Tentacles," a leading force in the alternative scene, were ultimately cleared when a mistrial was declared, but it ended the band, according to Robbins (1989).[13] A motion for retrial was denied by the judge.

The *Circle Jerks'* classic "Golden Shower of Hits" was banned from some radio stations as obscene although it only contained a medley of very well-known pop songs done in thrash style tracing a relationship from beginning to end: "Afternoon delight," "She's having my baby" and "D-I-V-O-R-C-E," etc. Presumably it was the name of the record that caused the reaction.

The band *Rapeman*—named after a Japanese comic — has recently broken up because of controversy surrounding the name (*Spin*, June 1989: 24). *Spin* also reported in the same issue (73) that the name *Fine Young Cannibals*—which we had deemed too mild for inclusion in our corpus—is being abbreviated to *FYC* to increase their pop appeal.

We do not pretend to have presented the definitive taxonomy of offensive band names, nor a complete list, nor to have even scratched the surface of potential areas of investigation within the rock scene. We hope that this brief article suggests some further avenues of interest and stimulates further research in the area.

FOOTNOTES

1. The authors thank, first of all, John Kirby, for inspiring this piece by his questions about offensive band names. *Phrogs*—Rick Rogers, Kendel Tilton, and The King—all helped with their detailed knowledge of the alternative scene. Thanks also to Frank Dent and Evan Finch of Bored Records. Any and all errors are naturally ours alone.

2. Fanzines are small-circulation publications focussing on science fiction, comics, or the alternative scene or some part of it. From *fan* + [maga]*zine*.

3. *Stiff's* motto is "If it ain't STIFF, it ain't worth a fuck."

4. Robbins (1983, 1989) mistranslates their name as 'wild animals,' although their album cover shows one horse mounting another and the band calls itself an 'electronic sex band.'

5. The research potential of the latter area is evidenced by the Los Angeles-based rap band *NWA* (*Niggers with Attitudes*) and their recent song "Fuck the Police."

6. Mass Giorgini, bassist for the band *Rattail Grenadier* (Roadkill Records), personal communication.

7. This clearly reflects a white and very ahistorical perspective about the position of jazz in American culture.

8. We have deleted initial definite articles from band names because of the tremendous variation in their use by the bands themselves.

9. Fluids can, of course, flow into the body as well as out, cf. *Claude Coma & the IVs*.

10. Note again that we do not deal with heavy metal, which deals extensively with death imagery (as well as Satanic imagery, etc.—rare in the alternative scene) and could be a study in itself.

11. *Joy Division* has become *New Order* since their lead singer killed himself, according to alternative scene legend, by putting his head in a

noose and standing on a block of ice until it melted. Death rock might be loosely characterized by relatively amelodic sound, slow heavy beat, often a predominately bass-oriented mix, and lyrics usually about death and dying.

12. The band which is most brought to mind by the word *rape* is the West Coast band, *The Mentors*, whose work has been called *rape rock*, based on their lyrics and stage show.

13. Wishnia (1987) points out that the choices of band and record label for prosecution were crucial. Major record labels have certainly released material equally worthy of attention, cf. e.g., *Judas Priest*'s "Eat Me Alive." Such labels commonly spend over $50,000 to record an album and could have comfortably spent far more than the $60,000 spent by *Alternative Tentacles* on Biafra's defense. Wishnia also cites sources involved in that case who think the prosecution did not reckon with Biafra's intelligence and articulateness, expecting rather "a bunch of blue-haired kids who didn't know what they were doing."

WORKS CITED

Hebdige, Dick. 1979. *Subculture: The Meaning of Style.* New York: New Accents/Methuen.

Robbins, Ira A. (editor). 1983. *The New Trouser Press Record Guide.* New York: Scribners. Most recent revised edition, 1989.

Wishnia, Steven. 1987. "Rockin' With the First Amendment: Of Punk and Pornography." *The Nation.* October 24: 444-446.

APPENDIX
Alphabetical List of Band Names

4-Skins
17 Pygmies
1,000 Homo DJs
Aborted at Line 6
Afterbirth
Agnostic Front
Alien Sex Fiend
Art Phag
Autistics
Baby Jesus Hitler
Bad Religion
Battered Wives
Beat Nigs
Bhopal Stiffs
Big Balls and the Great White Idiot
Bitch Magnet
Black Market Babies
Blessed Virgins
Bloody Mess and the Skabs
Blind Idiot God
Boat People

Bob on This
Bollock Brothers
Bone Orchard
Bulimia Banquet
Butthole Surfers
Buzzcocks
C*nts
Cancerous Growth
Capital Punishment
Carniverous Buttock Flies
Catholic School Boys from Hell
Chainsaw Dawg
Cheetah Chrome Motherfuckers
Christian Death
Circle Jerks
Claude Coma & the IVs
Clit Boys
Clive Pig & the Hopeful Chinamen
Closet Negros
Cocks in Stained Satin
Condemned to Death
Contractions
Coolies
Corpse Grinders
Cramps
Crippled Pilgrims
Crucifucks
Cycle Sluts from Hell
Dayglo Abortions
Dead Can Dance
Dead Hippies
Dead Kennedys
Dead Oswalds
Dead Milkmen
Death of Samantha
Death Piggy
Deep Wound
Deviants
Dicks
Discharge
Doggy Style
Drunk Injuns
Elvis Hitler
F-word
False Prophets
Fartz
Fearless Iranians from Hell
Fetus Productions
Flaming Fuckheads
Flaming Mussolinis
Foetus Interruptus
Freddy Fetus & the Abortions
Fried Abortions
Fudge-packers
FU's
GG Allin and the Scumfucs
Gay Cowboys in Bondage
Gaye Bykers on Acid
Geile Tiere
Gigolo Aunts
Hard-ons
Heads on Sticks
Hollywood Autopsy
Homo Picnic
Homosexuals
House of Freaks
Impulse Manslaughter
Inbred
Inca Babies
Jack Rubies
Jerry's Kids
Jesus Chrysler
Johnny Vomit
Killer Pussy
Killing Joke
Leather Nun
Les Blank's Amazing Pink Holes
Lesbian Dopeheads on Mopeds
Lost Cherees
Lubricated Goat
Man Sized Action
MDC
Meat Beat Manifesto
Mighty Sphincter
My Bloody Valentine
My Dad is Dead
My Life with the Thrill Kill Kult

Naked Raygun
Napalm Death
Necropolis of Love
Necros
Neurotic Arseholes
New Roger Diarrhea
Nurse with Wound
Part-time Christians
Peace Corpse
Penetrators
Peter and the Test Tube Babies
Phantom Limbs
Pink Fairies
Pope Paul Pot
Poster Children
Pussy Galore
Rapeman
Raw Meat
Retarded Elf
Reverb Motherfuckers
Revolting Cocks
Richard Hell & the Voidoids
Root Boy Slim & the Sex Change Band
Rotting Corpses
Sarcastic Orgasm
Schleimkeim
Scraping Foetus Off the Wheel
Screaming Dead
Screaming Fetus
Seemen
Severed Heads
Sex Gang Children

Sex Pistols
Sharon Tate's Baby
Sic F*cks
Single Bullet Theory
Slits
Slow Children
Smegma
Southern Death Cult
Soviet Sex
Specimen
Spermbirds
Spit
Stains
Stranglers
Strangulated Beatoffs
Stretch Marks
Suicidal Tendencies
Tar Babies
Tex and the Horseheads
Throbbing Gristle
Thrownups
Tragic Mulatto
Trotsky Icepick
Tupelo Chain Sex
Vatican Commandos
Verbal Abuse
Vibrators
Violent Apathy
Violent Children
Violent Femmes
Vomit and the Zits
Vomit Launch
Vomitorium
Yeastie Girls

RESULTS OF MALEDICTA POLL 1988

Reinhold Aman

Our first International Maledicta Poll (see MAL 9: 34-35) resulted in 871 labels for the persons listed below. Although I expected nouns (e.g. **jerk**) or combinations of adjectives plus nouns (e.g. **white trash**) with *negative* connotations, some respondents supplied adjectives only or nouns with *positive* connotations. Still, the results are very interesting in several ways.

Out of over 12,000 *Maledicta* readers, only 40 participated, of which 29 are from the USA, one is from England, and 10 are from Canada (most of those responses thanks to the efforts of Greg W., who supplied photocopies of the Poll to his fellow Torontonians). Female readers supplied 190 terms, males 681, for a total of 871. Our participants ranged from 23 to 79 years of age.

The reponses show that several foreign politicians are not well known in the USA. In addition to being "unknown," politicians and other celebrities have not left a strong impression on our participants ("no opinion"). It is amazing how few Americans know the Prime Minister of Canada, Brian Mulroney, or have much of an opinion of him. In contrast, almost all Canadians consider him a **jerk**.

Also, several celebrities have not left much of an impression, and others may be amazed by the low opinion we have of them.

It is interesting to note that some personalities have one very distinct trait, seen in the high frequency of the same label. Others have several characteristics, and still others have no definite trait. The most abusive and varied terms were applied to Jesse Jackson. (No, it's not really a "racist thing," as George Bush would say; Jackson is simply a grating, annoying, loudmouthed opportunist who is shooting off his mouth anywhere he can get publicity, like another reverend, Al Sharpton of New York, and thereby gets on our nerves.) Ron and Nancy Reagan also are not as belovèd as they might wish to be. Of the eight labels suggested to be used, our participants chose mainly **bitch** for women and **jerk** for men.

FEMALES

Corazon Aquino: unknown (2x), no opinion (4x), *bimbo* (9x), bitch (5x), courageous bitch (1x), broad (5x), frump (5x), *and one each* doomed; goody-two-shoes; heroine; out-of-her-league.

Bo Derek: no opinion (4x), *bimbo* (30x), bimbo's-bimbo, broad (3x), bitch (1x).

Jeane Kirkpatrick: unknown (6x), no opinion (5x), *bitch* (15x), bitch-plus (1x), frump (8x), broad (7x), *and one each* tough cookie; dragon-lady; rattlesnake-eyes.

Imelda Marcos: unknown (2x), no opinion (5x), *bitch* (17), bitch-plus (1x), crazy bitch (1x), bimbo (11x), ex-bimbo (1x), broad (4x), frump (2x), *and one each* oriental Lady MacBeth; shoe-fetishist; greedy whore.

Jacqueline Onassis: no opinion (2x), *bitch* (16x), vampire-bitch (1x), bimbo (11x), broad (9x), *and one each* clever; gold-digger; slut.

Nancy Reagan: no opinion (1x), *bitch* (25x), nouveau-riche bitch (1x), bitch-in-orbit (1x), bimbo (9x), frump (2x), *and one each* ambitious; broad; frigid cunt; zipless fuck (i.e. her facial expression); misunderstood; turd.

Joan Rivers: *bitch* (23x), bitch-plus (1x), scatological bitch (1x), broad (7x), bimbo (5x), frump (3x), *and one each* frigid, stupid, ugly cunt; rat-fart.

Gloria Steinem: unknown (3x), no opinion (6x), *bitch* (12x), bitch-bitch-bitch (1x), *broad* (12x), bitchy broad (1x), frump (5x), bitchy frump (1x), bimbo (2x), old hat (1x).

Margaret Thatcher: *frump* (22x), sharp frump (1x), bitch (15x), bitch (but what a bitch!) (1x), broad (6x), iron broad (1x).

Oprah Winfrey: unknown (1x), no opinion (7x), *broad* (16x), overweight broad (1x), frump (7x), queen-frump (1x), bimbo (4x), bitch (2x), black bitch (1x), black beach-ball (1x).

MALES

George Bush: no opinion (2x), *preppy* (22x), wimp (11x), jerk (4x), nerd (4x), *and one each* absence (i.e. non-presence); wimped asshole; fucking disgrace; fart-in-the-wind; white man's flunkie; pussy; Texas turd; white trash.

Jacques Cousteau: no opinion (10x), *nerd* (12x), nice, cute nerd (1x); jerk (3x), preppy (2x), wimp (2x), *and one each* admirable; all wet; dreamer; fish; frog; Mr. Adventure; obsessed.

Gary Hart: no opinion (1x), *jerk* (22x), super-jerk (1x), wimp (6x), nerd (5x), preppy (4x), *and one each* absolute flaming asshole; stupid bastard; sap; shithead; yuppie.

Jesse Jackson: no opinion (5x), *jerk* (15), insensitive jerk (1x), lying-scumbag-of-a-jerk (1x), nerd (5x), asshole (3x), preppy (2x), *and one each* anti-Semite; bull-jive artist; Christian; climin', rhymin', Hymin' Jackson; demagogue; mushmouth; neo-gadfly; opportunist; radical pig; racist; SOB; schwartze; slum-slick; thief; black trash; weasel; wimp.

Ted Kennedy: no opinion (2x), *jerk* (15x), indiscrete jerk (1x), super-super-jerk (1x), preppy (11x), nerd (7x), wimp (7x), *and one each* absolute flaming asshole; bullshitter; disgrace; jerk-off; murderer; fucking murderer; pretty; white trash.

Helmut Kohl: unknown (2x), no opinion (20x), *nerd* (10x), jerk (2x), preppy (2x), wimp (2x), colorless wimp (1x); rich pig (1x).

François Mittérrand: unknown (2x), no opinion (16x), *jerk* (8x), jerk-frog (1x), nerd (5x), preppy (5x), *and one each* frog-faced, snail-eating bushwhacker; primped French sot; wimp.

Brian Mulroney: unknown (9x), no opinion (10x), *jerk* (11x), nerd (4x), preppy (2x), *and one each* ambulatory asshole; ok; wimp.

Prince Charles: no opinion (2x), *preppy* (15x), nerd (11x), wimp (9x), jerk (4x), *and one each* boring; mamma's boy; pretty.

Ronald Reagan: no opinion (1x), *jerk* (18x), wimpish jerk (1x), nerd (8x), wimp (2x), *and one each* assfucker; asshole; world-class creep; disaster; fucking disgrace; dreamer; rich man's flunkie; would-be MF; out-of-it; shit-from-a-monkey's-ass; shithead; senile SOB; specimen; white trash; useless as a limp dick.

NEW TARGETS SUGGESTED FOR FUTURE POLLS

Our readers participating in the 1988 Poll suggested the individuals below for future polls. The numbers indicate how often they were nominated.

Bella Abzug
Alan Alda
Woody Allen
Yasser Arafat (5)
Jim Bakker (2)
Tammy Bakker (2)
Menachem Begin
Leonard Bernstein
Pat Boone
David Bowie
Boy George (2)
David Brinkley
Tom Brockaw (3)

William F. Buckley, Jr. (2)
Sonny Buono
George Burns
Barbara Bush (3)
Truman Capote
Joanna Carson
Johnny Carson (2)
Jimmy Carter (3)
William Casey
Fidel Castro (2)
Dick Cavett (2)
Neville Chamberlain

John Chancellor
Cher (4)
Connie Chung
Winston Churchill
Joan Collins
Perry Como
Dennis Connors
Bill Cosby
Mario Cuomo
Tony Curtis
Bette Davis
Charles de Gaulle
Elizabeth Dole (3)

Robert Dole
Phil Donahue (2)
Sam Donaldson (2)
Michael Dukakis (3)
Duke of Windsor
Clint Eastwood
Dwight Eisenhower
Jerry Falwell (3)
Farrah Fawcett
Sarah Ferguson (4)
Geraldine Ferraro
Jane Fonda
Gerald Ford (2)
Harrison Ford
Micheal J. Fox
Moammar Gadhafi
Uri Geller
Richard Gere
Mikhail Gorbachev
Raisa Gorbachev
Tipper Gore
Merv Griffin (2)
Florence Griffith-Joyner
Bob Guccione
Bryant Gumble
Jessica Hahn
Alexander Haig (2)
Fawn Hall
Patty Hearst
Hugh Heffner (2)
Jesse Helms
Pee Wee Herman
Shere Hite
J. Edgar Hoover
Bob Hope (2)
Julio Iglesias
Michael Jackson (3)
Mick Jagger
Peter Jennings
Lady Bird Johnson
Lyndon B. Johnson
Diane Keaton
Bobby Kennedy
John F. Kennedy

Ayatollah Khomeini (2)
Nikita Khrushchev
Henry Kissinger (2)
Edward Koch
Ted Koppel
Stan Laurel
Cyndi Lauper
Robin Leach
Cloris Leachman
David Letterman
Madonna (2)
Ferdinand Marcos (2)
Groucho Marx
John McEnroe
Ed McMahon (2)
Evan Mecham (2)
Ed Meese (3)
Golda Meïr
Bette Middler
Marilyn Monroe ("a broad who could be a bitch but was treated like a bimbo," Neil Crawford, U.K) (2)
Mr. Rogers
Mr. T
Bob Newhart
Brigitte Nilson
Richard Nixon
Oliver North (2)
Thomas "Tip" O'Neill
Yoko Ono
Daniel Ortega (4)
Dolly Parton
Jane Pauley (2)
Luciano Pavarotti
Sean Penn
Pope John Paul II
Elvis Presley (2)
Prince (2)
Prince Philip
Princess Di (3)
Dan Quayle (3)
Sir Randolph Quirk
Dan Rather (4)

Burt Reynolds
Donna Rice
Don Rickles
Oral Roberts
Pat Robertson (2)
Andy Rooney
Mickey Rooney
William Safire
Carl Sagan
Andrei Sakharov
Helmut Schmidt
Patricia Schroeder
George Schultz (2)
Arnold Schwarzenegger (2)
Willard Scott
Gene Shalit
Ariel Sharon
Rev. Al Sharpton
Brooke Shields
Beverly Sills
Paul Simon (senator)
Paul Simon (singer)
Grace Slick
Eleanor Smeal
Bruce Springsteen (2)
Sylvester Stallone (2)
George Steinbrenner
Jimmy Stewart
Meryl Streep
Barbra Streisand (2)
Jimmy Swaggart
Pierre Elliott Trudeau
Desmond Tutu
Barbara Walters (2)
Lech Wałęsa
Caspar Weinberger
Ruth Westheimer
Vanna White
Elie Wiesel
Bruce Willis
Deborah Winger
Jim Wright
Molly Yard
Pia Zadora

TATTLING THE RACIST LAUGHTER OF ALABAMA LEADERS, 1950-1967

Louie Crew

The air-conditioners hummed noisily as Rotarians in Anniston, Alabama, fiddled with their desserts at the YMCA, in August 1961. Their guest speaker humored them, as they expected him to do:

> A Negro dies and goes to heaven. St. Peter asks how things are on earth.
> "Fine. Segregation gone; integration works."
> "How is that?"
> "I decided to go to a white Baptist church. The ushers were cordial and took me down to the front seat. Preacher directed the sermon to me, opened the doors of the church, and urged me to join. It passed unanimous. Then they asked if I was baptized. I said no and they showed me a pool right behind the pulpit. Me and the preacher in robes go down in the water."
> The Negro paused and scratched his head.
> St. Peter asked, "What is the matter?"
> "You know, that is the last thing I remember."

Three months earlier, other Annistonians had physically attacked Freedom Riders and burned their bus. Anniston Rotarians would not have dared join these "rednecks," as they would have called them. Still, after the fact, the Rotarians happily fantasized that their Baptist preacher, archetypal spokesperson of values in Southern communities, could drown a black person who wanted to integrate the church.

"Have you heard about the Freedom-Rider Dolls? You

wind them up and they head straight for the white rest room." That got a big laugh on November 16, 1961, at the Rooster Club, a breakfast group to promote progress for Anniston. In August 1961, Rotarians laughed at:

> The son was scratching.
> The father, a Negro, said, "What's the matter?"
> Son: "I have chiggers biting."
> Father: "They not chiggers, son, but Chigroes."

While Freedom-Rider dolls and Chigroes aimed to trivialize the issues of social justice, ironically the second joke only faintly concealed another victory for the black victims. Ostensibly the Anniston leaders were rankled that they now had to say Negro. Most had already avoided *nigger* in polite company, but they had insisted on *nigra*, as their own, more polite term. In the joke, white Southerners acknowledged, grudgingly, that black people had won the right to do their own naming.

Five years later, in August 1966, Anniston Rotarians laughed about a joke in several ways the antithesis of the tale about the preacher who drowned the black integrationist:

> Over breakfast coffee, Delta Airlines passengers for flight number 640 to Boston read in the *Atlanta Constitution* that theirs will be the first flight piloted by a black man.
> Surely enough, after they are airborne, the voice comes over the p.a. system: "Dis is Joe Brown. We is flying at an altitude over 30,000 feet gwine nowth, nowtheast at 400 miles per hour. We due to arrive in Boston in 2 hours and a half. If you look out the window in about 10 minutes, you will see the Atlantic Ocean. Have a nice flight. Thank y'all for flying Delta."
> Fifteen minutes later, when the passengers are enjoying their coffee, the same voice comes back on again. "Folks, as I told you, now if you will look out the window you will see

the ocean. Way down dere they is this big yaller dot. Does you see it?"

The right wing of the plane dipped sharply and everyone glared down at the yellow dot miles below.

"And in that yaller dot dere bees a black dot. Does you see that 'en too?"

Most of the passengers nod. "Dat dere is yo pilot. Dis here is a recording."

The Rotarians laughed with a new twist: the joke was on them. In it, they drowned. Thereby the Rotarians quietly acknowledged that they had lost, that segregation had indeed gone with the wind.

Whites' Laughter at Blacks of the 1950s

In contrast, the jokes Anniston leaders told about blacks in the 1950s showed no respect at all for blacks as a political force. Instead, whites portrayed blacks as simple, harmless illiterates on whom the whites could heap their own fantasies:

> Two colored girls go to a photographer. He sits them down and gets his head under the black cloth.
> "What's he doin?"
> "He goin to focus now."
> "Whut? Both us?"

> Two colored girls meet.
> "Hi, Liza."
> "Hi, May."
> "How is you?"
> "I'se fine. I'se married now."
> "Who to?"
> "Sam Jones."
> "Don't you know he drinks too much. Dat drinkin' take the lead out of his pencil."
> "Huh. Don't worry me. He don't do all my scribblin' nohow."

Those gathered for the Alabama Hardware Convention in May 1950 laughed heartily.

In the more polite society of a noon meeting of Rotary, sexual stereotypes yielded to a demeaning innocence:

> Coffee salesman to a small colored boy: "Boy, do you drink coffee?"
> "Sho does, 'bout 12 cups every day."
> "Don't that much coffee keep you awake?"
> The boy answers with a yawn, "It helps."
> *(Rotary Club. October 17, 1950)*

Adult blacks fared no better. The Anniston Chamber of Commerce, which promoted the town as "The Model City," easily laughed at black adults as stupid:

> Policeman to colored driver: "You do not have your dimmers on."
> Driver: "Sho did. I have on all my ma put out for me."
> *(January 15, 1951)*

People at the same meeting of the Chamber had little respect for the black family:

> Negro from Selma "does" Detroit. Reports drift back about a Cadillac and a white wife.
> Truth gets told: old Cadillac. High-brown gal, with not a drop of white blood: one-half Negro and one-half Yankee.

Southern white jokers in the 1950s often affirmed the verbal cleverness and folk wisdom of selected blacks, namely those who stayed in their place:

> A Negro named Joshua was up for illegal liquor. The judge said, "So you are the Joshua who made the sun stand still?"
> The Negro replied: "No suh, I'se the Joshua who made the moonshine." *(Rotary Club. June 4, 1956)*

The joker here managed the Anniston Coca-Cola Co., bottler of legal potions.

In 1954 the United States Supreme Court decided *Brown vs. Board of Education* and demanded "all possible speed" to end the segregation of schools. Notice how unready Anniston leaders were to affirm the intellectual worth of the black pupils, as evidenced by the tale Anniston Rotarians circulated in their official newsletter on April 12, 1954:

A Not Uncommon Failing

A colored boy came to a white man's house in the country and said to the white man, "Boss, I'se hongry." The man said, "All right, go 'round to the kitchen." The boy said, "Boss, if you gimme sumpin to eat, I'll split up that stove wood in your back yard." The man said, "All right, all right, go and get your grub." A couple of hours later the man went to the back yard and noticed the boy who was just sitting and asked him, "Have you chopped up that wood?" The boy said, "Boss, if you let me rest around till dinner time, after dinner I'll chop that patch of cotton for you." The man said, "All right, but don't fool me no more." After the boy had eaten a big dinner he started to the cotton patch and he met a cooter (mud-turtle). The cooter said, "Nigger, you talk too much." The boy goes tearing back to the house and the man came out and said, "Nigger, have you chopped that cotton?" The boy said, "Lawd, Boss, I wuz on my way and I met a cooter and he started talkin' to me and here I am." The white man said, "Take me to that cooter, and if he don't start talking, I'm going to give you a beating." So they started for the cotton patch, and there in the middle of the road sat the cooter, but he never opened his mouth. So the man hopped on the boy and whipped him something scandalous and left for the house. Well, the colored boy was just about through brushing himself off when the cooter poked his head out and looked at him and said, "Nigger, I tole you, you talk too much."

Notice, too, how faintly the joker criticizes the man's physical violence towards the young black person: "So the man hopped on the boy and whipped him something scandalous and left for the house."

In January 1960, at the beginning of the new decade, Judge Coley clearly specified the limits for any trust of black intelligence:

> A lawyer appeared at a professional hearing with a large briefcase. An old friend kidded him, saying:
> "You know! When I first started out in life, my father gave me some good advice: 'Don't trust too much a preacher without a church and a nigger with a briefcase.'"
>
> *(The Rooster Club)*

Although whites' humor in the 1960s mirrored new political dimensions, many older notions persisted simultaneously. Even three years after the burning of the Freedom-Rider bus, President Wright of Samford University, a Baptist institution in Birmingham, felt it appropriate to tickle the Anniston Rotarians with these two:

> Mandy to lawyer on Monday morning: "I wants to get a divorce."
> Lawyer: "I didn't know you were married. When did you marry?"
> Mandy: "Saturday."
> Lawyer: "When did you meet the man?"
> Mandy: "Friday."
> Lawyer: "Met Friday, married Saturday, divorced Monday. Why?"
> Mandy: "Mister John, he's most over-introduced man I ever saw."

> A Negro gets a lawyer to take his case to sue another. The lawyer says that he will take the case on a "contingency basis." On leaving the office, the Negro asks the elevator operator what "contingency basis" meant. "If he loses, you lose; he don't get no money. If'n he wins yo case, you don't get no money."
> *(September 15, 1964)*

Dr. Wright implies: "I refuse to acknowledge the issues that are shaking this community, and I trust that you can laugh with me in the Amos & Andy way we used to before integration." Much other civic humor in Anniston during the 1960s shared Dr. Wright's quietism, as did the popular joke about a bridge party:

> Yes'm, ah quit dat job. Dat were de mos' ridiculous place I'se ebber been in! Dey played a game called bridge, an' las' night dere was lots o' fellas an' gals dere. Jes' as ah was fixin' to serve 'freshments ah heahs dis man say to a woman, "Take yo hands off mah trick!"
> Ah jes neah drapped daid when, bless mah bones, ah heahs annudder man say, "You sure got a nice bust!"
> Den annudder man say, "Lay down an' let me see what you got!"
> Den ah heahs dis woman say, "You forced me an' ah had to take you out when ah'd already been down twice!"
> Den dis udder woman say, "You jumped me twice when you didn't have stuff enuff fo' one good raise."
> An' den some woman say somep'n 'bout "coverin' her honor."
> Well, ah jist ups an' gits mah hat 'cause ah knowed dat ain't no fittin' place fo' me, an' just as ah was leavin', ah hope to die ef dis woman didn't say, "Well, ah guess we'll stop now, as dis is mah las' rubber," an' den—doggone ef she didn't say, "Lay down yo dummy an' let me pay on it!"
> No ma'amm, ah's a lady an' ah jes' couldn't stay there!

Compare this joke with a very different one about a domestic servant, as retold during a Rotary dinner conversation: "Leila Carrington's cook referred to the civil rights folks as 'late model niggers.'" Possibly the whites enjoyed the cook's derogatory "niggers" so much that they missed her ironic affirmation of the new breed.

Black drama of the sixties often celebrated just such maids who spoke the truth as clearly as they dared, to whites who simply refused to hear. Segregation may not have finally ended in the white imagination, but it surely had ended in the imagination of Leila Carrington's cook.

One sample tellingly mixes old stereotypes with the new political reality:

Negro's 23rd Psalm

Lyndon is my Shepherd. I shall not work.
He maketh me lie down in front of theatres.
He leadeth me into White Universities.
He restoreth my welfare check.
He leadeth me in the path of 'sit-ins,' for Communists' sake.
Yea, though I walk through the HEART OF DIXIE, I shall fear no police, for Lyndon is with me.
He prepareth a table before me in the presence of WHITE FOLKS.
He annointed my head with anti-kink hair straightener.
My Cadillac tank runneth over.
Surely the Supreme Court will follow me all the days of my life.
And, I will dwell in the house of the Federal Housing Project forever.

Amen

The Cadillac and the laziness stereotypes arrive right out of the white humor of the fifties; but the spite is new. Witness "anti-kink hair straightener." The laughers resent new black political clout—legislation, sit-ins, integration, government economic commitment. Nowhere does the parodist acknowledge common community even with the poorer whites, who comprised the vast majority of those whom the federal money helped in Anniston.

Then only about 10 percent of the 33,000 Annistonians were black.

Similar bitterness infests a joke circulated among employees who worked in local government in Anniston during the late sixties.

Subject: Decorating School for Christmas

We have been informed by the office of H.E.W. of Washington, D.C., that a white Christmas would be a violation of Title 11 of the Civil Rights Act of 1964.

These are the steps to be taken to comply:

1. All Christmas Trees must have at least 26.4% colored bulbs and they must be placed throughout the tree and not segregated in the back of the tree.

2. Christmas presents must not be wrapped in white paper unless colored ribbon is used to tie them.

3. If the manger scene is used, 21% of the angels and one out of the three Kings must be of minority race.

4. If Christmas music is played, "We Shall Overcome" must be given equal time. Under no circumstances will "I'm Dreaming of a White Christmas" be played.

5. Care should be taken in party planning. For example:
   (a) Use pink Champagne instead of white.
   (b) Turkey may be served, but only if the white and dark meat is on the same platter. There will be no separate-but-equal platters permitted.
   (c) Use chocolate ripple ice cream instead of vanilla.
   (d) Both chocolate and white milk must be served. There will be no freedom-of-choice plan. Milk is to be served without regard to color.

A team from H.E.W. will visit us on December 25th to determine compliance with the act. If it snows on Christmas Eve, we are all in trouble.

After 1967, my source recorded no more jokes about black people, though he continued to record many other jokes in civic clubs of Anniston until he retired, in 1977. Maybe blacks disappeared from civic-club humor. More likely, my source just lost interest in copying them.

In the 50s and 60s, my source served on the Anniston Board of Education. As chair for several years after the Little Rock decision, he told The Rev. Quentus Reynolds, the N.A.A.C.P. petitioner, that the Board would not integrate the Anniston schools. "I am sworn to uphold the Constitution of the State of Alabama," he insisted.

In 1965, President Johnson nationalized the Alabama Guard to abort George Wallace's stand against the integration of the University of Alabama. Federal law became Alabama law, and my source followed it. He went on to direct Johnson's poverty program in several northeast Alabama counties until he retired. At his funeral in 1982, The Rev. Quentus Reynolds—once his adversary, then his coworker, finally his successor at the Community Improvement Board—eulogized him for important contributions to the economic well-being of poor people in the community, white and black alike.

I visited him as he was dying in 1982. He asked generously about my black spouse, whom he had grown to respect during his last decade. Then he turned his eye to the ceiling above his bed.

"Son," he said, "when you have to throw things away, you might too quickly chuck a file marked *Jokes*, but you must not. I wrote down and dated all that I heard through the years. Some of them will hurt you, but you must write about them. They are part of what happened. I love you both."

Rest in peace.

DONORS NEEDED

Over the past 12 years, I have given away many copies of our books to readers who can't afford them or buy them because of currency restrictions: students, retired or unemployed folks, prisoners, scholars in Eastern Europe and Africa, etc. But there are more requests for free copies than I can afford — am I Croesus?

If you want to buy a gift of MAL for a scholar in Czechoslovakia, Poland, Russia, Yugoslavia, East Germany, or Nigeria, please send $15.00 for one MAL gift, indicate to what country you want it to go, and whether you wish to remain anonymous or want me to give your name to the giftee, so that s/he can write you a thank-you note.

BEYOND THE METAPHOR
CURSING IN ULSTER

Alan Crozier

In an analysis of words denoting sexual intercourse, Robert Baker (1981: 174-80) shows that the traditional view has always been of an active man and a passive woman: *Dick fucked Jane* and *Jane was fucked by Dick* (but not *Jane fucked Dick*).[1] For Baker this implies that the passive female is being harmed or taken advantage of, a claim which is based on the metaphorical use of *fucked* to mean "deceived, hurt or taken advantage of" and the use of *prick* as a term for "a person who hurts (and takes advantage of) others." Baker's conclusion may appear justified on the basis of his own American English usage.[2] However, by using evidence from another variety of English, and by carefully distinguishing dirty words used literally and dirty words used as maledictions, rather different conclusions can be drawn. The linguistic evidence in this article comes from my native dialect of County Tyrone, Northern Ireland (Ulster).

Dirty words are usually referred to in Ulster as *bad words*, and their use is known as *dirty chat* or *cursing* (the verb *swear* is used only in the strict sense of asseverating on oath). These words denote things which are not talked about openly in our society, coming from the usual tabooed spheres of sex and excretion. Most of Ulster's dirty words are known and used throughout the English-speaking world, and therefore need no explanation in the following list. Synonyms are given in parentheses:

Sex: fuck (tup, bull, buck, buff, ride, frig); wank; bugger.
Persons associated with illicit sex: whore, bitch; bastard (get); bugger.
Excretion: shite, skitter, turd; fart; pish.
Parts of the body associated with sex and excretion: cock (prick, dick, tool, wire, willy), (a dose of) the horn[3]; balls (ballocks); cunt (twat, fud, fanny, pussy); tit (diddy); ass (hole, asshole).

Some of these dirty words are of course perfectly innocent in certain contexts: dog owners speak freely of *bitches*, farmers' wives talk unblushingly of a cow's *tits*, and words like *tool* and *ride* occur frequently in everyday conversation in their clean senses.

There is another class of words which is prohibited in English, not because the words are dirty but because their use outside a proper religious context constitutes a breach of the third commandment and other biblical injunctions. They are used to invoke supernatural powers as witnesses to the truth of a statement (*swearing oaths* in the strict sense) or to invoke divine vengeance and condemnation (*cursing* in the strict sense) or as exclamations of anger and surprise, uses which also have a religious origin. To distinguish them from the *dirty words* classified above, these words will here be called *swearwords,* and the utterances in which they are used will be called *oaths* (as a general term) or *maledictions* (when it is necessary to distinguish *cursing* from *swearing*). Ulster's swearwords are:

God; Lord; Jasus; divil; hell; damn.

In their proper religious context *Jesus* and *devil* are pronounced in the standard way, whereas as swearwords they retain older dialectal pronunciations (rhyming with *blazes* and *civil*). There is also a range of dialectal asseverations which, although scarcely stronger than *indeed,* are clearly of religious origin and therefore oaths:

> in faith; in soul; in troth; in sang.

The last of these means "by the blood (of Christ)." The meaning of the others is obvious, but it should be noted that they retain dialectal pronunciations, rhyming with *death, owl,* and *cloth* respectively. The *in* which begins each oath is optional. The expressions may also be combined:

> Faith in soul I'm not drunk.
> Deed in troth you are.

The adjective and adverb *bloody* also belongs to the class of dirty words. In origin it is more likely to be a mere intensive rather than a corruption of *by our Lady,* but it may derive its offensiveness from supposed religious connotations (oaths by *God's blood* and *sang*) as well as sexual associations.

All dialects have ways of toning down and disguising swearwords (Aman 1980), often by changing everything except the first two phonemes (*crumbs* for *Christ; goldarn* for *God damn*). The words may also be disguised semantically rather than phonetically, often by the use of antonyms (*heaven* for *hell; bless* for *damn*). The commonest disguised Ulster swearwords are:

> Gosh, goodness; Jakers, Japers, Jove, Jingo; Cripes, Crimety; dickens; heck, heaven, earth; dang, bliss; blinking, blooming.

The strict distinction observed here between swearwords and dirty words can lead us to the conclusion that a person who exclaims *My goodness!* is swearing, whereas a person who says *He fucked her* is not. Most people feel that *goodness* is a harmless exclamation but the use of *fuck* is swearing. Dirty words and swearwords can be associated because the use of both classes of words is prohibited. The shared feature of prohibition allows dirty words to be used in oaths. Thus a person who trips and falls may release his anger in an oath in which not only swearwords may be used (*Christ! Damn! Hell!*) but also dirty words (*Fuck! Shite!*), on the analogy that these words are also prohibited. The transfer of dirty words to the class of swearwords of course occurs in all dialects of English, but different dialects may allow different words to be transferred. Similarly, different languages allow different dirty words to be used as swearwords. A French speaker can express anger with *Putain!* and a Spaniard can say *¿Qué coño?*, but no English dialect, as far as I know, uses **Whore!* or **What the cunt?* On the other hand, Scandinavian languages allow hardly any transfer between the two classes of tabooed words, swearing only with the equivalents of *damn, hell*, and *devil* (Einarsson 1981: 31-34; Ljung 1986: 39-48).

When dirty words are used in oaths they can be phonetically disguised in the same way as swearwords. Ulster people disguise *Fuck!* as *Fluke! Flute! Flip!*, while *Shite!* can become *Sugar!* These forms cannot be substituted for *fuck* and *shite* in their literal use as dirty words. It is impossible to say **He fluked her* or **I'm dying for a sugar*. Dirty words used in their literal sense are rarely disguised phonetically.[4] People instead substitute Latinisms (*copulate, defecate*) or euphemisms (*to sleep with, to go to the toilet*) or slightly less offensive words (*ride, dung*).

Dirty words can be employed in oaths because they give the swearer the satisfaction of releasing aggression by breaking a ban on the use of prohibited words. Swearwords like *Christ* and *damn* can be used harmlessly in religiously contexts, but a word like *fuck* is wholly bad, and therefore has the advantage of giving greater satisfaction to the swearer and greater offence to anyone who is meant to be offended.

Oaths such as *Fuck!* and *Shite!* show the dissociation of word and thing. Satisfying oaths depend on dirty words as words and not on the tabooed things they denote. *Copulate!* and *Excrement!* would make poor oaths. They could conceivably be used for humorous effect, but the humor only serves to show that dirty words as oaths are not meant to be taken literally, and that they are not even meant to be taken figuratively.

There is a common tendency to take swearwords and maledictions as metaphors. Such figurative explanations may often appear persuasive, offering significant psychological and sociological insights. For example, the use of *bastard* as a term of abuse could be explained as a metaphor developing through the following stages:

1. *Denotation*: A person born out of wedlock.
2. *Connotation*: The unwanted product of illicit sex, and consequently a legally inferior and socially undesirable person.
3. *Metaphor*: A person who is not illegitimate but is nevertheless undesirable.

The first two uses are literal; the third shows a figurative transfer of the negative moral and social overtones of bastardy without the central fact of illegitimate birth. As a fresh metaphor, *bastard* has two referents: it says something about the traditional status of bastards in the past, and it says something about the person who is the object of the insult. Frequent figurative usage leads to a further stage, *Lexicalization*, when the dead metaphor *bastard* actually takes on the sense of "evil, unpleasant person," denoting this as much as (if not more than) "a person born out of wedlock."

Bastard can therefore be compared to a word like *pig*: the connotations of greed and dirt are transferred to greedy and dirty people, even though they obviously lack the central feature of animality. The dead metaphors *pig* and *bastard* take on a life of their own, applied for instance to fascists in a way which is quite unfair to innocent animals or people whose parents happen to be unmarried. There is, however, one important difference between *bastard* and *pig*. *Bastard* is a dirty word. In its literal senses it can be euphemized into *illegitimate person*. In its use as a malediction it becomes a swearword and cannot be so euphemized; the English disguise it phonetically as *basket*. *Bastard* derives its abusive force not only from the negative implications of illegitimate birth but also from the fact that it is a forbidden word. Metaphor is the transfer of meaning, whereas malediction is the transfer of the offensive force of a prohibited word, regardless of its meaning.

To elaborate this point, we may look at the strongest single-word insult used in Ulster (and the rest of the British Isles), namely *cunt*. This is applied only to men (like *bastard* and *whore*; the strongest insult for a woman is *bitch*). If the use of *cunt* is a metaphor, we must look at the negative connotations of the vulva which make it appropriate as a term of abuse. Some might claim that men view the vulva as the lowest, vilest, ugliest thing on earth, but I doubt that this is the case. An Ulsterman who is called a *cunt* is likely (if he does not resort to violence) to shrug and say "A cunt's a useful thing." The strength of *cunt* as an insult depends less on the thing and its associations and more on the offensive nature of the word itself. The validity of this claim can be tested by looking at other words for the vulva and seeing if they have the same abusive force. *Twat*, a slightly less offensive name for the same organ (and consequently included in the *Oxford English Dictionary*), is a slightly less offensive insult than *cunt*. It designates extreme stupidity rather than evil. More affectionate names such as *pussy* and *fanny* have no force as insults, nor have the medical terms *vulva* and *vagina*. Of the names for the male organ, only *prick* is commonly used as a term of abuse. The fact that it is a relatively mild insult in Ulster, denoting insignificance and stupidity, is probably due to the fact that *prick* (unlike *cunt* and *twat*) has a range of entirely innocent uses alongside its application to the penis. Being only in part a dirty word it has a relatively low degree of offensiveness as an insult. An obstinately stupid person may also be called a *ballocks* (or simply a *balls*), a slightly more offensive term than *prick*.

The difference between *cunt* and *prick* as terms of abuse has nothing to do with the relative status of the organs in question; it is due to the relative offensiveness of the words. *He is a cunt* is not a metaphor in the same way as *He is a bastard* can be explained as a metaphor. The development of *cunt* can be outlined thus:

1. *Denotation*: Female organ of reproduction.
2. *Connotation*: An organ associated with sex (sin, shame, taboo, etc.).
3. *Prohibition*: The name of a tabooed thing, and therefore a tabooed word.
4. *Malediction*: An unspeakable word, and therefore used to condemn unspeakable people.

The prohibition of *cunt* as a word has two consequences. First, it means that those who are forced to talk about the thing must find a respectable word, like Latin *vulva*. Second, it allows the dissociation of the prohibited word from the thing which it denotes. The application of *cunt* to unspeakably vile men derives its offensive force not from the vulva conceived as an unspeakably vile organ, but from *cunt* as an unspeakably vile word. *Cunt* as a malediction cannot be taken figuratively.

Let us now look at the non-literal uses of our strongest and most versatile taboo word, *fuck*. There are cases where it can be used metaphorically. Kanin (1979) has explained the use of *fucked* to mean "cheated, maltreated, deceived, exploited" as a reflection of the techniques of premarital seduction. *I've been fucked* develops thus:

1. *Denotation*: A man has copulated with me.
2. *Connotation*: A man has deceived me into copulating with him, and thereby devalued and exploited me.
3. *Metaphor*: I've been cheated, exploited.

Note that senses 1 and 2 could only have a woman as the speaker, whereas the subject of 3 is most likely to be a man; a woman could hardly use this metaphor for fear of being taken literally.

This sense of *fuck* (also seen in the riddle about the difference between the lawyer and the angry hen who clucks defiance) is specifically American, but unknown in Ulster, where *fuck* has other uses, some of which may be metaphorical, but many of which are purely maledictory. *I'm fucked* can mean "I'm exhausted" and might be a figurative allusion to post-coital exhaustion (like the British synonym *shagged out*). What then of *This engine's fucked* "The engine is utterly useless, can no longer function"? Is this really how men view the condition of a woman with whom they have just had sexual intercourse? Baker evidently thinks so, since he interprets *fuck* as a metaphor for "harm" (1981, p. 177), and such uses as *fuck you* as a way of "telling someone that you wish to harm him." He has missed the point that *fuck you* (like *damn you*) is a malediction, not a metaphor. The prohibition of the word *fuck* means that it can be dissociated from its reference to sexual intercourse and associated instead with prohibited swearwords. There are thus two *fuck* words. *Fuck¹* means literally "to copulate with," with possible figurative senses like "to deceive." *Fuck²* has no intrinsic meaning, but has an offensive force which means it can be freely used in oaths and maledictions.[5] A dictionary entry for the Ulster uses of *fuck²* might look like this:

fuck *n* Word which can be substituted in oaths for swearwords with nominal function.
  a) For GOD: *I swear to fuck it's true. For fuck's sake, keep quiet. I wish to fuck you'd shut up. What in fuck's name does he want? Fuck only knows what will happen now. Surely to fuck you're not serious. (Holy) Fuck!* (exclamation of suprise).
  b) For HELL: *Go to fuck! This country's away to fuck altogether. Where the fuck do you think you're going? Run like fuck! You're as lazy as fuck. Like fuck I am! Fuck!* (exclamation of anger).
  c) For DAMN: *It's not worth a twopenny fuck. He doesn't give two fucks about anything.*

fuck *v*
  a) Word which can be substituted in maledictions for DAMN: *Fuck the bit he cares. You know fuck all about fuck all. I'm fucked if I know. He's as lazy as be fucked. Fuck you (for a whore's bastard)! Fuck the Pope/Queen. Fuck me!* (exclamation of surprise). *Fuck it!* (exclamation of anger).
  b) Used in a few other maledictions where DAMN does not occur: *Fuck up!* "Be silent!" *Fuck off!* "Go away!" whence *He's fucked off.* "He has absquatulated."
  c) As an equivalent to DAMN in senses such as "destroy, ruin": *If you're not careful you'll fuck the whole thing.* Hence *fuck about* or *around* "to mess about," *fuck up* "to spoil, ruin."

fucking *attrib adj & adv* Equivalent to DAMNED/BLOODY in condemnatory senses, "infernal": *The fucking engine is useless. You're a fucking liar.*[6] Equivalent to DAMNED/BLOODY as an intensifier, "extremely": *She's fucking beautiful. You think you're fucking smart. You know fucking well what I mean. It serves you fucking well right.*

fucked *predic adj* In condemnatory senses such as "damned, destroyed, finished, useless": *One more mistake like that and we're fucked. The bastarding engine's fucked.*

fucker *n* A condemnatory term corresponding to BASTARD/CUNT, applied to basically evil people unless qualified by adjectives denoting less malicious characteristics: *That fucker shot my brother. Such a stupid fucker I've been. The poor fucker got the blame for everything.*

> **fuck-up** *n* used like BALLS-UP/COCK-UP to mean a "mess, fiasco, mistake": *The British government has been responsible for the one fuck-up after the other.*

The use of *fuck²* as a substitute for such opposites as *God* and *hell* shows the lack of intrinsic meaning. *Fuck* is most commonly substituted for *damn* (whence such senses as "destroy, ruin"), but again with no intrinsic meaning, since *damned* can be replaced by both the active *fucking* and the passive *fucked*. The difference in the distribution of the two words is a purely formal one between attributive and predicative uses. The traditional conception of sexual intercourse is, as Baker shows (1981: 174-77), an active man who fucks a passive woman. The distinction is irrelevant to the use of *fuck²*, which has no intrinsic meaning; in Ulster it is possible to say *The fucking engine's fucked*. Baker says that "When one man fucks many women he is a playboy and gains in status; when a woman is fucked by many men she degrades herself and loses stature" (1981: 179). If *fuck²* reflected this difference in attitudes, we might expect *fucker* to be a term of praise, since the word is used mostly by men. However, the active *fucker* is just as negative as the passive *fucked*. *Fuck²* and its derivatives tell us nothing about our traditional attitudes to sex except for the obvious fact that it has long been forbidden to talk about sexual intercourse in direct terms. The connection between *fuck¹* and *fuck²* is not metaphorical, since it is not a question of the transfer of meaning but merely of the transfer of the offensive maledictory force which results from the prohibition of the word *fuck*.

NOTES

1. Baker notes (1981: 181) that American English usage is now beginning to admit active female constructions such as *Jane laid Dick*. This suggests that we are not prisoners of language to the extent that Baker claims.

2. Baker seeks to draw conclusions of general validity from his own linguistic usage, conclusions which may be questioned when other linguistic evidence is taken into account. His belief, for instance, that sexual egalitarianism can be achieved by the use of a neutral third-person pronoun (he suggests *person*!) is not borne out by the example of a country like Turkey, where the neutral pronoun *o* "he" and "she" has scarcely improved the position of women in society. Baker also fails to consider the difficulty of introducing neutral third-person pronouns in languages with grammatical gender.

3. "An erection"; note that this is treated like a sort of illness, with the typical Ulster use of the definite article as in *I have the toothache*. In rural Ulster, where certain individuals are still believed to have magical charms to cure such ailments as sprains, loose women can be described as having "a cure for the horn (but you have to keep going back)."

4. The only phonetically disguised dirty words which I can think of are *buff, dick, diddy,* and *pee* (for *buck, prick, tit,* and *piss*).

5. This parallels the division of *fuck* into two distinct lexical items by Quang (1969: 46).

6. In this usage Ulster also has the analogically formed *bastarding* and *cunting*.

REFERENCES

Aman, Reinhold. 1980. "Clean Up Your Fexing Language! Or, How to Swear Violently Without Offending Anyone." *Maledicta* 4: 5-14.

Baker, Robert. 1981. "'Pricks' and 'Chicks': A Plea for Persons." In *Sexist Language: A Modern Philosophical Analysis,* ed. Mary Vetterling-Braggin, pp. 161-82. Totowa, N.J.: Littlefield, Adams and Co.

Einarsson, Jan. 1981. *Fult och fint: Anteckningar om språk och kön.* Språk och kön i skolan, 3. Lund: Lunds Universitet, Institutionen för ämnesmetodik och ämnesteori, Avdelning för svenska.

Kanin, Eugene J. 1979. "The Equation of Coital Vulgarisms with Personal and Social Transgressions." *Maledicta* 3: 55-57.

Ljung, Magnus. 1986. *Om svordomar i svenskan, engelskan och arton andra språk.* 2nd ed. Stockholm: Akademilitteratur.

Quang Phuc Dong. 1969. "Phrases anglaises sans sujet grammatical apparent." *Langages* 14: 44-51.

OFFENSIVE WORDS IN DICTIONARIES
IV. ETHNIC, RACIAL, RELIGIOUS, AND SEXUAL SLURS IN AN AMERICAN AND AN AUSTRALIAN DICTIONARY

Reinhold Aman

*In loving memory of Don Laycock,
a learnèd and lusty friend*

When in 1988 the Third College Edition of *Webster's New World Dictionary* appeared, I was happy to see that finally many standard obscenities, vulgarities and assorted slurs were included in this new edition. The book censors of many school libraries will, of course, condemn such honest recording of real language, but now that even the "worst" words are in all but some simple-minded, bowdlerized dictionaries, the schools either will have to order honest reference dictionaries or shortchange their students with castrated junk.

Looking for ethnic, racial, religious, and sexual slurs in WNW3, I was struck by three peculiarities of that dictionary: (1) several very common and high-frequency slurs are missing, e.g., *chink*, *coon*, *dago*, *guinea*, *Hebe*, and *Polack*; (2) the usage labels are very inconsistent and some are absent, e.g., *frog* and *kraut* are not labeled "vulgar" or "hostile" but others are; and (3) two anti-Semitic slurs—and these two only, *kike* and *to jew* (*down*)—are marked with the special label "vulgar"; and *nigger* only is labeled "viciously hostile." One does not expect a general dictionary to contain all slurs, but one should be able to find the most common ones labeled consistently in such a comprehensive work.

I have compared the entries in the third edition, edited by Victoria Neufeldt, with those in the second edition, edited by David B. Guralnik. Terms absent in the earlier edition but found in the third edition are marked with a bullet (•). One notes that the second edition lacked many ethnic slurs, including the common *kike* and *nigger*, due in part to the opinion of Mr. Guralnik (and his colleagues) who considers such slurs "the true obscenities."[1] Further, in the third edition, anti-homosexual slurs now feature "warning labels," whereas the second edition labeled them merely *slang*. The labeling of such terms as "hostile," "derisive," "contemptuous," or "offensive" follows the current trend of being "sensitive" to the feelings of certain groups, also observed by the Random House dictionary Editor in Chief, Stuart B. Flexner.[2] Ms. Neufeldt probably will get a tongue-lashing from fanatical feminists for not labeling **bird** ("young woman," U.K.), **broad** ("woman"), and **chick** ("young woman," U.S.) as "sexist," "hostile," or "vulgar and offensive."[3]

The entries **Eskimo**, **Gypsy**, (American) **Indian**, **Negro**, **cripple** and **leper** show no usage label. Despite the efforts by pressure groups of self-appointed socially "sensitive" bullies to outlaw these words, it appears that we can still use them without having to feel overly guilty and being branded "insensitive" Neandertalers.[4]

While I did not *look* for inconsistencies in the labels, I did notice that some labels are qualified by "generally," "often," "sometimes," or "usually," without any discernible reason for these differences. Such differences are not noticed when one looks up a word here and there, but they become obvious when one sees them in a listing like this one. I would prefer the modifiers "usually" or "generally" used in all labels for slurs, as so much depends on the context—who is using the term with whom and with what intentions? Similarly, minor inconsistencies are seen in the use of the article (*a* term vs. *term*), in the use of *and* and *or* (*contempt and derision* vs. *contempt or derision*), as well as in the use of *contempt, derision,* and *hostility*: some slurs are labeled with one of these nouns, others with two, again with no obvious plan why one slur is "contemptuous," another "hostile," and a third is both. Also, some slurs are labeled *a contemptuous term*, while others are *a term of contempt*. To be sure, such inconsistencies can occur in a dictionary with some 170,000 entries, but I do notice such nitpicking details and report them. My intentions are not to embarrass dictionary editors (also in *Maledicta 9*, where I quoted the newest unabridged *Random House Dictionary* repeatedly for flaws in its definitions, etc.) but to report oversights to be corrected in their next editions.

Following below are the words listed by group (to show the inconsistencies; *see,* e.g., HOMOSEXUALS) with the warning labels from the definitions or usage notes, followed by some comments mostly about the American dictionary. This list is, of course, just a sampling of various slurs, not a comprehensive inventory.

Since this is a tribute to my Australian friend Don Laycock who, on his last visit to Wisconsin, gleefully pointed out the prudery in *The Macquarie Dictionary*,[5] I am comparing the terms and labels from this newest American "college size" dictionary with the most recent edition of a standard, similar-sized Australian dictionary, *The Macquarie Dictionary* (revised edition 1985). To distinguish between the American and the Australian entries, the American ones are shown in this **Palatino** typeface, whereas the Australian terms, definitions and labels, following the American entries, are shown in **Helvetica**. Note the difference in capitalization in these two dictionaries, as well as the more liberal (or less "sensitive") labels in *Macquarie,* which uses only the label *colloquial* and sometimes adding (*usually*) or (*often*) *derogatory* but lacking such subjective labels as *con-*

temptuous, derisive, hostile, offensive, patronizing, viciously hostile, or *vulgar* found in its American counterpart.

ASIANS

Chinaman: "a contemptuous or patronizing term." This is the only slur labeled *patronizing*.
Chinaman: "a native or a descendant of a native of China; a Chinese." No label.
chink: missing.
Chink: "a Chinese." *Colloquial. Derogatory.* Also, **Chinkie**.
Jap (a Japanese): "a hostile term." No label in the 2nd ed.
Jap: "a Japanese." *Colloquial.*
slant-eye: missing, though fairly common.
slant-eye: "a person of a Mongoloid race, as Chinese, Tibetan, etc." *Colloquial. Derogatory.* Also, **slant**, **slanthead**.
zip (esp. a Vietnamese): missing.
zip: missing.

GERMANS

heinie: missing, though fairly common.
heinie: missing.
hun: "term of contempt applied to German soldiers, esp. in World War I."
Hun: 1. "a German soldier, unit, aircraft, or the like, in World Wars I and II." 2. "any German." *Colloquial.*
•**kraut**: "a derogatory term." Just *derogatory*, not *hostile, contemptuous* or *vicious*?
kraut: "a German." *Colloquial. Usually derogatory.*

HISPANICS

•**spic**: "offensive term of contempt and derision." Why add *offensive*?
spic: 1. "any person of European descent." 2. *U.S.* "a person from a Spanish-speaking community." Also, **spick**, **spik**. *Colloquial.*
wetback (esp. a Mexican): no usage label; warning label needed.
wetback: *U.S.* "an illegal Mexican immigrant." No label.

HOMOSEXUALS

dyke: "a lesbian, esp. one with pronounced masculine characteristics." *Slang*, but no warning label in the 2nd and 3rd editions.
dyke: "a lesbian." *Colloquial.*
fag: "a term of contempt and hostility." No warning label in the 2nd. ed., only *Slang* "a male homosexual."
fag: "a homosexual." *Colloquial.*
faggot: "term of contempt." Is this term less *hostile* than **fag**? No label in the 2nd. ed.
faggot: "a male homosexual." *Colloquial.*
fruit: "term of contempt or derision." No label in the 2nd. edition.
fruit: "a male homosexual." *Colloquial.*
homo: "often a contemptuous term." Just *often*, not *usually*? No label in the 2nd. ed.
homo: "a homosexual." *Colloquial.*
pansy: "an effeminate man; esp., an effeminate male homosexual: often a contemptuous term." Just *often*? No label in the 2nd. ed.
pansy: 1. "an effeminate man." 2. "a male homosexual." *Colloquial.*
•**poof**: "often an offensive term." *Brit., etc. Slang*. Also, •**poofter**, •**pouf**, •**pouff**, •**pouffe**. Why *often*, instead of *usually*?
poof, poofter: 1. "a male homosexual." *Colloquial.* 2. "a person, esp. one who is weak and cowardly." *Colloquial. Derogatory.* Also, **pouf, pouffe**. Why is sense 2 "derogatory" but sense 1 is not?
queer: "term of contempt or derision." Is this term not very hostile, like **fag**? No label in the 2nd. ed.
queer: "a homosexual." *Colloquial.*

ITALIANS

dago: missing, though very common.
dago: 1. "a Spaniard or Portuguese." 2. "a person of Latin race." *Colloquial. Derogatory.*
guinea, ginney: missing, though common.
guinea, ginney: missing.

- **wop**: "an offensive term of hostility and contempt." Is *offensive* necessary?
wop: "an Italian or any foreigner thought to be of Italian appearance." *Colloquial. Usually derogatory.*

JEWS

Hebe: missing, though common.
Hebe: missing.
Hymie: missing, even though it has been much in the news for years (Jesse Jackson).
Hymie: missing.
- **JAP** (a Jewish-American Princess): "a mild term of derision, contempt, etc." The dozen or more Jewish women who in 1987 and 1988 have published articles to condemn this term and those who have experienced *JAP-bashing* don't think this is a *mild* term.
JAP: missing.
- **to jew (down)**: "a vulgar and offensive usage, even when not consciously expressing an anti-Semitic attitude." Why is this word *vulgar* but **queer** and **frog** are not?
to jew, to jew down: missing.
- **kike**: "a vulgar term of hostility and contempt." See comment about *vulgar* under **to jew (down)**.
kike: "a Jew." *U.S. Colloquial. Derogatory.*
- **Yid**: "a very offensive term of contempt." Why is this term *very* offensive?
Yid: "a Jew." *Derogatory.*

NEGROES

coon: missing, even though very common.
coon: "a dark-skinned person." *Derogatory.*
jungle-bunny: missing, even though common.
jungle bunny: "a name used by some white people to describe Aboriginals, Melanesians, Negroes, etc." *Colloquial. Derogatory.* An unusual definition.
- **nigger**: "acceptable only in black English / virtually taboo / a viciously hostile epithet." This is the only slur labeled *"viciously* hostile." I believe that **kike** and **queer**, for example, are equally vicious.

nigger: 1. "a Negro." 2. "a member of any dark-skinned race." *Derogatory.*
spear-chucker: missing, even though fairly common.
spear-chucker: missing.
Zulu: missing.
Zulu: missing.

OTHERS

• **abo** (an Aborigine): "an offensive term." *Australian Slang.*
Abo: "an Aborigine." *Colloquial. Often derogatory.*
bohunk (a Central or East European): missing, though fairly common.
bohunk: missing.
Canuck (a Canadian, French Canadian): "sometimes a disparaging term." No label in the 2nd. ed.
Canuck: "a Canadian, esp. a French Canadian." *Colloquial.*
cracker: 1. a poor white: "contemptuous term." 2. a native/inhabitant of Georgia or Florida: "a humorous usage." Call a Georgian a *cracker* and see if he laughs.
cracker: *U.S.* "one of a class of poor whites in parts of the southeastern U.S."
mackerel-snapper (a Roman Catholic): missing.
mackerel-snapper: missing.
• **frog** (a French person): "term of contempt or derision." Is this not also *hostile* or *vulgar* or both?
Frog: "a Frenchman." *Derogatory.*
goy (a gentile): "often used contemptuously." No label in the 2nd. ed.
goy: "a non-Jew; gentile." No label.
half-breed (often an American Indian plus other race, usually white): "generally regarded as an offensive term because often used contemptuously." Too wordy; *offensive* or *derogatory* suffices. No label in the 2nd. ed. for the noun, but the adjective is labeled as "sometimes regarded as a hostile or contemptuous term."
half-breed: "the offspring of parents of different races; one who is half-blooded." No label.
• **honky** (a white person): "a term of hostility and contempt."
honky: *U.S.* "a white man." *Colloquial. Derogatory.*

Kiwi (a New Zealander): *Colloquial.*
Kiwi: 1. "a new Zealand soldier or representative sportsman, esp. a Rugby League representative." 2. "any New Zealander." *Colloquial.*
limey (an English person): no usage label.
limey: 1. "a British sailor or ship." 2. "an Englishman." *Colloquial.*
Mick (an Irishman): missing, though common.
Mick: 1. "a Roman Catholic (esp. of Irish extraction)". 2. "an Irishman." [Also, "female pudendum"] *Colloquial.*
mickey (an Irishman): *British Slang.*
Mickey: "a policeman." *Colloquial.* [Plus additional meanings].
Newfie: (Newfoundlander): missing, though very common in Canada.
Newfie: missing.
ofay (*black English*: a white person): missing.
ofay: missing, except as an alternative for *au fait.*
Polack: missing, though very common.
Polack: *Chiefly U.S.* 1. "a person of Polish descent." *Derogatory.* 2. "a Pole." *Archaic.*
redneck (a poor, white, rural Southerner): no usage label; warning label needed.
redneck: *U.S.* 1. "a southern U.S. white farm labourer, esp. one who is ill-educated or ignorant." 2. "any uneducated prejudiced person, usually a manual worker." *Colloquial. Derogatory.*
• **shiksa** (a female gentile): "term of mild contempt." This term is quite derogatory, not just *mild*. Also, it should be spelled **shikse̲**.
shikse: missing.
WASP: no usage label.
WASP: *Orig. U.S.* "a member of the establishment conceived as being white, Anglo-Saxon, and Protestant." No label.
• **whitey:** "a usually hostile term of contempt."
whitey: "a white man." *Colloquial. Derogatory.*

FOOTNOTES

1. In *Maledicta 8* (1984-85): 131-132, David Guralnik explained in great detail why his Second Edition lacked almost all sexual, excretory, and ethnic/racial slurs.

2. See Mr. Flexner's complete comments in *Maledicta 8* (1984-85): 130:

> In the past we have labeled certain words for homosexuals, including such old ones as *pansy, fag*, etc., as *slang*; however, I am increasingly adding the label *derogatory* and/or *offensive* to such items, because for the last decade or so we have become aware just how offensive these words are to gays. In like manner, we are...slowly changing our labeling of such words as *broad* to show that it is more than slang, that it is considered offensive by a great many women.

3. I sent an advance copy of an earlier version of this article to Ms. Neufeldt to get her comments or corrections, but she did not reply.

4. This spelling is preferable to *Neanderthals*, derived from *Neandertal*, the valley of the Neander river near Düsseldorf, Germany, where the skeletal remains of those prehistoric people were first found. The old-fashioned spelling *Thal*, now *Tal* ("valley, dale"), was used for the 19th-century scientific designation *Homo sapiens neanderthalensis* and became the basis for the English term. As someone from London is a *Londoner* (not a *London*), someone from the Neandertal is a *Neandertaler* (not a *Neandertal*), with the added place-name-origin suffix *-er*. *Neanderthal* is wrong, as it means "Neander (river) valley." The only correct terms are *Neandertal man* (although "sexist") and *Neandertaler*, as they mean "Neandertal person," in their literal and figurative senses. Of course, one could argue that *Neandertal* is the short version (just as *Phillips* is the short version of *Phillips screwdriver*), with *man* (and *screwdriver*) understood. Spelling it without the obsolete and never-pronounced *h* also prevents the ignorant pronunciation *-thôl* instead of the correct *-tôl*.

5. As Dan pointed out, in earlier editions the "dirty" headwords are replaced by "clean" words of preceding and following entries: in the 1982 edition, on p. 721, the headword is **fuchsite** (instead of **fuck**), and on p. 722, it is **fucoid** (instead of **fuckable**). See illustrations on page 135. During his last visit, we also discussed one of his great interests, Pidgin English, and an article about terms of abuse in that language.

NOTE

A similar version of this article will appear in *A Memorial Volume for Donald C. Laycock*, edited by Tom Dutton, Darrell Tryon and Malcolm Ross, to be published by the Linguistics Department at the Australian National University in Canberra. On 27 December 1988, Don suddenly died of leukemia. A cheerful man who loved life, he cherished *Maledicta*, bawdy songs, and Pidgin English. We miss him greatly.

721　　　　　　　　　　　　　　　　　　　　**fuchsite**

frumpish /'frʌmpɪʃ/, *adj.* dowdy and unattractive. – **frumpishly**, *adv.* – **frumpishness**, *n.*
frumpy /'frʌmpi/, *adj.*, **-pier**, **-piest**. →**frumpish**. – **frumpily**, *adv.* – frumpiness ~~~~~~~~~~~~~~~~~~~
fuchsite /'fuksaɪt/, *n.* a green variety of muscovite in which some of the aluminium is replaced by chromium. [named after J. N. von *Fuchs,* 19th-century German geologist]
fuck /fʌk/, *Colloq.* –*v.t.* **1.** to have sexual intercourse with. **2.** to treat (someone) unfairly, deceive, or cause inconvenience, distress, etc. to (oft. fol. by *about, around,* etc.). **3. fuck up,** to make a mess of; ruin. –*v.i.* **4.** to have sexual intercourse. **5.** to behave stupidly or inanely (oft. fol. by *about, around* etc.). **6. fuck off,** (*oft. offensive*) to go away; depart. –*n.* **7.** a person, as the object of the sexual act: *a good fuck.* **8.** the act of sexual intercourse. **9. not give a fuck,** not to care at all. **10. the fuck,** (an intensive): *who the fuck are you?* –*interj.* **11.** (an offensive exclamation of disgust or annoyance, often used as a mere intensive). **12. what the fuck!** (an exclamation of contempt, dismissal, or the like). **13.** (an exclamation of wonder or delight). [? ME, of uncert. orig.; but cf. G *ficken,* lit., to strike, F *foutre,* L

u = pool　ɜ = pert　ə = apart　aɪ = buy　eɪ = bay　ɔɪ = boy　aʊ = how
ʒ = measure　tʃ = choke　dʒ = joke　ŋ = sing　j = you　õ = Fr. bon

 **fucoid**　　　　　　　　　　　　　　　　　　　722

futuere, Gk *phyteúein*]
fuckable /'fʌkəbəl/, *adj. Colloq.* sexually desirable.
fuck-all /fʌk-'ɔl, 'fʌk-ɔl/, *n. Colloq.* very little, nothing: *they've done fuck-all all day.*
fucked /fʌkt/, *adj. Colloq.* **1.** exhausted. **2.** ruined, done for. **3.** broken; out of order. **4. get fucked,** (*offensive*) go away; leave (one) alone.
fucker /'fʌkə/, *n. Colloq.* **1.** one who fucks; one much given to fucking. **2.** a contemptible person or thing. **3.** (*not necessarily offensive*) any person.
fucking /'fʌkɪŋ/, *Colloq.* –*adj.* **1.** (an intensive signifying approval, as in *it's a fucking marvel* or disapproval, as in *fucking bastard*). –*adv.* **2.** very; extremely: *fucking ridiculous.*
fuck-up /'fʌk-ʌp/, *n. Colloq.* confusion; ruin; miscalculation; mistake.
fuckwit /'fʌkwɪt/, *n. Colloq.* a nincompoop.
fuckwitted /'fʌkwɪtəd/, *adj. Colloq.* foolish; stupid.
fucoid /'fjukɔɪd/, *adj.* **1.** resembling, or allied to, seaweeds of the genus *Fucus.* See **fucus**. –*n.* **2.** a fucoid seaweed.

The latest revised ed. of *The Macquarie Dictionary* (1985) avoids the problem by placing **fuck-** entries in the center of p. 711.

☛ Fortunately, that excellent Australian dictionary can now be bought in the U.S.A., too. It is available exclusively through **Facts On File**, 460 Park Avenue South, New York, NY 10016. ISBN 0-949757-23-3, 2009 pages, $45.00. If your bookstore does not handle "special orders," inquire at F.O.F. directly for total price.

LETTER TO A PENNSYLVANIA POSTMASTER

Reinhold Aman

In March 1988, when *Maledicta* 9 appeared, I sent a rush copy by Priority Mail to the editor and book reviewer of an Easton, Pennsylvania, newspaper, expecting that our *Festschrift* for their local celebrity, Lillian Mermin Feinsilver, would be reviewed or mentioned. The newspaper ignored *Maledicta* and Mrs. Feinsilver. (May that editor and book reviewer get huge boils on their bums!) The postal peabrains returned the first rush shipment, because the newspaper had moved to another part of town. On 4 April 1988, I sent the following letter to the Postmaster at Easton, with a copy to the Postmaster General.

To: The Postmaster, Easton, PA 18042

Thank you, you inconsiderate, lazy bastards, for returning my Priority Mail RUSH package, instead of handing it to the correct carrier.

It should not surprise you that many postal customers think your "service" sucks, like many of your imbecilic employees who "just follow orders."

I don't care so much that I had to spend another $2.40 to get the package back to your town, but I'm furious because your manure-brained employee wasted a precious week.

I hope that insensitive, ignorant, lazy son-of-a-bitch who returned my *urgent rush* package falls on his fat ass and breaks his coccyx when he picks up his next paycheck. Falling on his head would do him no harm, as a brainless, solid-bone skull can't be damaged.

Sincerely Up Yours,

R. Aman

THE PECKERWOOD POETS
A TRIBUTE

Sanford H. Margalith

It was Fort Knox, Kentucky, December, 1941. I, a 15-year-old private, reported for duty in a flimsy tarpaper shack which was to billet my battery of the newly formed 91st Armored Field Artillery Battalion, 1st Armored Division. I was to live in that freezing wreck of a barrack with a small group of foul-mouthed, whiskey-swilling, brawling, womanizing Regular Army soldiers until I was discharged as under age in the spring of 1942. Later, I joined the Navy and served until the war ended in 1945. But none of the hundreds of men I fought alongside through U-boat attacks and two invasions impressed me as much as those loud-farting, scrotum-scratching country boys of Battery B. A tissue of oxymoronics, they were tolerant racists, intrepid poltroons, trustworthy thieves, honorable prevaricators and loyal-to-the-death deceivers. They lived by an anachronistic code of the downtrodden and dispossessed of 17th-century Britain. They were mostly from West Virginia, Kentucky, Tennessee, and Louisiana, with a sprinkling of the flotsam of ground-down towns, closed-down mines and blown-away farms of other states. Their surnames sounded of peckerwoods, hollows and hardscrabble homesteads: Beasley, Suggs, Sykes, Vernon, Waters, Birdwell, and a sprinkling of names beginning with Mc and Mac. Ethnically, they probably were mostly a mix of Celt and Saxon and, if some of their names be any guide, a little of many others: Fleming (from Flanders), Holland (from the

Netherlands), Beecham (from the French *Beauchamp*), Tolliver (from the Italian *Tagliaferro*), Jewett ("little Jew"), not to mention a number of names of Viking origin.*

My life-long love for these raw-boned career soldiers sprang from their language. It was as different in spirit from my Eastern speech as Chinese from Arabic. To overhear a conversation was an entertainment. Their speech was a mosaic of surprises: an insult concealed in a sentence like a terrorist's bomb, a racist sentiment gift-wrapped in hilarious image, a delicate poetic image coupled with a brutal expression, a judgment at the end of a sentence that tells you all—"Louisville? Well, now, jest get on that road over yonder and keep going north until you smell shit." Every one of them was "expert beyond experience."

It began the very first moments we joined the battery. Huddled in our olive drab great-coats around the primitive Franklin stove in the center of the barracks, we were regaled by a pompous, posturing, rotund first sergeant named Pauker. Immediately after he finished speaking, a half-frozen face topped off by hair the color of Kentucky corn bread, turned to me and said, "That guy's got more shit with him than a thundering herd of cattle." I was enchanted.

From then on similes and imagery in a vast variety of forms were spat around me unceasingly. The simplest statement was embroidered by the creations of some backwoods poet.

If it were cold, it was "As cold as a well digger's ass." If it were *very* cold, it was "As cold as a well digger's ass *in Alaska*." Sometimes it was cold enough to "Freeze the balls off a brass monkey."

If you had too much to do, you were "Busier than a

---

* Some of the names have been changed to avoid embarrassing former members of Battery B or their survivors.

one-armed paper hanger." If you were *very* busy, you were "Busier than a one-armed paper hanger *with the crabs.*"

Should they not be overjoyed to see Pvt. Smith, he was "As welcome as a turd in a punchbowl." Or perhaps they would just recite a little poem to him: "The wind blew, the shit flew, and in walked Smith."

Nearly every criticism or admonishment, or even sometimes an innocent request, was met with the retort, "Blow it out your ass!"

"Hey, you're creasing my blanket."
"Blow it out your ass!"
"I'll never go honky-tonkin' with you again."
"Blow it out your ass!"
"Pass the ketchup, please."
"Blow it out your ass!"

One could never have trouble inserting a device of any sort into a receptacle without being told by the onlooker, "Bet you'd get it in if it had a little hair around it." And to say something that annoyed would sometimes provoke the listener into grabbing his penis with a ferocious grip and cry: "How can you talk when I have you by the throat?"

What is today expressed as "I couldn't care less" came out as, "Fuck 'em all but six and save them for pallbearers."

To be jittery was to be "Nervous as a whore in church."

If you were from a remote rural area, you "Lived so far back in the hills they have to wipe the owl shit off the clocks to see what time it is."

If someone were unconvincing, "He couldn't sell cunt in the state penitentiary."

A man who told tall tales was "Full of shit like a Christmas Goose."

A friend of mine once remarked to me of an unusually offensive honky-tonk bee girl: "I wouldn't piss in her cunt if her ovaries were on fire." I considered his remark unique until I heard it said of a disliked comrade: "I wouldn't piss on his ass if his piles were on fire."

An uppity girl was referred to as "She thinks she shits strawberry icecream." I also heard it said of one such woman: "She thinks her shit comes out wrapped in cellophane."

A man who was stupid "Couldn't tell asshole from tin cup," which has to be admitted is very stupid indeed.

A particularly crude character was sometimes described as "the kind of guy who would shit in the bathtub and kick it out with his feet." Also: "He'd fart in the bathtub and bite the bubbles as they come up."

It was often said of a desired woman: "I would eat a *yard* of her shit just to get up to bite her ass." Or even more directly: "I would eat the peanuts out of her shit."

If you weren't much help, you were "As much use as teats on a bull."

If someone left abruptly, he "Took off like a big-assed bird."

Then there was always the man who "Talks like he has a paper asshole."

When surprised, they dipped into an entire library of exclamations, like the alliterative, "Great puddles of pink panther piss!"

Battery B boys did not often tell jokes. When they did they usually had a farm setting and concerned biological functions (as British humor often does to this day). "Where's Virgil?" the farmer asks. "The pigs ate him," is the reply. Says the annoyed farmer, "I'll be goddamn if I'm going to work all day and fuck all night to support them pigs."

One never knew which expressions were created on the spot or were the passed-along products of some rustic genius. An example: When a comrade and I were ordered to bore sight (check the barrel) of a 105mm howitzer, my friend remarked wistfully, "I'd rather be bore-sighting a mule's ass." And indeed to a plow boy there was a vague similarity.

The word *wimp* was unknown then. Even if it were known, I am certain no Battery B man would stoop to using so wimpish a term. He would say, rather, as he often did of men whose manhood he doubted, "I'll bet he squats to piss." The word *motherfucker* had little currency among white soldiers until around 1944 when they had had more contact with blacks from whom they had been segregated their entire peacetime lives.

A soldier once complained to me after a night of honky-tonking that he felt as if he had been "Shot at and missed and shit at and hit."

There were hundreds more. Most, unhappily, have been lost in the labyrinth of my brain or murdered by ten thousand pre-prandial cocktails. Unhappily, because I have always thought that their speech was underground folk poetry worthy of collection and study. They offer insight into what the lowest classes in Elizabethan Britain thought amusing and creative. Their speech is a reflection of a creative plain-speaking and brutal people; just the sort to go out and conquer a quarter of the world. Their humor is not very different from that of the literati of the Elizabethan England. Shakespeare's plays are sprinkled with much the same humor. He wrote his share of similes and play-on-words obscenities, as in *Hamlet*, Act III, Scene ii:

Hamlet:	Lady, shall I lie in your lap?
Ophelia:	No, my lord.
Hamlet:	I mean, my head upon your lap?
Ophelia:	Ay, my lord.
Hamlet:	Do you think I meant country matters?

The word *country*, of course, is spoken, *cunt* (pause) *ry*.

Their facility with language is even more impressive when one considers that their speech was almost 100 percent Anglo-Saxon, while most literate Americans have at their command the vast potential of the three languages that live side by side in English: Anglo-Saxon, Norman French, and Latin.

Somehow one gets the feeling that more than mere persiflage is going on in country-boy humor. There is anger, protest and frustration in some of it. There is often a desire to shock, to wound and to bind, too.

This is, after all, mostly the humor of the indentured servant, the white slaves brought to America to work the plantations of the pre-Revolutionary-War aristocracy. It reflects, as well, a technique of social leveling—"We're all at the bottom of the heap together, so don't put on any airs with me, friend." Some of it seems to mock the Norman French and Latin pretenses of the aristocracy, much the way the black slaves mocked the carriage of their white masters with the cakewalk. Some, too, seem a pitiful attempt to remind each other that they may be on the bottom, but not on the *very* bottom. So "coons" (blacks), "chopcocks" (Jews) and "dagos" (Italians) came in for special bashing. While waiting in a long chow line one day, a soldier said to me, "I'm so hungry I could eat the asshole out of a dead nigger." When I asked one man how he had done in a card game, he replied, "I made out like a Jew bandit in a junkyard." Women didn't escape, either. "Keep 'em knocked up and barefooted; they stay out of trouble that way," was one commonly expressed sentiment. Another, which again revealed their love of alliteration, was, "Find 'em, feed 'em, feel 'em, fuck 'em and forget 'em."

I have, over the years, heard an occasional try at country-boy similes: "Tight as a bull's ass in fly time" or "Quiet as a fish's fart." They are okay. Worth a chuckle or two the first time you hear them. But they lack the bite, the anger, the impact of Battery B speech.

I had long feared that authentic country-boy speech was dead, killed by television, literacy and better times.

That is, until one day a young Texan came to work for the company that employed me. He was a pleasant, likeable boy whose country-boy facial features had been smoothed by meat and vegetables instead of corn bread and chittlins, disco dancing instead of plowing and two years of junior college instead of six-grades-and-into-the-fields to try to make a living out of land so poor a Battery B boy would have said, "You could't raise a ruckus on it."

He had come into my office one Monday morning looking weary. As a matter of politeness I asked him if he had had a rough weekend. When he replied, his eyes twinkled and his accent reverted to its country origins. He was about to talk about real-world things, and that was no time for radio-announcer general American. "Yeah, I'm plum tuckered out. I met this gal at the Palamino. I tell you, man, I'm still pulling the sheets out of my asshole." Pure Battery B, 91st Armored Field Artillery, 1st Armored Division.

On February 14, 1943, near Side-bou-Zid, Tunisia, North Africa, Battery B was surrounded and overrun. Many died in the alien desert sand 6,000 miles from Appalachia. Pauker, the pompous first sergeant, refused to surrender and was bayonetted to death.

Answer from page 35:

An art-vark

1990 ATTORNEY-HUNTING SEASON AND BAG LIMIT

1. Any person with a valid Alaska hunting license may harvest attorneys.
2. Taking of attorneys with traps or deadfalls is permitted. The use of currency as bait is prohibited.
3. Killing of attorneys with a vehicle is prohibited. If accidentally struck, remove dead attorney to roadside and proceed to nearest car wash.
4. It is unlawful to chase, herd, or harvest attorneys from a snow machine, helicopter or aircraft.
5. It shall be unlawful to shout "Whiplash!", "Ambulance!" or "Free Scotch!" for the purpose of trapping attorneys.
6. It shall be unlawful to hunt attorneys within 100 yards of BMW, Saab or Mercedes dealerships.
7. It shall be unlawful to use cocaine, young boys, $100 bills, prostitutes, or vehicle accidents to attract attorneys.
8. It shall be unlawful to hunt attorneys within 200 yards of courtrooms, law libraries, health spas, whorehouses, gay bars, ambulances, or hospitals.
9. Stuffed or mounted attorneys must have a state health department inspection for AIDS, rabies, and syphilis.
10. It shall be illegal for a hunter to disguise himself as a reporter, drug dealer, legal clerk, sheep, accident victim, physician, bookie, or tax accountant for the purpose of hunting attorneys.

BAG LIMITS

Yellow-bellied sidewinder	2
Two-faced tort-chaser	3
Back-stabbing divorce litigator	4
Small-breasted ball-buster (female only)	3
Big-mouthed pus-gut	2
Cutthroat	2
Back-stabbing whiner	3
Brown-nosed judge-kisser	2
Hairy-assed civil libertarian	7
Silver-tongued drug defender	$500 bounty
Honest attorney	EXTINCT

I have received several such permits, the first from David B., Arizona, March 1988; from Elsa K., Indiana, July 1989; and the latest from attorney William E., Iowa, Oct. 1989. His version was published in the *Alaska Bar Rag* (Feb. 1988, p. 15). In the different versions, there are changes in wording, and the year and state of the hunting license differ, depending on their origin. There is also a primitive imitation, a *Hunting Permit for Porch Monkeys* (Negroes) from Arizona, allegedly signed by Governor Evan Mecham.

EGYPTIAN ARABIC ABUSE

Dilworth B. Parkinson

INTRODUCTION

Egyptian Arabic (hereafter EA), defined as that variety of spoken Arabic used in the greater Cairo speech community, provides its speakers with an incredibly large number of terms of address in general, and of terms of abuse specifically.[1] This was substantiated by research performed in Cairo[2] in which a large body of naturally occurring speech data on terms of address was gathered by several workers, most of them native EA speakers, together with relevant social data about the speech events involved. Supplementary information was also provided by an interview about terms of address that was conducted with nineteen native speakers of EA, representing all social classes and ages and both sexes. In all, 530 terms of address were gathered, over 125 of which would be considered abusive. Of these latter, 25 were relatively common.

The EA word **šitiima**, 'abuse, vilification' refers to words that imply something (usually very) negative about the addressee of a speech event. In English, while it is possible to use abusive terms as terms of address (as in 'Hi, stupid') it is much more common to simply "call" someone something, using patterns such as 'You____!' ('You idiot') or 'You are a(n) ____!' ('You are a creep!'). The opposite is true in EA. While on a very few occasions I did hear terms of abuse as the predicate of equational sentences (**'inta xawal** 'You are a homosexual,' **'inti ibn kalb** 'You (f.) are a son of a dog'), by far the most common practice is to use them as terms of address, preceded by the vocative particle **ya**.

Despite this, it is true that many instances of abusive term usage come closer in meaning to 'You [term]!' than to 'O [term]!' In these cases they often appear almost unconnected to surrounding discourse, and function solely, or almost solely, to attribute features of the term to addressee, rather than functioning as regular terms of address on the discourse level to get addressee's attention, mark turn changes, etc. I will refer to this kind of use as the "name-calling" function of term of address usage.

In other cases, terms of abuse are used as regular terms of address, surrounded by other speech and performing discourse functions. Even in these cases, however, the name-calling aspect of the meaning can be quite important. This is frequently played with by EA speakers who may insert an abusive term in a discourse otherwise marked as respectful in order to emphasize sarcastically its effect, as in this piece of natural data, gathered in Cairo:

> 1. A young man approaches a coffee house where he is greeted by a friend who says with a polite and friendly voice:
> **'ahlan ya siidi itfaḍḍal itfaḍḍal yabn ilwisxa!**
> *Hello, sir, have a seat, sit down, you son of a whore!*

EA speakers use terms of abuse both in **hiẓaaṛ** 'sarcastically' and seriously. They use them sarcastically to friends, especially among youthful peer groups, in which case the abusive meaning is not taken at face value. When asked why he had used a fairly "heavy" term of abuse to his best friend, with whom he had not been angry or annoyed, one informant replied that the term meant **'inta ṣaḥbi 'awi** 'you are really a close friend.' In other words, since he would never use abusive terms in this way to any addressee with whom he had a formal or respectful relationship, his using the terms freely and sarcastically to close friends actually marks intimacy and friendship.

The terms are used seriously to express anger, annoyance, disgust or disapproval of addressee. As an extension of this, parents and teachers use abusive terms to instill "correct" values into their children and students. When I first arrived in Cairo, I was surprised to hear a father use what I had been told was an extremely vile term to his two-year-old son who had fallen off a chair and was crying. I therefore asked informants during the recorded interview why a father would call his own son a **xawal** 'homosexual playing the female role' in such a situation, and almost all of them responded that he did it to inculcate in the child the values of **ruguula** 'manliness,' which are considered to be the opposite of the values associated with the term **xawal**. Likewise, almost all teachers (including the very polite ones) use terms like **ḥumaar** 'donkey' that imply stupidity specifically in order to get their students to act and perform intelligently. I believe that this pattern of usage is closely related to the well-known Arab child-raising practice of creating shame on the part of the child. Using these terms of address is felt to be an important way of creating feelings of shame in the child and therefore of instilling in him the proper values.

RANKING EA TERMS OF ABUSE

Interestingly, all of the common abusive terms, and most (possible all) of the less common terms, have associated with them a ranking on what I will call the "heaviness" scale. In discussing particular terms, informants often classed them as **ti'iil** 'heavy' (=strong) or **xafiif** 'light' (=mild), and they were often willing to rank two terms, claiming one to be heavier than the other. Other words used to describe light terms include **raaqi** 'refined' and **basiiṭa** 'simple,' while other words used to describe heavy terms include **gamda** 'solid,' **bayxa** 'degenerate, very bad,' wiḥša 'bad,' and **baladi** 'local, working class, of the illiterate masses.'

Informants stated that for any one speaker, the angrier or more annoyed he is the lower down the scale he is likely to go to choose an abusive term. They also stated that the more a speaker is speaking "down" (in social class or age) the lower the term would most likely be.

Seven of the terms of abuse were discussed in the interview, and a clear social class gradation of these terms emerged. Informants were presented with a term and asked: "Do you ever use this term?" Three categories of terms emerged: those claimed only by *upper class* speakers, those claimed only by *working class* speakers, and those claimed by *all classes* of speakers. The upper class terms were judged light and the working class terms as heavy by all informants. The terms used by all classes were ambiguous, with working class informants calling them light, and upper class informants calling them at least somewhat heavy. I have labelled this category of terms as "medium."

Working class speakers claimed normally to use the heavy terms when angry, but might also use the medium terms in "polite" settings (as, for example, to a fellow student in school in the presence of a teacher), or when they want to imply sarcastically that the addressee is not a "real" man and therefore could not take the heavy terms. The term **gabaan** 'coward' was considered by these informants to be very light, almost feminine, and when asked to give examples of its use, they inevitably put on a female voice and used it in a way that implied that addressee had female characteristics.

Upper class speakers claimed normally to use the light terms, but they also might drop down to the medium terms in situations involving real anger. For them, **gabaan** is a rather heavy term.

Middle class speakers, especially males, have the whole

range of terms available, using light terms in polite or formal settings, medium terms with friends and in annoyance, and heavy terms when truly angry or to a working class, younger addressee.

It should be noted that two upper class male informants pointed out that upper class males, in peer groups, delight in using the heavy terms, but that this is taken as a "mimicking" of working class usage rather than as reflecting on the speakers themselves.

It should also be noted that some upper class speakers, both male and female, find the heavy terms to be so **bayxa** 'degenerate, rotten, vile' that they simply cannot bring themselves to pronounce them, much less use them. In other words, for these speakers a taboo reaction is in evidence for the heavy terms. No taboo is involved with the medium or light terms for any speaker, as far as can be determined, and working class speakers demonstrate no feelings of taboo even for heavy terms.

To summarize, then, the whole EA term of address system appears to form a continuum. Only a few speakers control the whole continuum while most speakers use only a section of it. The section a particular speaker uses is closely related to that speaker's view of himself, his own social class, age and sex. The portion of the part of the continuum he does control that ends up being used in a particular situation is determined by the social class and other characteristics of addressee, by their general relationship, and by aspects of the specific situation, including whether the interchange is serious or sarcastic, friendly or angry, etc. All speakers move toward the heavier end of their own section of the continuum when angry or when speaking "down" to an addressee of lower social class and/or age than themselves, and move toward the lighter end of the continuum in more formal or polite situations, when not very angry, and when not speaking "down."

THE NATURAL DATA

The natural data on the abusive terms support the above general analysis taken from the interview data. The data divide very neatly into three groups: (1) those terms used exclusively by middle and upper class speakers, (2) those terms used by all classes of speakers, and (3) those terms used exclusively by middle and working class speakers. The first category includes the terms judged by informants as light and the last category the terms judged by informants as heavy. All of the heavy terms, it should be noted, have some sexual content, either actual or metaphorical. Only one heavy term was used by upper class speakers, and this is almost certainly a case of upper class speakers' "mimicking" working class usage, in jest. The corpus of natural data on EA terms of abuse is summarized in the Table below, by group.

Differences in term use for the various ages are not statistically significant, but differences for speaker's social class, speaker's sex and addressee's social class are highly significant (to a .005 level) and differences according to addressee's sex are somewhat significant (to a .05 level).

The natural data, therefore, do support the analysis below of the EA term of address system. Female and upper class speakers are more likely than male or lower class speakers to either give or receive light terms of abuse, and male and lower class speakers are more likely to give and receive heavy ones. Middle class speakers pattern between the two extremes.

TABLE
Data Summary for the Terms of Abuse, by Group

WC = working class, MC = middle class, UC = upper class
M = male, F = female, Y = young, MA = middle aged, O = old

	Speaker's Social Class			Addressee's Social Class		
	WC	MC	UC	WC	MC	UC
Light Terms	0	10 (.182)	42 (.525)	2 (.023)	19 (.333)	31 (.500)
Medium Terms	25 (.347)	21 (.382)	36 (.450)	32 (.364)	19 (.333)	31 (.500)
Heavy Terms	47 (.653)	24 (.436)	2 (.025)	54 (.614)	19 (.333)	0

	Speaker's Sex		Addressee's Sex	
	M	F	M	F
Light Terms	30 (.192)	22 (.431)	40 (.242)	12 (.286)
Medium Terms	60 (.385)	22 (.431)	59 (.358)	23 (.548)
Heavy Terms	66 (.653)	7 (.137)	66 (.400)	7 (.167)

	Speaker's Age			Addressee's Age		
	Y	MA	O	Y	MA	O
Light Terms	40 (.282)	8 (.160)	4 (.267)	49 (.265)	2 (.105)	1 (.333)
Medium Terms	52 (.366)	22 (.440)	8 (.533)	74 (.400)	6 (.316)	2 (.667)
Heavy Terms	50 (.352)	20 (.400)	3 (.200)	62 (.335)	11 (.579)	0

DESCRIPTION OF THE TERMS

In the next section of this article, EA terms of abuse are divided into categories, listed and discussed.

Light and Medium Terms of Abuse

Upper class informants stated that they use a much larger number of abusive terms than working class speakers do, precisely because their parents have trained them not to use the "truly expressive" (heavy) terms available to working class speakers. Upper class speakers have therefore proliferated the terms of abuse greatly, so that they will have a large number to choose from for any particular occasion. The main categories from which they have chosen words to become terms of abuse are: (1) names of animals, (2) names of low professions (with the exception of professions relating to sex), (3) names of physical defects, (4) names of moral defects, (5) names of mental defects, (6) names of lowly objects, (7) words implying that addressee is a child, and (8) words implying that addressee has purposely been avoiding speaker. These categories will be discussed individually.

(1) *Animals*

Animal terms occurring in the data include **kalb** (f. **kalba**) 'dog,' along with **ibn ilkalb** 'son of a dog' and several variants, **mi'za** 'goat,' **ṭoor** 'bull,' **waḥš** 'wild animal,' **'igl** 'calf,' **ḥuṣaan** 'horse,' **gamuusa** 'water buffalo,' **ḥayawaan** 'animal,' and **ḥumaaṛ** 'donkey.' Of these, only **kalb**, **ḥayawaan** and **ḥumaaṛ** are common.

The first, **kalb**, when used by itself, is definitely a light term, disavowed by working class informants and claimed by upper class informants. Its relative politeness is probably to be attributed to the fact that it contrasts directly with the most common term of abuse in EA, **ibn ilkalb** 'son of a dog,' which is not considered to be so polite. Several variants of **ibn ilkalb** appeared: **bint ilkalb** 'daughter of a dog,' **wilaad ilkalb** 'children of a dog,' **ibn diin ilkalb** 'son of the religion of a dog,' **bint diin ilkalb** 'daughter of the religion of a dog,' and **bint sittiin kalb** 'daughter of sixty dogs.' All of these are considered to be medium terms of abuse, used by all classes. They seem relatively light for working class speakers but quite heavy for upper class speakers. This, of course, contrasts with **kalb** alone, which is light for all classes of speakers.

The term ḥayawaan 'animal' appeared only in classroom settings in the natural data, in all cases being used in anger. Its use implies that addressee is not acting like a human being (i.e., is not obeying classroom etiquette).

The term ḥumaaṛ 'donkey,' and the rare **ibn ilḥumaaṛa** 'son of a female donkey,' imply a lack of intelligence. The former term is used frequently in classroom settings, like ḥayawaan, by both fellow students and teachers. Informant statements about this term illustrate the position of medium terms generally. One upper class male informant claimed to use ḥumaaṛ to his close friends, adding that use of low terms in this way could imply intimacy. A middle class informant from a working class neighborhood, however, claimed to use it only to a friend who was **muḥtaṛam šiwayya** 'a little respected,' rather than to really close friends. A working class informant claimed to use it only "in school." The term, then, appears as fairly heavy for upper class speakers, but quite light for middle and working class speakers.

(2) *Low Professions*

The terms taken from names of low professions include **ibn il'aṛbagi** 'son of a donkey-cart driver,' **bint ilġassaala** 'daughter of a washwoman,' **miṛaat il'askari** 'wife of a soldier' (this one apparently implies that addressee is fat), ḥaṛaami (f. ḥaṛamiyya) 'thief,' **bint ilḥaṛamiyya** 'daughter of a thief,' **bint innattaaša** 'daughter of a pickpocket,' **bint il'owantagi** 'daughter of a con-man,' **mugrim** (f. **mugrima**) 'criminal,' **ibn ilmugrima** 'son of a criminal,' and **bint ilmugrima** 'daughter of a criminal.'

Of these, only **mugrim** and its variants are relatively common. All of them are light, and are usually used to young children, neighbors, siblings and one's own children. In many cases they are used with a tone of voice that causes them to be taken as **dala'** 'terms of endearment' rather than **šitiima** 'abuse.'

(3) *Physical Defects*

The abuse terms which have been taken from words for physical defects include **'a'ma** 'blind,' **bint il'amiyya** 'daughter of a blind woman,' **'aṛa'** 'bald,' **bint il'aṛ'a** 'daughter of a baldwoman,' **'a'wag** and **mu'wiga** 'stooped,' **ṭurš** 'deaf' (pl.), **tixiina** 'fat,' and **gaṛbaan** 'leprous.' All of these terms, with the possible exception of **'a'ma** 'blind,' are light and also not common. Several informants of all classes claimed that **'a'ma** is used to strangers who bump into them in the street or who don't look before crossing the street. Informants also claimed that the term for deafness is used in school to students who do not catch something the first time. A further term, **laẓlaẓ**, was reported by one informant to mean 'fat,' but it did not occur in the natural data.

(4) *Moral Defects*

The abuse terms taken from words implying some moral defect include **ṭifiṣ** (f. **ṭifṣa**) 'stingy,' **diniyya** 'stingy,' **'aliil il'adab** 'impolite,' **ibn tarbiyit iššaari'** 'son of street education' (i.e. unrefined, impolite), **bayxa** 'vile, of low morals,' **nadl** 'vile,' **muftari** (f. **muftariyya**) 'ruthless, bad,' **gabaan** (f. **gabaana**) 'coward,' **wisix** (f. **wisxa**) 'dirty,' **bint ilmihazza'a** 'daughter of a dirty woman,' and **ibn ilyahuudi** 'son of a Jew' (i.e. 'stingy').

Of these, only **gabaan** occurred more than a few times. It is used by all classes and is therefore a medium term. Working class speakers apparently use it in its "true" meaning, to imply that addressee is acting like a coward, while upper class speakers use it as a more general term of abuse for anything bad. For example, an upper class man who was knocked off his motorcycle by a truck illegally turning left got up and screamed **ya gabaan!** at the truck driver. In a sense, **gabaan** is the upper class equivalent of working class **xawal**. The term **xawal** 'homosexual' is the opposite of **gada'** and everything it stands for in the way of macho manliness. While **gabaan** does not have a positive term opposite it as **xawal** does, for speakers of the upper classes it appears to be the opposite of their somewhat less macho ideal of manliness and "humanness."

The other moral defect terms appear to be mainly light, although **wisix** and **bayxa** are most likely medium.

(5) *Mental Defects*

The terms taken from words for mental defects include **magnuun** (f. **magnuuna**, pl. **maganiin**) 'crazy,' **bint ilmagnuuna** 'daughter of a crazy woman,' **bint ilmahwuusa** 'daughter of a mad woman,' **liibi** 'Libyan'(i.e. crazy), **'abiiṭ**, (f. **'abiiṭa**) 'stupid,' **ibnil'abiiṭ** 'son of a stupid man,' **bint il'abiiṭa** 'daughter of a stupid woman,' **'ahbal** (f. **habla**) 'stupid,' **ibn ilhabla** 'son of a stupid woman,' **ǵabi** (f. **ǵabiyya**) 'stupid,' **'ahwaš** 'slow to understand,' **ṣi'iidi** 'Upper Egyptian'(i.e. slow, stupid), and **fallaaḥa** 'farmer' (i.e. slow, unmannered, stupid).

Of these, the most common are **magnuun** 'crazy,' which is a very light term, and three of the words for 'stupid': **ġabi**, **'ahbal** and **'abiiṭ**. For some reason, the first two are light, while **'abiiṭ** is medium. It is not clear why this should be so.

(6) Lowly Objects

The terms of abuse taken from words for objects considered lowly include **gazma** 'shoe,' **zift** 'asphalt,' and **ṛaxam** 'rubbish.' While **ṛaxam** appears to be a medium term, **zift** is clearly one of the lightest terms of abuse. The feminine **zifta** also occurred, as did the form **si zift** 'sir asphalt,' a sarcastic combination of an old-fashioned term of respect with a **šitiima**.

(7) Terms Implying That Addressee Is a Child

The term **'ayl** 'child' and its plural **'ayaal** appeared in the data, always used to imply that addressee has just done something not in keeping with his supposed level of maturity. Both forms are considered to be fairly light.

(8) Terms Implying Purposeful Avoidance

Three terms were used to imply that addressee has been purposefully avoiding speaker: **haṛṛaab** (f. **haṛṛaaba**) 'fleer,' **maxfi** 'hidden,' and **ḍay'a** 'lost.' It should be noted that one of the most common ways of greeting a friend whom speaker has not seen for about two days is with some expression implying that addressee has been avoiding speaker. Both try to say it first so as to avoid being accused by the other. Use of one of these three terms is only one of many possible ways of expressing the same idea. For example:

> 2. A young woman comes to visit a friend at the friend's house. The latter greets her with:

izzayyik yaxti ya ḍayʻa? kull da ġiyaab?
How are you, my sister, O lost one? All this absense?

to which the young woman responded:

hiyya 'ana illi ḍayʻa walla 'inti? 'ana kunt 'andik imbaariḥ wis'al 'ummik!
Am I the lost one or are you? I came by yesterday, just ask your mother!

Other Light and Medium Terms

The reader will have noticed by now that there truly are a large number of light and medium terms of abuse. A few that do not fit any of the categories mentioned up until now include **bahlawaan** 'clown,' **balaawi** 'catastrophe,' **midawwixni** 'you who are mixing me all up,' **miṭanniš** 'you who are ignoring (me)' and several terms that imply that speaker is going to injure addressee in some way: **maḍruuba** 'hit' (i.e. 'you who are going to be hit'), **'ataʻ ra'abtak** 'your neck cut off' (i.e. 'you who are going to have your head chopped off'), and **maksuur irra'aba** 'broken neck' (i.e. 'you whose neck I'm going to break'). All of the latter were said as threats to get young children to do something.

Strong Terms of Abuse

The heavy terms of abuse that appeared in the natural data include **šarmuuṭa** 'rag' (i.e. whore), **bint iššarmuuṭa** 'daughter of a whore,' **ibn il'aḥba** 'son of a whore,' **ibn ilwisxa** (lit. 'son of the dirty [woman]') 'son of a whore' (f. **bint ilwisxa**, pl. **wilaad ilwisxa**), **ibn ilmara ilwisxa** (lit. 'son of the dirty woman') 'son of a whore,' **ibn ilwasiixa** 'son of a whore,' **xawal** 'male homosexual playing the female role,' **ibn ilxawal** 'son of a homosexual,' **'arṣ** 'male homosexual playing the male role,' **'arṣa** 'lesbian' (?), **mitnaaka** 'fucked' (f.) (pl. **mitnaakiin**), **kuss ummak** 'your mother's cunt' and **bint ilmi'arraṣa** 'daughter of a pimp.'

These are "fighting words" for all classes of speakers,

although it will have been noticed that upper class speakers almost never use them. Some upper class speakers refuse even to pronounce some of them. Working class speakers (as well as some middle and upper class young men) also use these terms in a friendly way, often as part of a **šitiima** battle in which two friends trade insults in a competitive way, each trying to better the insult of the other. Two examples of such semi-friendly exchanges follow:

> 3. Two young male working class friends are playing cards at a coffee house. One keeps getting distracted and the other yells in fake annoyance:
>
> **ma til'ab yabn ilwisxa!**
> *Come on, play your card, you son of a whore!*
>
> The other replied:
>
> **ya ṭayyib ya kuss ummak 'iḥna waṟaana ḥaaga?**
> *What's your problem, your mother's cunt, do we have anything else to do?*
>
> 4. A working class young man pauses at the door of a small shoe factory where his friend works and says:
>
> **izzayyak ya sulum, izzayyak yabn ilwisxa?**
> *How are you, Sulum* (nickname for Sulayman), *how are you, you son of a whore?*
>
> Sulum replies:
>
> **itfaḍḍal yaaḍ ya 'aṟṣ ya lli 'ummak bitaklak!**
> *Come in, my boy, you homosexual, you whose mother eats you!*
>
> The first then comes back with:
>
> **bass ya xawal!**
> *That's enough, you homosexual!*

As one informant stated, these terms that imply that there is something sexually wrong with addressee or with his mother or father would probably never be used to a "real" homosexual or a "real" son of a prostitute except in cases of extreme anger. Thus, as in the examples cited above, the message is often 'inta ṣaḥbi 'awi 'you are my good friend.' In other cases, of course, the message involves real anger. The terms are used in anger to strangers, friends, neighbors, and to one's children. Two examples of use to children follow:

> 5. A two-year-old working class girl wet her bed and her mother spanked her. As she stood there crying, a neighbor lady walked in and went over to pick her up and comfort her. As she was doing this, the mother told the neighbor lady what the girl had done. She immediately threw the girl to the floor in disgust and exclaimed:
>
> **ya wisxa! ya kalba! ya šarmuuṭa!**
> *You dirty thing! You dog! You whore!*
>
> 6. A working class mother told her 19-year-old daughter to sweep the courtyard. The daughter argued, and the mother, angered, yelled:
>
> **imsaḥi ya bint iššarmuuṭa ya mitnaaka! imsaḥi kwayyiis badal ma 'aagi 'aṭalla' 'ineeki!**
> *Sweep, you daughter of a whore, you (who have been/will be) fucked! Sweep well or I'll come and tear your eyes out!*

The terms **ibn ilwisxa** and **xawal** are by far the most common of the heavy terms, with **kuss ummak** and **ibn il'aḥba** also being relatively common. As stated above, the term **xawal** appears to be a catch-all term for working class speakers, used whenever speaker wants to imply that addressee does not measure up to the ideals of macho manliness in whatever way.

SUMMARY

We have seen that EA has a large number of terms of abuse, even though the great majority are not common.

Terms are marked in the lexicon as light, medium or heavy, with the largest number of terms being light and medium since these two categories include all of the creative categories of various kinds of defects, animals, etc., and with only the sexual terms being marked as heavy. How speakers use the terms of abuse is determined both by social class and by individual degrees of "politeness." A majority of speakers (only the very polite being exceptions) have about two-thirds of the continuum in their active vocabulary, almost all speakers using the medium terms, but only upper and middle class speakers using the light terms and only middle and working class speakers using the heavy ones. Women tend to use a lighter portion of the scale than do the men of their social class. Friends use the lowest terms in their repertoire in a relatively friendly way to each other. Upper class males occasionally use the very heavy terms: some do this among themselves because mimicking working class usage is now "in style," and others do it only in fights, especially to working class addressees (for example, according to one informant, an upper class young man may give a heavy term to a taxi driver, if the taxi driver has "descended to the same level of abuse"). All parents use terms of abuse to aid in raising their children, but again, usage is very strictly correlated to social class; upper class parents generally use only light terms to their children, middle class parents may have a slightly broader range, and only working class parents use the heavy terms to their children.

Informants, without hesitation, labeled light terms as **raaqi** 'refined' and heavy ones as **bayxa** 'vile,' **baladi** 'local, of the masses,' etc., clearly recognizing that how one uses his terms of abuse is a sensitive marker of his social status. On a pragmatic level, then, using and interpreting terms of abuse involve several different levels of meaning: who speaker thinks he is and who he thinks addressee is, how angry he is with addressee, whether addressee is a close friend or not, as well as the surface level of the "dictionary" definitions of the terms and the implications of these dictionary definitions. Finally, it should be pointed out that terms of abuse are expected in certain situations, and therefore, since they are expected, they do not carry the angry force they may seem to carry to an outside observer. For example, teachers are expected to use terms of abuse to students. I believe that most middle class American speakers of English would be rather surprised to hear a term of abuse from a teacher, and if they did hear one they would assume that it expressed extreme anger. EA speakers, on the other hand, expect to hear (relatively light) terms of abuse from teachers, and they therefore hear the terms when used by teachers as expressing slight annoyance, or merely a simple correction of a student. This also applies to the use of terms to one's friends, children, and in various other situations. It is certainly not too much to claim that an instance of EA term of abuse usage cannot be properly interpreted without knowing the social class and sex of speaker and addressee, how well they know each other, the tone of use, what kind of situation they are in, and whether (and which) terms of abuse are expected in that situation.

NOTES

1. An earlier version of this article appeared as a chapter of my dissertation, "Terms of Address in Egyptian Arabic," University of Michigan, 1982.

2. This research was performed under the auspices of a Fulbright-Hayes Dissertation Grant during the 1978-79 academic year.

EDITOR'S NOTE: The IPA symbols were graciously supplied by Ecological Linguistics (see p. 42). When fonts are mixed, e.g., Palatino and IPA or Georgian, right-hand justification is sometimes poor.

INSTRUCTIONAL GRAFFITI

*Rosetta Stone

In the spring of 1989, I noticed a six-inch high by two-foot long graffito written on the wall in a stall of the women's restroom, third floor, at the University of Maryland Art building.

Someone else had corrected the spelling by crossing out **O** and writing **Oops** beneath it. This dialog graffito made me wonder whether anyone else would respond to instructional graffiti, as I call this type. For the first time in my life I wrote a graffito on a bathroom wall (see boldfaced graffito ⑤). Following below is the result of my experiment. Each graffito is written by a different hand. The numbers show the sequence in which the graffiti appeared.

> ANDROG̶O̶NY ♀ ♂

① **Oops**

② Why do you want everyone else to be androgynous? Some are heterosexual, some are homosexual, some bisexual. Whatever floats your boat. But what's the purpose of writing your sexual preference on a bathroom wall? If you're trying to desensitize society, that's not the way to do it! Perhaps your first triumph would be learning how to <u>spell</u> your sexual preference, hu?

③ *Before <u>you</u> criticize others, you should get <u>your</u> facts straight. Androgeny is not a sexual preference. It refers to the socialization process.*

④ By the way, <u>you</u> spelled "androgyny" wrong, too. Why don't you <u>both</u> look it up in a dictionary?

⑦ Please write more. I've been coming here for 3 months, and no additional statements have been made.

⑧ Your additional statement is at the bottom.

⑥ *Because we need to communicate and teach and there are lots of places besides our sacred halls in the academe, just as good or better!*

⑤ **This is not a sexual preference, Dr. Ruth. It is the state of being the adjective "androgynous" <u>irrespective</u> of sexual preference. Sex, gender and sexual preference are three entirely different concepts. Homosexual, heterosexual and bisexual refer to <u>sexual preferences,</u> <u>not</u> gender identity or sex role characteristics like being androgynous. Learn how to think before you tell someone else "learn how to spell."**

⑨ |WHO CARES!|

LINGUISTIC TABOOS, CODE-WORDS AND WOMEN'S USE OF SEXIST LANGUAGE
A DOUBLE BIND

Sol Saporta

One of the privileges men enjoy in a sexist society is the greater latitude in the use of emotionally charged words. This inequity presumably is merely one example of a general situation, namely the demands on women to accede to norms of propriety.

Contemporary women, struggling to achieve a more egalitarian society, have resisted this asymmetry, and hence, one is now more likely to hear women use an expletive like *shit* in lieu of less forceful—what Lakoff (1975, p. 10) has called 'trivializing'— forms, like *Oh dear* and *goodness*. However, many of these emotionally loaded words are themselves sexist. Hence, the double bind: either women refrain from using such expressions, thereby legitimizing men's privilege, or they do not refrain from using them, and thereby participate in their own degradation. The result is the incongruous situation whereby women who are indignant at the use of a word like *chairman* have nevertheless 'reclaimed' the word *bitch*. A related issue is the struggle to influence men in their linguistic usage, the current debate about pornography being essentially the logical extension of this position.[1]

The presence of a taboo word typically results in a proliferation of synonymous expressions, both euphemisms and emotionally charged words. So, for example, in certain segments of our society, the word *die* is avoided, being replaced by euphemisms like *to pass away* or *to go home*. Not surprisingly, there also exist frivolous or irreverent synonyms like *to croak* or *to kick the bucket*.

Similarly, then, for words referring to sex: the euphemisms are expressions like *to sleep with someone* or *to go to bed with someone* alongside epithets like *fuck*. Incidentally, the euphemisms, but not the epithets, tend to have symmetrical syntax: *He sleeps with her; She sleeps with him*, whereas *fuck* tends to occur with a male as grammatical subject.[2]

Another linguistic device available in lieu of the taboo words is the use of 'code-words.' One common type of code-word is a word phonetically similar to the taboo word, e.g., *shoot* for *shit*, *fudge* for *fuck*. Paradoxically, the code-word can be substituted only for the expletive use, not the literal use of the taboo words. Thus *Oh shoot!* but not *I have to take a shoot*.

The use of phonetically similar code-words is not limited to English. Spanish speakers often use *miércoles* 'Wednesday' for *mierda* 'shit' and even contrived *mi hermosa patria* 'my beautiful fatherland.'

The code-word may be a phonetically similar nonsense syllable: *frig* for *fuck*, *heck* for *hell*.

The code-word may be one part of a compound: *mother* for *mother-fucker*; *sucker* for *cocksucker*. Or the code-word may be an abbreviation: *s.o.b.* for *son of a bitch*. Even relatively innocuous terms are sometimes abbreviated, as in *b.m.* for *bowel movement* or *v.d.* for *venereal disease*, which seem to be abbreviations of expressions which are themselves euphemisms.

Occasionally, the code-word is completely arbitrary, as in the use in 'nursery' language of the expressions *number one* and *number two* for bodily functions.

A particularly insightful (and inciteful) use of a code-word was Lenny Bruce's recorded comedy routine, called

"Blah Blah Blah." Bruce had apparently been arrested the previous evening during a performance at a club for having used the word *cocksucker*. He then reported on his appearance before the judge, and in order to avoid being arrested again, advised the audience that he would not repeat the word, 'a ten-letter word, beginning with *c* and ending with *r*.' In the course of the monologue, Bruce points out, first that the judge and police officers 'like to say blah blah blah,' and also, that the meaning of the word does not limit its use to male homosexuals, as the police imply, that is, the word is sexist in a rather unique way. What we have here, is a kind of word-magic, in which one use of the taboo word results in incarceration, whereas repeated use of the code-word is absolutely innocuous.

To make certain obvious distinctions explicit: not all taboo words are sexist: *bitch* presumably is; *shit* is not. There is a difference between a taboo word and a taboo act. Incest is a taboo act; the word *incest* is not a taboo word; the word *mother-fucker* is.

There are, then, three issues: first, the nature of linguistic taboos, which are not limited to, but often are sexual in their reference, and sexist in their usage. Consider uniquely female activities like pregnancy and menstruation. In addition to expressions like *to be expecting* and *to be unwell* one finds *to be knocked up* and *to have the rag on*.

Second, women and men may differ in their choice of expressions. If women tend to be more 'proper,' they are more likely to use more innocuous terms, euphemisms and code-words.

Third, the emotionally charged words, in contrast to the euphemisms, tend to be sexist, both in their assymetrical syntax and in their distinctive connotations: calling a woman a *cunt* is not the same as calling a man a *prick*, the former having much stronger sexual and moral connotations than the latter.

Now, the political strategy suggested by these observations remains an open question. Bruce is almost explicit in claiming that the existence of taboo words is itself pathological, and that repeated use of a taboo word will eventually defuse it of its emotional charge, a consequence he clearly considers desirable. This is a position that is shared by many contemporary young people who consider themselves progressive. But breaking a taboo is not the same as eliminating it. Given the fact that taboo words persist, women seem to be in a double-bind, because the two desirable consequences are mutually exclusive. They cannot simultaneously deny men their linguistic privilege and refrain from using sexist language.

The pornography issue can now be rephrased: Can a sexist society sustain an erotic language (or literature or art) which is not sexist?

FOOTNOTES

1. Consider the form *cuntionary*, introduced presumably as a feminist alternative to a *dictionary*. The political effectiveness is not measured by the linguistic ingenuity.

The dilemma that women face is not unlike the situation confronting Blacks who speak a stigmatized dialect of English. Learning the prestige dialect, what is usually referred to as bidialectalism, is, in effect, legitimizing the bias of a racist class-conscious society. Refusing to learn the prestige dialect has obvious social and economic consequences.

2. The semantic and syntactic analysis of *fuck* is unclear. Specifically, whether the feature of 'penetration' is critical is open to debate, precisely because of the use of the word with a female subject. The issue may be clarified by considering an analogous case. The fact that one can say "She's one of the boys" does not invalidate that the word *boy* includes the feature 'male.'

REFERENCE

Lakoff, Robin (1975). *Language and Woman's Place*. New York, N.Y.

CHALLENGER SHUTTLE JOKES

Reinhold Aman

INTRODUCTION

Much wound-healing time has passed since the *Challenger* exploded in 1986. As *Maledicta* honestly chronicles everything, regardless of how terrible it may be, I will now present the most complete collection of "shuttle jokes," together with some commentary. Now, four years later, we are able to look at the material with less emotion. But do skip this article if you were upset by the "Ethiopian Jokes" in *Maledicta* 8: 37-42. Several longtime members stopped reading our journal because of the Ethiopian jokes; one cancelled his subscription "before the next MAL gives me all the 'jokes' related to the exploding space shuttle." A German orientalist called Christopher's Ethiopian jokes "absolutely revolting, tasteless, thoughtless, impertinent and shameless." And Gershon Legman, to whom I tried to explain the importance of publishing the Ethiopian and *Challenger* riddles (during his visit with Wisconsin Maledicta members), called us "sadistic cocksuckers."

One reason why the European professor and Europe-based Legman *cannot* understand that Americans can joke about such tragedies as the Ethiopian famine and the shuttle explosion is this: unlike them, we Americans and Canadians are saturation-bombed by media coverage of such tragedies; especially television shows us again and again the dying, fly-covered Ethiopian babies and old ones. For months and months we see—and can't escape from—the same story about dying babies presented by network anchors and whiney has-been actors and actresses. This overexposure was one reason why Ethiopian jokes became popular. True, telling such "jokes" functions as a coping mechanisms to drain off our anxieties corncerning our own mortality (and whatever shrinks come up with), but simply put, the common man and woman became fed up with seeing the same emaciated, fly-covered, skull-like faces staring at them, week after week, month after month. Enough, already!

Two days after the space shuttle *Challenger* exploded on 28 January 1986, killing all seven astronauts, I flew to Europe. Discussing the shuttle tragedy with MAL readers in Europe, I was certain that no jokes would appear about the explosion, because the tragedy was too horrendous to have anything funny about it—even if to relief one's anxieties—and because we cannot identify with flying in space (unlike AIDS which *could* happen to anyone).

But I was wrong, terribly wrong. When I returned, I received a telephone call from Eric, a Michigan grade school student who wanted to be the first to report a shuttle joke, and letters had arrived in the meantime with one or more jokes. The first joke was what NASA stood for, found in almost all submissions. The first letter with six shuttle jokes was dated January 30—two days after the accident had happened. Other letters arrived steadily over the months, helping me chronicle this phenomenon; they contained usually two to six jokes, often preceded by an apology for sending such "terrible, awful, tasteless, sick" jokes.

Several newspapers published stories about why people are telling "all those astronaut jokes," such as *The Daily Item* of Sunbury, PA (20 March 1986: 15) but none printed any. The only mainstream publication I know of that printed four actual riddles was *The New Republic* (24 March 1986: 14, sent by John Th.), in Nicholas von Hoffman's "Shuttle Jokes" in his *The Press* column.

"Shuttle jokes" arrived in this chronological order from the following places:

January 30: Los Gatos, CA
February 7: Dearborn, MI
February 13: Arlington, VA
February 15: Worcester, MA
February 16: Kirkland, WA
February 21: Cleveland, OH
February 28: Richford, VT
March 1: Lawrence, MA
March 2: Las Vegas, NV
March 5: Berlin (U.S. soldier)
March 7: Alliance, NE
March 10: Washington, DC
March 10: Philadelphia, PA
March 11: Cleveland, OH
March 15: Philadelphia, PA
March 15: Brabant, Holland
March 18: New York, NY
March 18: Chapel Hill, NC
March 25: Livonia, MI
March 25: Huntingtn.Woods, MI
March 26: Philadelphia, PA
March 27: Boulder, CO
April 1: Ontario, Canada
April 2: Las Vegas, NV
April 4: Concord, NH
April 6: Victoria, Australia
April 9: Chicago, IL
April 10: Concord, NH
April 10: Inverness, CA
April 13: Richmond, VA
April 16: New York, NY

After April 16 I stopped recording date and place.

Before presenting the riddles, I wish to comment on two articles that appeared after the *Challenger* explosion to show you what would-be scholars do. A third one, by Smyth, is intelligent and needs no comment. Two of the articles were published in *Western Folklore* 45/4 (October 1986): Willie Smyth, "Challenger Jokes and the Humor of Disaster," pp. 243-260, and Elizabeth Radin Simons, "The NASA Joke Cycle: The Astronauts and the Teacher," pages 261-277. Patrick Morrow's "Those Sick Challenger Jokes" appeared in the *Journal of Popular Culture* 20/4 (Spring 1987), pp. 175-184 (sent by Michael W., Seattle).

The article by Elizabeth Simons is narrow-minded, biased, self-serving, and full of flawed logic. The authoress, a secondary school teacher, uses the *Challenger* explosion to voice her anti-Reagan sentiments, claims that the jokes are meant to show that teachers are stupid, and overinterprets jokes told by ignorant kids.

For example, according to her, telling *Challenger* jokes "was an opportunity to strike out at teachers, the symbol and perceived cause of the failure of the American public school system" (p. 277). Such a statement is simply paranoid and hysterical. If the first civilian in space had been a lawyer or a journalist instead of a teacher, there would have been lots of jokes based on the stereotypes of those professions.

Simons also overinterprets jokes. For example, on page 269 she cites a joke told by a Texas boy:

What do you call seven astronauts at the bottom of the sea?
— A good beginning.

This is clearly a stupid, screwed-up, senseless "joke," but according to her, the boy's joke "suggests getting rid of NASA altogether." No, for Christa's sake! The boy is just a twit who heard a similar joke and screwed it up. The standard wishful-thinking riddle has members of *disliked* minorities or *hated* professions drown, e.g., the wish that a thousand Negroes or feminists or lawyers die or "be at the bottom of the ocean." Before writing such a nonsensical interpretation, Simons should have asked herself: How could the drowning of seven *admired* people be "a good beginning"? Who would be sick enough to wish that seven innocent people die in such a terrible way? Would a boy hate (those) astronauts so much that he wished they were dead? Of course not. The boy or whoever told him the joke remembered a joke about some other group, tried to turn it into a *Challenger* joke, but blew it. That little dork surely does not have enough brains to imply that we get rid of NASA altogether.

The article about the shuttle explosion by Patrick Morrow, a Full Professor of English in Alabama, is even worse, but for different reasons: he needed a horde of collaborators for his short piece (six pages text, one page jokes, one page bibliography, and two pages of illustrations); he wanders off on some tangent; he doesn't understand the jokes; and he screws up several jokes and tells them poorly.

In footnote 6, Morrow thanks *ten* males and females "for help with gathering, selecting, verifying, and editing Challenger jokes." He further thanks two females for typing, and he's "very much indebted to Dr. Joyce Rothschild" for help with editing. So, "his" article about 14 jokes is the product of 14 people, all of whom should stay out of joke analysis and go into tree surgery.

For instance, jokes No. 3 and No. 12 are essentially the same, thus do not illustrate different issues. Several jokes are told so poorly one could scream:

> What were the last words of the Challenger crew?
> — OK. OK! *Bud* Light.

Not OK! Not OK! Punch line fucked up! It should be "No! No! (I said a) BUD Light!"—after Christa mistakenly flicks her lighter instead of handing the commander a beer. Whoever told or edited that joke needs a good rap on the head.

Like other commentators, Morrow adds highfaluting cacademic bullshit that impresses only a mousebrained university administrator:

> Thus Challenger jokes, using McAuliffe as hostility object, the one astronaut on the mission who was a civilian, thus prone to error like the rest of us mortals, serves as a punching bag, absorbing our deflected vituperation against the technological powers-that-be. (p. 181)

Pure barf. Such verbiage and its writer become non-deflective hostility objects for me. There is more nonsense in Simons's and in Morrow's multi-authored and co-edited quickie, but this gives you a taste.

If you want to read intelligent comments on shuttle

and other disaster jokes, you will have to leave the professionals and turn to a journalist. Nicholas von Hoffman's brilliantly snide essay on *Challenger* jokes puts the academics to shame. He exposes the television networks' handling of the tragedy, from their relentless repetition and insincere solemnity to the anchormen Rather, Jennings and Brockaw fingering their "space phalluses" [models of the shuttle] and to finding "the crackpottiest shrink-ologists to give on-air instructions for saving the nation's [traumatized] schoolchildren." His conclusion: When joksters quip about taboo topics, they are merely saying, "Enough, already!" to the unending solemnity and monstrous repetition of media news.

In reports on the *Challenger* explosion, the bureaucrats at NASA outdid themselves with insulting and disgusting euphemisms. The National Council of Teachers of English awarded them their "Doublespeak Award" for using **anomaly** (the explosion), **recovered components** (bodies of the astronauts), and **crew transfer containers** (coffins for astronauts), MJ, 28 Nov. 1986: 12D. Now I ask you: what is more callous and obscene, the jokes about the explosion or such a barbaric dehumanizing of those who died?

Most jokes are about Christa McAuliffe; only three are specific references to the Negro astronaut (Ronald McNair) or to the Japanese astronaut (Ellison Onizuka). There are no riddles referring to Judith Resnik's Jewishness.

Why the stress on Christa McAuliffe? Because the media went crazy with their damned "First Teacher in Space" hype that got on people's nerves. At our Wisconsin meeting, Legman claimed that the jokes about Christa were anti-woman; no, they were not, because there are no references to her as a "sex object"; most references deal with her profession, a teacher. *USA Today* dubbed her **Teachernaut** (1 May 1986: 3A).

THE RIDDLES

I have added a few jokes from the two articles in *Western Folklore* we didn't have and marked them with *. The riddles, with variants, are grouped by topic. Several items have two topics but are recorded under their main topic only.

NASA

What does NASA stand for?
— *Need* [or *Needed:*] *Another Seven Astronauts*
— *Need Another Seven Assholes*
— *Need Applications for Seven Astronauts*
— *Now Accepting Seven Applications*
— *No, Another Shuttle, Asshole!*
— *Not Another Soul Alive**
— *No Aging Survivors Agency**
— *National Aquatic Sports Agency**
— *Not A Seal Anywhere**
— *Not Another Space Accident* (from Canada)
— *Not As Someone Anticipated* (Canada)
— *Nice Air Show, Assholes* (Canada)

Christa McAuliffe and Teacher

What were Christa McAuliffe's last words?
— *"Now which button am I supposed to push?"*
— *"Hey, what's THIS button for?"*
— *"And what does THIS botton do?"*
— *"I'm so excited I could just explode!"*
— *"Oh, shit! The rubber burst"!* [Reference to O-ring]

What were Christa's last words to her husband?
— *"You feed the cats* [or *dogs, kids*], *and I'll feed the fish."* [In a variant, these are also commander Francis Scobee's last words]

Where is Christa taking her vacation this year?
— *All over Florida.*

What's the new McDonald's specialty in Florida?
— *Christa McNuggets.*

Did Christa make it into space?
— *No, but she made a splash.*

What's the new name for Cape Canaveral?
— *Corpus Christa.*

What did Christa McAuliffe say to her students?
— *"I'll be back in a flash."**

What is Christa doing now?
— *Teaching schools of fish.**

How many teachers can you get into a Volkswagen?
— *Seven. Three in front, three in back, and Christa in the ashtray.* [Recycled. Also told about Turks, Auschwitz, Michael Jackson, etc.]

How many astronauts can you get into a Volkswagen?
— *Eleven: two in the back seat, two in the front, and seven in the ashtray.*

What was the proximate cause of Christa's death?
— *Teacher burnout.*

What's the worst case of teacher burnout on record?
— *Christa McAuliffe.*

What do Donna Rice and Christa McAuliffe have in common?
— *They both went down on the challenger.* [Reference to Gary Hart. See MAL 9: 273]
— *Both were spread all over the Caribbean.*

What color were Christa's eyes?
— *Blue. One blew right and one blew left.*
— *Blue. One blew this way, the other blew that way.*
— *Blue. One blew east and one blew west.* (Canada)
— *Blue. One went right, one went left.*

The teller of the last joke didn't understand the wordplay: *blue* versus *blew*, thus ruins the riddle. Also told about Judith Resnik. The joke also circulated earlier about John F. Kennedy when he was shot in Dallas. Also told in Australia, recycled; see Australia section in "Kakologia," p. 305.

Why was Christa chosen Teacher of the Year?
— *Because she blew up only once in front of her class.*

Why did Christa's students love her so much?
— *Because they saw her blow up only once.*

What happened to Christa despite seven months of training?
— *She still went to pieces.*

What kind of teacher was Christa?
— *In the early morning she taught physics, but by late morning she was history.*
— *She used to teach science, but now she's history.*

What is Christa teaching now?
— *History.*

What is the next profession that's going up on the *Challenger*?
— *Substitute teachers.*

Who will replace Christa?
— *A substitute teacher.*

What did they tell Christa's children when they asked where mommy was?
— *There, there, there, there....* [Point in various directions]

What new law of physics did the *Challenger* crew discover?
— *What goes up must come down, unless it's Christa.*

Why won't Christa's family get a NASA pension?
— *Because she got fired.*

How come Christa got fired?
— *Her boosters were fired first.*

What was the last thing that went through Christa's mind?
— *The instrument panel* [or *control panel, sheet metal, her ass*. Recycling of riddle about a bug hitting a windshield]

What was the last thing that went through the teacher's head when the shuttle blew up?
— *Her arsehole*. [from Australia]

What was the last thing that went through the minds of the astronauts?
— *The left rocket booster*.

Did you know that Christa had dandruff?
— *They found her head and shoulders on the beach*. [Told earlier about Vic Morrow and others, see MAL 7: 304. *Head & Shoulders*® is an anti-dandruff shampoo]

What did Christa use for shampoo?
— *Head and Shoulders*.

How did the investigators learn Judy Resnik had dandruff?
— *They found her Head and Shoulders washed up on the beach*.

What did the reporters ask Christa's husband?
— *"Apart from that, Mr. McAuliffe, how did you enjoy the launch?"* [Recycled Abraham Lincoln joke]

Did you hear about the teacher in space?
— *She learned her lesson.**

What song was playing on the shuttle radio when it blew up?
— *"Hot for Teacher."*

How do you get rid of a teacher?
— *Challenge her.**

What did the bumper sticker say on the piece of salvaged *Challenger* fuselage?
— *"If you can read this, thank a teacher."*

Astronauts

What's the weather forecast for Florida?
— *It'll be raining astronauts for seven days.*

Why wasn't it important that the astronauts didn't shower before take-off?
— *Because they washed up on the beach afterwards.* [Told earlier about Natalie Wood and Leon Klinghoffer]

Why didn't they put showers on the *Challenger*?
— *Because they knew everybody would wash up on shore.**

What are redfish eating these days?
— *Blackened astronauts.*

What did TWA award all the astronauts?
— *100,000 bonus miles, posthumously.*

What do astronauts do on their vacation?
— *Deep-sea diving in parts.*

Negro and Japanese

What do you get if you lock three soldiers, two women, a Jap, and a nigger into a space shuttle?
— *They have a blast.*
— *Quite an explosion.*
— *A gang-bang.*

Why was there only one black on the *Challenger*?
— *Because they didn't know it was going to explode.*
— *Because nobody knew it was going to blow up.*

Did the NASA rescue team find a piece of the black astronaut?
— *No, it was just a radiator hose from an old Chevy.*

Bud Light Beer

What were Commander Scobee's last words?
— "No! No! I meant a BUD Light!"

This refers to the Budweiser Light Beer commercial in which a tavern patron, wanting a "light" beer, asks for it generically and is given some extravagant "light": a flaming baton, a fiery hoop through which costumed dogs jump, etc., whereupon he exclaims, "No, a *Bud* Light!"

What were the last words of the commander?
— *"Not that button, bitch!"**

Drinks and Food

Why do NASA officials drink only Coke these days?
— *Because they couldn't get Seven-Up.*

Why is Sprite NASA's official soft drink?
— *Because they couldn't get 7-Up.*

What is NASA's favorite drink?
— *7-Up with a splash.**

What's the latest drink around the Bahamas?
— *Seven-Up with a dash* [or *splash*] *of Teacher's.* [A brand of scotch]

Why isn't NASA serving Tang any more?
— *Because they have switched to Ocean Spray.* [Both are fruit drinks]

Why did the *Challenger* blow up?
— *Because the crew was freebasing Tang.*

What truth was revealed about Richard Pryor?
— *He was in astronaut training.* [Pryor nearly burned to death some years ago freebasing "controlled substances"]

What is the official NASA cereal?
— *Space Crispies.**

What's the latest deli specialty in Florida?
— *Launch meat.*

What do the sharks call astronauts?
— *Launch meat.*

What did the people watching the lift-off with their mouths open get?
— *A free meal.*

Body Parts

Did they find the astronauts' remains?
— *Yes, they found a head and two hands.* [Stick your index fingers into your ears and close eyes tightly, as if hearing an explosion. Heard in Holland]

What's worse than finding half a worm in your apple?
— *Finding bits of an astronaut in your canned tuna.*

What do you call a burnt penis washed up on the Florida coast?
— *A shuttlecock.**

What's the name of the new restaurant in Florida?
— *Pieces of Seven.*

Seal and O-Ring

What do you call a retarded NASA executive?
— *O-ring-utan.* [Reference to the faulty O-ring]

What do a sea lion, Tylenol, and the *Challenger* have in common?
— *They all need a tight seal.* [Reference to the pain-relief medication now protected with a seal against poisoning by criminals]

What *one thing* do NASA, the makers of Tylenol and Flipper want?
— *A tight seal.*

Miscellany

How's the weather at Cape Canaveral?
— *It's raining dogs and hot pussy.*

What was the forecast for Florida on the day of the launch?
— *Cloudy with scattered shuttle.*

What's another name for the *Challenger* explosion?
— *Shuttle scuttle.*

What was the purpose of the *Challenger* mission?
— *To explore the Big Bang theory.*

Where is the new Florida NASA amusement park located?
— *In a submarine.*

What do the New England Patriots and the *Challenger* have in common?
— *They both were good for one minute, 13 seconds.* [A football team that lost in the 1985 Super Bowl to the Chicago Bears]

What's the theme song for the space shuttle?
— *"I ain't got no body."*
— *"I cover the waterfront."*

What is the positive side of the *Challenger* disaster?
— *It went out with a bang instead of a whimper.*

The following two jokes are from *Jim's Letter* 13 (April 1986: 4, sent by Sandy B., Minnesota), a newsletter by Jim Murray, New York City:

What did Henry Kissinger say to Reagan after the explosion?
— *"Let me head the inquiry. I'll prove it didn't happen."*

Why did Reagan refuse?
— *"Those Texans don't talk to Jews."*

The following riddles were collected in Ontario, Canada; none of these Canadian riddles was told by Americans.

What's the new American cereal?
— *Challenger Bits.*

When is the next shuttle going up?
— *On the Fourth of July.*

What new club is being formed at the NASA headquarters?
— *The shuttle booster club.*

What cutbacks is NASA imposing on future shuttle missions?
— *Next time, they'll use a supply teacher.* [U.S. *substitute teacher*]

Who convinced Christa to go on the shuttle?
— *Her students. They kept calling her a space cadet.*

SHUTTLE JOKES & FOLKLORISTS
A Sarcastic Epilog

Our journal records these gruesome "jokes" and is maligned for chronicling this aspect of humanity. Folklorists and others in academia, however, gain fame & fortune by publishing learnèd treatises on the same material.

Basing my conjecture on past publications—JAP jokes, Polack jokes, Auschwitz jokes, and the like—I predict that a famous Californian folklorist (he's so famous he's *famed*) will publish several articles with psychological interpretations about shuttle jokes in *Western Folklore* or *The Journal of American Folklore*, "proving" that all male Americans telling such jokes are homosexual, latent rapists, anally fixated, or combinations thereof. The Famed Folklorist will push our noses into such Freudian symbols as:

(1) **homosexual**: shuttle (=penis); shooting up into the air (=entering another male's rectum); exploding into a ball of white clouds and streaks (=ejaculation and squirting of semen); debris falling back on earth (=semen splashing on buttocks).

(2) **rapist**: shuttle (=penis); shooting up into the atmosphere

(=penis forcibly entering vagina); exploding (=ejaculation); burst rocket falling back on earth (=spent penis, now turned flaccid).

(3) **anally fixated**: shuttle (=turd); leaving earth (=rectum) in a cloud of smelly gas (=crepitus); explosive burst (=diarrhea) caused by broken seal (=loose anal sphincter).

The Famed Folklorist may further "prove" that the *Challenger* disaster was really *caused by Jew-hating, excrement-fixated Germans*: if the Nazi engineers had not developed their rockets in the 1940s, there would be no *Challenger*, thus no tragedy. Through research materials supplied to the Famed Folklorist by pinko colleagues in Berlin, he will be able to trace the invention of space rockets to two Nazis, Adam von Steifenschwanz and Eva von Eierstock-Mittelschmerz, who once forced the Famed Folklorist's grandfather, Shlomo Raketenkopf of Frankfurt/Main, to develop rocket blueprints in their toilet (*nota bene*) converted into a poorly ventilated laboratory.

Furthermore, the Famed Folklorist may prove that *the shuttle explosion was a sinister plot by male chauvinist pigs to kill two brilliant, educated women* who might otherwise have become a threat to those insecure phallocratic swine. By sabotaging this space mission with two women aboard, the Chauvis were able to kill two birds with one bang. The victims were the unmarried scientist Judith Resnik, who never suffered the shackles of that "obscene" institution, marriage (Simone de Beauvoir, who just went to Dyke Heaven), and first-teacher-in-space Christa McAuliffe, whose martyrdom as a married woman was intensified by a fourth K-chain: in addition to the traditional KKK-chains of married women, *Kinder* (children), *Kirche* (church) and *Küche* (kitchen), she endured the additional chain of *Klassenzimmer* (classroom).

As a result of such brilliant psychological-folkloric speculations and publications, the Famed Folklorist normally would be rewarded with a large salary increase. However, already having reached the maximum salary allowed by the University of California ($175,000 per academic year), the Folklore Department will be renamed "The Dunce-Nacktarsch Center for Folklore & Folklife," and the Famed Folklorist will be appointed Executive Director, with an annual salary of $350,000 plus liberal fringe benefits, perks, and 365 rolls of extra-soft toilet paper.

Non-academic folklore scholar Gershon Legman, upon learning of that obscene salary, will foam and curse the Famed Folklorist with his forefathers' traditional outburst, the Hungarian "**Lófasz a seggedbe!**" ("A horse's cock up your ass!"). Informed by Philadelphia folklore colleagues of this new Legmaniacal outrage against him, the Famed Folklorist will see to it that Legman will never again be invited to lecture at any campus of the universities of California and Pennsylvania.

G. LEGMAN NEEDS BOOK
In order to finish his last volume of unexpurgated folkloric Xeroxlore and Miscellanea, G. Legman "will pay its weight in silver and gold" for a small 400-page American humor book (about 1915) he needs for folksong research, entitled: *Select Reading (Profusely Illustrated) for Gay Girls and Naughty Boys*. Mr. Legman can be reached at 8, chemin Camp-Cordéou, La Clé de Champs, F- 06560 Valbonne, France.

---

* PEREGRINE PENIS *
An Autobiography of Innocence
by G. Legman

About halfway between Casanova's *Memoirs*
and *My Secret Life*.
But "not degenerate enough," alas,
for any commercial publisher.
Forty-five chapters of 50 manuscript pages each • Quarto

An Immoral History of This Century, as Seen by an Insider:
The New Freedom — How It Came, How it Went.
Private computer-printout *Samizdat Manuscript* Edition, limited to **12 copies only**. For more information, write to above address.

SLOGANS TO PROMOTE NATIONAL CONDOM WEEK

Reinhold Aman

The following list is a composite of Xeroxlore received from our readers. Most sheets had 20-25 slogans. The first copies arrived in May 1988 from Roy M., Ohio, and Brian P., Illinois. The next batch was sent in October by Roberta U., Michigan, and Michael F., Illinois. Two came in November, from Chas. H., Illinois, and Joe S., Arizona (in prison). In December, three more versions: from Tom M., Kansas, Jackie Y., Wisconsin, and George K., Connecticut. In February 1989, from Michael W., Washington; in March from Frank N., Kentucky, and the last one in July 1989 from John M., Canada.

In March 1989, *Playboy* magazine (pp. 43-44) published 20 common slogans.

The German news magazine *Der Stern* (No. 14, 30 March 1988: 74) shows a photo of the red-light district in Kiel with the poster: **NUR EIN DUMMI MACHT OHNE GUMMI**, "Only a dummy does [it] without [a] rubber."

- Cover your stump before you hump.
- Before you attack her, wrap your whacker.
- Don't be silly, protect your willy.
- When in doubt, shroud your spout.
- Don't be a loner, cover your boner.
- You can't go wrong if you shield your dong.
- If you're not going to sack it, go home and whack it.
- If you think she's spunky, cover your monkey.
- It will be sweeter if you wrap your peter.
- If you slip between the thighs, be sure to condomize.
- She won't get sick if you wrap (cap) your dick.
- If you go into heat, package (wrap) your meat.
- While you are undressing Venus, dress up that penis.
- When you take off her pants and blouse, suit up your trouser mouse.

- Especially in December, gift-wrap your member.
- Never (never) deck her with an unwrapped pecker.
- Don't be a fool, vulcanize your tool.
- The right selection? Check (sack) your erection.
- Wrap in foil before checking her oil.
- A crank with armor will never harm her.
- Before you blast her, guard your bushmaster.
- Before you bag her, sheath your dagger.
- To save embarrassment later, cover your 'gator.
- She'll be into fellatio, if you wrap your Horatio.
- There's still cunnilingus with a shielded dingus, but she'll pass on fellatio if you've wrapped up Horatio.
- Befo' da van start rockin', be sho' yo' cock gots a stockin'.
- Before you let it all hang out, be sure to wrap your trouser trout.
- Before you bang her, engulf your wanger.
- Encase your porker before you dork her.
- If you really love her, wear a cover.
- Don't make a mistake, muzzle your snake.
- Sex is cleaner with a packaged wiener.
- If you can't shield your rocket, leave it in your pocket.

The last version received, circulating on a campus in Newfoundland, had additional, different slogans:

- No glove, not love.
- Urge for a f**k, reach for a latex.
- When in doubt, leave it out.
- Want to activate the cock, put on the sock.
- When you are in charge, collect your discharge.
- When there is a flutter in your pants, get the rubber in your hands.

CONDOM COUPLETS

The preceding catchy slogans inspired some New Yorkers to compose their own creations. The first five are by **Mary and Preston K.**, and the remaining copious discharge is by **Joseph Tunick Strauss**, with the help of **Matthew Bulger** and **Paul Murley**.

- Between the sheets or in the yard
  Wear a condom when you get hard.
- Before you take a dive
  Wear a condom; stay alive.
- Before you start to copulate
  Wear a condom, protect your mate.
- Before you pop that chick
  Be sure to cap your dick.
- If you're gonna get some
  You better wear a condom.

- Wear a condom when using any orifice
  To prevent there from being less or more of us.
- Oral, anal, or conventional
  Condomize to be preventional.
- In the event of an accepted proposal
  Be sure to have protection at your disposal.
- Proper protection is very fitting.
  No joke, but the punch line is: No Kidding!
- If he refuses your request to sheath it,
  Just tell him to leave you alone and beat it.
- Having sex? Don't leave those condoms on the shelf,
  Unless, of course, you're all by yourself.
- Put on a condom even if she fights,
  'Cause she's a virgin—you know she's tight!
- Whether oral, doggie, or up the dirt road,
  Use that condom before blowing your load.
- Put on a condom when your dick's hard as steel,
  Then take it off later and give her a meal.
- Before you take it in the ass, cunt or ear,
  Make him wear a rubber if he's a queer.
- If you ever end up in any prisons,
  Make him wear a condom before he jisms.

- If you don't wear a condom before taking a dip,
  You may wear one later because of the drip.
- When you're out of D cells and look for live fun,
  Make sure they wear condoms before they come.
- If you're like me and like your hair,
  A condom will keep sperm from landing there.
- Better wear a condom at family affairs,
  Lest your sisters and cousins start bearing your heirs.
- If she ever tells you to get lost and leave her,
  Pull out a condom and penetrate her beaver.
- If you use a condom you'll never wish
  That your dick didn't smell like stale fish.
- A condom is your best friend
  When penetrating the anal end.
- Wear a condom, she'll think you're super,
  Why, she'll even let you do her pooper!
- Wear a condom and make it black,
  After that she'll never go back!
- Wearing a condom on your stiff rod
  Prevents your johnson from smelling like a cod.
- Wearing a condom is smart, even when you shoot a blank.
  Who knows what animal's been slamming that skank?
- If John C. Holmes had worn a rubber on that 10-inch dick,
  He'd still be around to star in another porn flick.
- When I'm doing the entire hockey team,
  I make them wear rubbers before they cream.
- Be a real swell guy and don't be a toad,
  Wear a rubber before blowing a load.
- Slip on that condom when you're about to hum,
  You won't have time right before you come.
- When you're not going oral, and she's about to scream,
  Just roll on that spiked condom and cream, cream, cream!
- Get the rubber out of your pocket and don't be a fool,
  Whenever you know that you'll use your throbbing 8-inch tool.
- When you're moving in and out of the old anal chasm,
  Better slip on that condom before your first spasm.

- Better put on your condom in case of attack,
  Remove it later if you want to come on her back.
- A condom will always look better on you
  When your 10-inch dong splits her in two.
- A condom will always look better on you,
  Especially if your dick might get covered with poo.
- By using a condom you'll always be wiser
  Before taking it up the pooper from your advisor.
- Make sure to always have a condom on your hog,
  You never know who else has already had your dog.
- Wearing a condom is a sign of class,
  Especially when someone is stuffing your ass.
- Better put on the condom sooner than later,
  Since you might be a premature ejaculator.
- Slip that condom on your throbbing member
  And give her a night she'll always remember!
- Wear a condom and she'll never say good-bye
  Even if you shoot your load right in her eye.
- Wearing a condom can never hurt,
  Make sure you get it on before you spurt.
- Wear a spiked condom and make her say "ouch!"
  When you give her the high hard one on the couch.
- Please heed the advice to procure latex domes
  So we won't be subjected to these crummy poems.

Who Will Move Out First?

Yvonne's Whorehouse	Fred's Home Realty
Arnie's Medical Clinic	Mark's Barbershop

See answer on page 202

CATULLUS XXXIII

Translation and Notes
by
Joseph S. Salemi

    O furum optime balneariorum
    Vibenni pater et cinaede fili
    (nam dextra pater inquinatiore,
    culo filius est uoraciore),
    cur non exilium malasque in oras
    itis? quandoquidem patris rapinae
    notae sunt populo, et natis pilosas,
    fili, non potes asse uenditare.

Tops among the bath house thieves,
Vibennius and your faggot boy
(Daddy's hand plays dirty tricks
While sonny's bottom swallows pricks)
Go to some godforsaken place
Where no one knows your little ploy.
Dad, the record's too well known
Of all your ripoffs, and your son's;
And Junior, you won't get two cents
For spreading wide those shaggy buns.

NOTES

The Latin text is from *Catullus: The Complete Poems for American Readers*, ed. Reney Myers and Robert J. Ormsby (New York: E.P. Dutton, 1970), p. 40.

    The scene is a Roman bath house. The father (Vibennius) is a pickpocket or a locker-room rifler who works while victims are engaged in anal intercourse with his pathic homosexual son.

    cinaede fili: "effeminate son." *Cinaedus* derives from the Greek κίναιδος (sodomite) and is a favorite Catullan insult (see poems

XVI, XXV, and LVII). As a noun *cinaedus* means "pervert, homosexual" but as an adjective it has the wider meaning of "effeminately lewd." In translations of this poem the term has been variously rendered as "fairy" (Myers and Ormsby), "pansy" (James Michie), and "Princess of the May" (Frank Copley).

Nam dextra...uoraciore: "The father has a very filthy hand; the son has an equally voracious bottom." **Inquinatus** means "polluted, sordid," while **uorax** means "gluttonous, voracious." The rhyme of these paired comparatives accents the complicity of father and son. The comparative degree in Latin can have an auxiliary derogatory connotation (cf. our use of "somewhat" or "rather" in expressions like "He is somewhat dull" or "This portion is somewhat small").

malas...in oras: "into evil regions." Catullus may have in mind the expression *in malam rem ire*, which means "to go into an evil thing, to go to hell."

non potes asse uenditare: "You can't sell [them] for an *as*." The *as* was a small coin of little value; hence the expression is comparable to our "They're not worth two cents."

The same Latin poem translated by

Randal Ford

Thieves known well
Among the bath houses:
Father Vibennius,
For his sticky fingers,
And his queer-bait son,
For his hungry asshole.
Why don't you two eat shit
And die? Everyone knows
Your pilferings, papa,
And sonny boy can't sell
His hairy-hog butt here anymore.

MARTIAL XI.99

*Translation and Notes
by*

Robert Wind

De cathedra quotiens surgis—iam saepe notavi—
    pedicant miserae, Lesbia, te tunicae.
quas cum conata es dextra, conata sinistra
    vellere, cum lacrimis eximis et gemitu:
sic constringuntur magni Symplegade culi
    et nimias intrant Cyaneasque natis.
Emendare cupis vitium deforme? docebo:
    Lesbia, nec surgas censeo nec sedeas.

TO LARGE LESBIA
I've noticed often when you rise
Your undies give obscene surprise.
Right hand, left, push, pull—no use—
Tears, groans—ah! They're loose.
How tight they're squeezed between those nates,
Gigantic gates to dark estates!
How might we end this ugly bit?
You mustn't stand. You mustn't sit.

NOTES
This epigram of the Roman poet Martial (first century C.E.) ridicules a pseudonymous Lesbia's chronic problem with the "wedgie"—surely the first such mention in western literature. Pretending to give some friendly advice to Lesbia, the poet first caricatures her as the victim of an indecent assault by her personified undies (*tunicae*), and then shifts his sympathies to the undies, now seen as heroic.

2. **pedicant:** "to bugger" (sodomize)

5. **magni Symplegade culi:** literally, "Symplegades of a big ass." The Symplegades were those great clashing rocks in the sea that in myth challenged the heroism of Jason and the Argonauts. The English translation makes do with the suggestion of heroic adventure: explicit and necessarily long reference to the myth here and in the next line would mistranslate the Latin poem's brevity.

6. **nimias intrant Cyaneasque natis:** literally, "They enter the huge Cyanean buttocks." The reference is to Symplegades again (Cyaneas, "blue rocks"?).

The same Latin poem translated by

Joseph S. Salemi

When you rise up from a chair, Lesbia
(I've seen it happen frequently)
You get buttfucked by your skirt.
The damned thing catches in the narrow crack
Between those massive buns of yours,
Those ship-crunching Pillars of Hercules.
You pull with your left hand, you pull with your right,
Wincing and grunting till it comes loose.
An unladylike *faux pas*, to say the least.
Want a tip on etiquette, Lesbia?
Don't get up, and don't sit down.

AN IRISHMAN'S LETTER TO THE DHSS IN RESPONSE TO RECEIVING THE AIDS LEAFLET

Dear Sir

I have just received the AIDS leaflet through my door and would like to apply straight away for AIDS.

I have been on the dole for the past ten years and have been living on Supplementary Benefit and every other state aid I could get. It now seems I will be getting aid for sex. It's a pity this AIDS has come so late as I have already got 15 children and wondered if you will be making any back payments?

Your leaflet states that the more sex I have, the more chance I have of getting AIDS. My only problem here is persuading the wife, who is not so keen after 15 kids. Several years ago I bought some sex aids but she showed little interest and they were hardly used — would there be any chance of a refund for the £17.28p I paid for these gadgets?

Anyway I will now explain to her that the Government will now be paying us for all the sex we have and I'm sure she will agree that we can't let a chance like this slip by.

You also state that I can pass my AIDS on, but as you will appreciate, with a wife and 15 kids to feed, there won't be much left to pass on. If by any chance there is a bit left though, I will pass this on to my poor old mother-in-law, who only has her pension.

I understand from your leaflet that I can get AIDS through a blood transfusion and I intend to write to my local hospital straight away to see when I can have one. Will the AIDS I get from the hospital be deducted from the AIDS I get from you? Perhaps you will write and let me know.

I am a firm believer in getting every aid from the Government that I can and I'm sure you will agree that, by my past performance, I do qualify for this one.

Could you let me know how much I will get paid each time and will it be paid weekly or monthly?

> Yours faithfully,
> *Shamus O'Toole*

P.S. Your advert is great. I certainly won't die of ignorance. — I know my rights!

DHSS = Department of Health and Social Security. British Xeroxlore sent by Tim H., South Yorkshire, in April 1987. A similar version circulates in Canada as "Newfie's Letter to the Minister of Health after Receiving the *AIDS* Leaflet," sent by John M., Newfoundland, in Jan. 1989. The Canadian version is somewhat shorter, worded differently, and signed by *Shamos O'Toole*. The "AIDS leaflet" seems to be similar to the pamphlet sent by Surgeon General Koop to most US households.

What Is This?

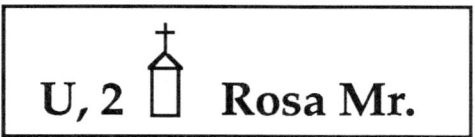

See answer on page 202

William A. Leavell, editor of the monthly **Washington Report** newsletter [P.O. Box 10309, St. Petersburg, FL 33733] had in his December 1989 issue wishful-thinking Christmas gifts for politicians and others in the news. His "gift" for Jim Bakker, who was sentenced to 45 years: "We give you a 300-pound minority cellmate that talks with a lisp." Translated into *non-sensitive* English: a 300-pound homosexual Negro.

WHOSE ANUS?
URANUS

Dennis R. Preston

At about 6:45 A.M. on January 12, 1984, a meteorologist (weatherperson) came on the air for WJR in Detroit and began to explain that our solar system was in the fairly unusual situation of having several planets lined up on one side of the sun. Listeners were encouraged to take advantage of this sight quickly since cloudy weather was forecast.

Of course a weatherperson does not get to explain such oddities every day nor is such a great amount of time usually devoted to "weather news." He warmed to his task and even began to speak poetically of the view, finally remarking that the configuration of planets as they were soon to be was "leading to a fascinating view of Uránus [*yerÁnus*]." Without pause or giggle he immediately corrected himself, "...Úranus [*YÉRunus*] I guess it's pronounced."

Our enthusiastic meteorologist had fallen into a phonological trap—one pronunciation of *Uranus* sounds like "your anus."

Though I was among the teenagers in the 1950s who noticed this nice homophony (and made something of it), I was not, at least in my younger days, aware of the innocent pronunciation. With the years (and more serious linguistic matters to attend to), I forgot this fundamental phonetic planetary prank. I was reminded of it a few years ago, however, when I saw the movie *The Groove Tube*. The film spoofs American commercial television and contains a good many ribald scenes based on sit-coms, news, and commercials. One particularly effective bit makes fun of antiseptic giant corporate ads, implying that all may not be well behind their slick surface. In this particular case the company name was *Uranus*, but what it made or sold was, at least at first, ambiguous; it was simply presented as a leader in new (and, we were led to expect, "technological") products. As the ad progressed, however, a stainless steel tube appeared at the top of the screen and the soporific voice began to speak of a new product. A moist (but substantial), brown, unmistakable substance started to fall from the end of the tube, dirtying the previous clean-room atmosphere of the ad. A hand even reached into the screen area and began to test the consistency of the product between thumb and fingers. Finally, we were told that the "new product" was "Brown 45." And, of course, it was "from *Uranus*." And, of course, the pronunciation was *yer-Anus*.

Although that little scene revived my memory of the humorous homonomy, I was aware by now of the other pronunciation, but, for some reason, I had come to regard it as a principally British form. Webster's *Ninth New Collegiate Dictionary* (1983) gives both pronunciations and does not mark either as having a specific geographic provenience. Similar treatments are given in *The American Heritage Dictionary of the English Language* (1969) and *The Random House College Dictionary* (1975). On the other hand, *Webster's New World Dictionary of the American Language* (1953) and Kenyon and Knott's *Pronouncing Dictionary of American English* (1944) give only the clean form—the pronunciation I had taken to be British. The mighty *Oxford English Dictionary* (1884-1928) gives only the clean pronunciation, but the *Concise Oxford Dictionary* (sixth edition, 1976, which claims to give only the "pronunciation ... associated especially with Southern England") gives both.

Is there any preference in American and British usage? If the clean form is older (as seems obvious from the *OED*'s citation of only that pronunciation), when did the dirty version appear? Did it appear first in England or America? The two older American sources cited above clearly reveal that it was not "standard" enough to have been given any citation at all in the 1940s and 1950s, although the later citations (in both England and America) show both pronunciations.

It is not hard to see that the clean form is the historically prior one. If the word had been borrowed into Old English, it would have had been stressed on the first syllable, in keeping with the Germanic stress rule (e.g., *Hólofernus*—compare Modern English *Holoférnes*). If it had been borrowed into Middle English, it would have preserved the Late Latin stress pattern (e.g., *Zépherus*—compare Modern English *Zephyr*, but *Neptúnus*, compare Modern English *Néptune*). In the case of *Uranus*, the Late Latin form would have been on the model of *Zépherus*, that is, stressed on the first syllable. Certainly, the older English pronunciations would have stressed the first syllable, and that is substantiated in the *OED* and older American dictionaries.

On the other hand, it is not hard to see how the dirty form arose. The general rule in Modern English is to stress the syllable with the first tense (i.e., long) vowel, moving left from the end of the word. If the *a* in *Uranus* is analyzed as a lax (i.e., short) vowel (as it would have been in Late Latin) and if the last *u* is also so analyzed (also the case in Late Latin), then the first *u* in the word is the first tense vowel encountered, and the older stress pattern is again predicted. A number of short *a* words were, however, reanalyzed as long *a* in Middle English (after Old English long *a* had already moved to the vowel in *caught* or *law*), and they later moved to the pronunciation in *name*. If, therefore, we take the *a* in *Uranus* to be a long vowel, the *Uránus* pronunciation emerges, predictable by the above rule. There is no doubt that just this pronunciation had great popularity in the United States. It was the only pronunciation I was familiar with as a child and young man, and many others my age or thereabouts (35-55) report the same.

Professional astronomers are aware of the joke but indicate they are tired of it (perhaps as much as linguists are of *cunning linguist*). Several Michigan astronomers with whom I spoke note that their professional use is divided, although they are more often users of the clean pronunciation in lectures.

A small number of people interviewed (who were surreptitiously discovered to be *YÉRunus* users) agreed in a number of interesting ways. They were nearly all younger speakers (under thirty) and nearly all reported having been made aware of the dirty phonological potential by *The Groove Tube*. The surprise, however, is in the source of their new-found pronunciation. All had been viewers of Carl Sagan's "Cosmos" series on public television, and nearly all reported remembering his use of the clean variety of *Uranus* and basing their current usage on that model. In fact, all these young southeastern Michigan residents remember using the dirty version before that cosmic experience. That public television from the East could have such a striking influence on Midwestern pronunciation is not too hard to imagine, given the general American high index of linguistic insecurity and mania for correctness.

If the cleaned-up version is on the increase in the United States, we may, at least in part, attribute a re-awareness of the maledictive phonological parallelism to one popular culture event and a corrective device to another.

It remains to be seen which form will win out; since the old form (now perhaps a euphemistic one) had even more public exposure with the Voyager flyby, you may stand in danger of losing Uranus.

URANUS • 199

EDITOR'S NOTE

Jacqueline Y. sent me a copy of *Science 86* magazine (May 1986) showing on its cover a photograph of Uranus with the headline

URANUS REVEALED

One of the "funny" lapel buttons (see page 203) asks, "Could I see Uranus tonight?"

From Cliff A. (Chicago) I received a copy of *Sidney Suppey's Quarterly and Confused Pet Monthly* (July 1983: 12) featuring the illustration below:

Illustration © 1988 by Wim van Piggelen. It appeared in the excellent Dutch language monthly *Onze Taal* 57/5 (May 1988): 69, in a good review of *Maledicta*. That entire issue is dedicated to Dutch insults, swearing, curses, and taboo-words.

DEPARTMENTAL COUNSELING SHEET

Under the Freedom of Information Act and the Federal Privacy Act of 1974 I understand that my behavior and work performance is being documented. I have the right to examine and copy documentation, I have the right to review and discuss differences in order to resolve them and I have the right to request amendments to or modification of any documents.

NAME	RATING	SS NUMBER
Knowledge		The son of a bitch really knows his shit.
		Knows just enough to be dangerous.
		Only has half a brain and is dangerous.
		Fucking brain-damaged. His coffee cup has a higher IQ.
Accuracy		Does excellent work if not preoccupied with pussy.
		Pretty good. Only occasionally blows it out his ass.
		Couldn't count his balls and get the same number twice.
		This guy could fuck up a train wreck.
Reliability		Really a dependable little cocksucker.
		Can rely on him at evaluation time.
		Can rely on him to be the first out the door.
		Totally fucking worthless.
Attitude		Extremely cooperative (if you kiss his ass frequently).
		Brown-noser in good standing.
		Often pisses off co-workers, thinks it's his ship.
		Doesn't give a shit, never did, never will.
Appearance		Extremely neat, even combs his pubic hair.
		Looks great at evaluation time.
		Flies leave fresh dog shit to follow him.
		Dirty, filthy, smelly son-of-a-bitch.
Performance		Goes like a son of a bitch if there's money in it for him.
		Does all kind of good shit at evaluation time.
		Works only if kicked in the ass every two minutes.
		Couldn't do less work if he were in a coma.

Leadership	Carries a chainsaw and gets excellent results.
	Better leader than fucking MacArthur at evaluation time.
	Occassionally gets told to get fucked.
	Mother Teresa told him to get fucked.

I understand that I have been counseled and know my rights under the Privacy Act of 1974. I further acknowledge that I am as fucked up as a football bat and will attempt to correct my deficiencies.

Signature of Supervisor / Date   Signature of Employee / Date

Xeroxlore • Michigan • March 1989 • Sent by Fred R.

Compare the above version (recent adaption by the Navy?) with the following one (original, Army?), sent by Lon H., California, February 1989.

EMPLOYEE PERFORMANCE APPRAISAL

Name _____ Date _____
Job_____ Last Rating _____
Department ____Supervisor _____ Hire Date _____

Accuracy
_ Does shitty work and constantly fucks up.
_ Doesn't give a shit if output is right or wrong.
_ Pretty good, only an occasional screw up.
_ Does good work, if not pre-occupied with sex.

Rate of Work
_ Doesn't do a fucking thing all day.
_ Works only if kicked in the ass, very often.
_ Does a lot of work at review time.
_ Goes like a son-of-a-bitch if he thinks he'll get a raise.
_ Fastest, if not pre-occupied with sex.

Dependability
_ Completely incompetent jack-off jerk.
_ Needs frequent threats and ass chewings.
_ Conscientious only if sex urge is satisfied.
_ Usually dependable at review time.
_ Really reliable, if not pre-occupied with sex.

Cooperation	_ Piss-poor attitude. Thinks he's being shit on. _ Often pisses off co-workers. He's a loner. _ Cooperative only if his ass is kissed frequently. _ Brown-noser (in good standing). _ Cooperative, if not pre-occupied with sex.
Knowledge	_ Stupid. Doesn't know his ass from a hole in the ground. _ Knows just enough to be dangerous. _ Adequate brain power, but doesn't use it. _ Knows most phases of the job. _ Really knows his shit, if not pre-occupied with sex.
Orderliness	_ Sloppy, Dirty, Filthy! _ Pisses in ash trays, shits in the corner. _ Sometimes empties ash trays and sweeps the corner. _ Neat and orderly. _ Extremely neat and orderly, if not pre-occupied with sex.
Handling and Developing People	_ Constantly pisses off the troops. _ Frequently gets the finger. _ Occasionally gets told to get fucked. _ Only the janitors obey him. _ Carries a hatchet and gets excellent results, if not pre-occupied with sex.

Employee Comments:

Employee Signature	Date	Supervisor/Manager Signature

My Signature Indicates Review Has Been Discussed

Answer from page 188:

Arnie's Medical Clinic, because there is too much fucking overhead.

Answer from page 194:

An Italian Wedding Invitation:
"You comma to church. Rosa missed her period."

TALK DIRTY TO ME
SASSY SAYINGS ON BUTTONS, CARDS, T-SHIRTS, AND RUBBER STAMPS

Reinhold Aman

After a genteel young lady from Houston, Texas, sent me a button—the round, 1.5-inch-kind worn on the lapel—reading CUNNING LINGUIST, I wrote for some catalogs to see what other sayings, slogans, and bold statements are available. The folks at Masterpiece Button, Inc. in South Orange, New Jersey, sent me their dealer catalog showing buttons with 756 different texts, from which I selected the funniest and nastiest ones, listed alphabetically below. There is something for everyone who wants to make a statement — or a fool of himself or herself:

Age is not important unless you're a bottle of wine.
Another brillyant mind diztroyed by the New York edukashun sistum.
Are you going to come quietly or do I have to use earplugs?
Asshole by birth.
Bastard by choice.
Beat me, whip me, pay me.
Bitch by birth.
Blink if you're horny.
Can I touch your tits?
Come near me and I'll kill you.
Condoms are for faggots.
Could I see Uranus tonight?
Deep, considerate, sensitive, and horny.
Dial 911—make a cop come.
Do you find it hard getting up in the morning?
Don't even think about fucking me.
Don't even think of fucking me without a condom.

Don't try to understand me, just fuck me.
Don't you dare even *think* about me when you masturbate.
Eat well, stay fit and die anyway.
Eat, Fuck, Kill.
Everyone needs to believe in something. I believe I'll have another beer.
51% Sweetheart, 49% Bitch.
Fuck Dr. Ruth.
Fuck me or I'll try to sell you insurance.
Fuck that shit.
Fuck you very much.
Give me a quarter or I'll touch you.
Go fuck yourself. Without a condom.
Haven't I fucked you before?
How can I love you if you won't lie down?
How can I say I ♥ you if you're sitting on my face?
How do you spell relief? M-a-s-t-u-r-b-a-t-e.
I accept tits.
I can't decide whether to commit suicide or go bowling.
I don't give a shit. I don't take any shit. I'm not in the shit business.
I don't have PMS, I'm always a bitch.
I don't like your negative attitude, asshole.
I don't want a love affair, just a blow job.
I have trouble remembering names. Can I just call you "asshole"?
I know you just want to get into my pants but I already have an asshole in there.
I love every inch of you.
I love it when you talk dirty.
I may be fat but you're ugly, and I can diet.
I need more money and power and less shit from you people.
I smell shit. Is there a lawyer in here?
I taught Dr. Ruth.
I think I could fall madly in bed with you.
I tried to drown my troubles, but my husband learned to swim.
I want to thank all the little people who kiss my ass.
I wish your breasts were larger.
I wish your penis was harder.
I would look good on you.
I wouldn't eat you if you were between two slices of bread.
I wouldn't fuck her with your dick.
I'd like to get something straight between us.
I'd like to see more of you.
I'd slap you but shit splatters.

I'll only hurt you in the end.
I'll shake your hand when you take it out of your nose.
I'll sleep with you if you're rich or famous.
I'm a worthless piece of shit. What's your excuse?
I'm not deaf, I'm ignoring you.
I'm not prejudiced. I hate everybody.
I'm not your fucking therapist.
I'm witty, charming, handsome and above average in length.
I've seen better heads on a pimple.
If I can't find true love then I'll settle for sex with you.
If I was alone on an island with you I'd masturbate.
If you don't smoke, I won't fart.
If you like sex and travel, go take a fuckin' hike.
Inconsiderate, insensitive bastard seeks girl like you to dominate.
It's a bitch being a queen.
It's American to be pissed off.
It's been lovely but I have to scream now.
It's been so long since I've had sex I can't remember who gets tied up first.
Jew him down!
Kiss me or I'll masturbate.
Life is a bitch and so am I.
Liquor in the front, poker in the rear.
May I fuck you?
Mother Teresa is better in bed than you are.
My condoms or yours?
My erections last longer.
Never too drunk to fuck.
No more Mr. Nice Guy: on your knees, bitch.
Not all men are fools. Some are bastards.
Not recently laid.
O.K. But wash it first.
Only a bastard like me could love a bitch like you.
Seven days of sex makes one weak.
Sex is like everything else. If you want it done properly, you have to do it yourself.
Shit happens.
Shut the fuck up.
Shut up and fuck.
Sit on my face and let me eat my way to your heart.
Size does count.
Spread your legs.
Stop staring at my tits.

Survey says: go fuck yourself.
Talk dirty to me.
The difference between genius and stupidity is that genius has its limits.
The meek shall inherit shit.
There are many ways to say I LOVE YOU but fucking is the best.
There is nothing like lipstick around my dipstick.
Those of you who think you know everything are very annoying to those of us who do.
Too ugly to live, too weird to die.
Trust me. I'm a lawyer.
Usually I'm very caring. As for you, I don't give a shit.
Vicious power-hungry bitch.
Warning: I scream when I come.
We cheat tourists & drunks.
When I want any shit out of you I'll squeeze your head.
When I'm with you I feel crazy. Sometimes I feel nuts.
Whip me, beat me, bite me, come all over my body. Tell me you love me, then get the fuck out.
Who farted?
Who needs this shit?
Who says I'm too short?
Who the fuck do you think you are?
Winning isn't everything but losing sucks.
With friends like you who needs enemas?
Women who come close to me know how big I can be.
You are who you eat.
You come first.
You have to fuck a lot of frogs in order to find a prince.
You must be walking backwards. All I see is an asshole.
You piss me off, you fuckin' jerk.
You're the reason my children are so ugly.
You're ugly and your mother dresses you funny.
Your breasts are bigger than your brains.
Your face or mine?
Your lips are too rough for oral sex.
Your penis reminds me of the man I love.
Your silly appearance coupled with your vile and unctuous skin makes you truly nauseating.
Yuck Fou.

Similarly irreverent texts are also found on bumper stickers, greeting cards, and T-shirts. Below is a list of texts on shirts marketed by Mellow Mail of New York:

Be kind to animals. Take a bitch to dinner.
Born-again bitch.
Feel safe tonight. Sleep with a cop.
Having sex is like playing bridge. If you don't have a good partner, you'd better have a good hand.
I don't have an eating problem. I eat. I get fat. I buy new clothes. No problem.
If I wanted to hear from an asshole I would have farted!
Instant asshole...just add alcohol.
It would be easy for me to make it hard for you.
Life is a bed of roses, but watch out for the pricks.
Life is like a shit sandwich. The more bread you have, the less shit you have to eat.
Life's a bitch and then you die.
Life's a bitch, then you marry one.
Moody bitch seeks a kind, considerate guy for a love-hate relationship.
The person wearing this shirt is a police officer. Lie flat on your back and do everything the nice officer tells you.
Wanted: Meaningful overnight relationship.
What are you staring at, dickhead?
Women like the simplest things in life...men.
Yes...but not with you.
You don't know anything about a woman until you meet her in court!
You're twisted, perverted & sick. I like that in a person.
Your father should have pulled out early.

Rubber stamps are another medium for one's message. The Inkling Stamp Co. in Santa Barbara, CA (Box 40195, ZIP 93140) sells illustrations and sayings on rubber stamps, most of which are quite inoffensive:

A dirty mind is a terrible thing to waste.
A morner is like a nooner, only sooner.
Beware of religions that have waterslides.
Can I do it 'til I need glasses?
Chaste makes waste.
Chastity is its own punishment.
It was hard when I kissed her goodbye.
Lie down, I think I love you.
O Lord, help me to be pure, but not yet.
Polymer physicists are into chains.

Running is an unnatural act, except from the enemy and to the bathroom.
Sex is not the answer; sex is the question. "Yes" is the answer.

Finally, a San Francisco wholesaler, Ephemera Buttons, probably has the most outrageous buttons, bourgeoisie-taunting-wise. Here is a sampling of their buttons:

Do you fuck, suck, swallow & take it up the ass—or am I wasting my time on a Jesus Freak?
Fuck the Real World—I'm an Artist.
I had better sex in prison.
I make money the old-fashioned way. I'm a whore.
I peed on Santa's lap.
I'd like to give you what you deserve, but my dog's constipated.
I'm not very smart, but I'm real good with zippers.
I've got the time if you've got the kneepads.
If we are what we eat, I could be you by morning.
Intolerant self-righteous castrating bitch with PMS.
It wasn't your brains that attracted me, so shut the fuck up.
Jesus loves you. Everyone else thinks you're an asshole.
Men are such assholes.
Mr. Rogers: "Can you say 'Cunnilingus'?"
Pardon me, but you're standing on my penis.
Show me a successful woman & I'll show you a frustrated bitch.
Sure, I'm ugly. But, I can really fuck.
Thank you for not jacking off on the furniture.
Thank you for not smoking, spitting, bleeding, dropping scabs, or excreting any pus.
The solution to your problem is in my pants.
You have a nice face—but that fat ass has got to go.

PIT, TIT, CLIT

A young Midwest lady calls her lover, who attaches his mouth with the fierceness of a pit bull to her breasts and nipples, *tit-bull*. She also calls him *clit-bull*, as he is "the best cunnilinguist west of Brest" who is down on his knees faster than a zealous monk and doesn't let go of her yummy labia minora and clitoris until she has reached at least three major orgasms. (Readers unsure of their knowledge of world geography are advised to consult a map of France and find Brest, a seaport located at the nipple of Brittany, which sticks out into the Atlantic Ocean like a firm breast.)

GOD CURSE YOU, AND THE CURSE IS THAT YOU BE WHAT YOU ALREADY ARE!
SWAHILI CULTURE, POWER, AND BADTALK

Marc J. Swartz

This article[1] examines teasing, curses, obscenities, and abuse (what I am calling "badtalk") among the Swahili of Mombasa and seeks to explain their use by reference to the group's culture. Particular importance is attributed to culturally-based differences in power and the relationship between these differences and the kinds of badtalk used.

The central hypothesis here is that for the Swahili badtalk is mainly a device of the powerless and this is true regardless of the kind of badtalk considered. *Teasing* is used by members of gangs of boys against destitute elderly people, with the latter replying with curses calling on God to defend the otherwise isolated and powerless old people against the boys who are themselves mistreated by their teachers and dependent on their parents. *Mixed curses* that combine a call for divine assistance and punishment while at the same time attributing undesirable qualities are used by women in dealing with other women. *Obscene badtalk* is used by boys, young men, and women dealing with others of the same status and by mothers in dealing with their children, especially their daughters.

It is notable that mature men, especially those of the upper caste and class, do not use badtalk at all even though as young men and boys they did use it.[2] These men, who control most property, jobs, and money, carry their avoidance of badtalk to the extent that when they bang their own thumbs with a hammer or find their cars to have flat tires, their most common exclamation is the beginning of a Koranic verse meaning "Nothing is either good or bad but that God makes it so." Having power, as these high-status men do, is associated with the avoidance of badtalk, while not having power, as women, old people, and dependent, propertyless young males do not, is associated with using badtalk. It may be that the powerful men use badtalk in privacy with their wives, but since it is a serious breech of dignity for them to do so, and since wives may talk or someone may overhear, it seems likelier that they do not use it at all.

The Swahili of Mombasa are a traditionally urban, Sunni Muslim people who founded the city they live in centuries ago. The group is sometimes referred to as *ThenasharaTaifa* or Twelve Tribes or as *Wamvita* (Salim 1973) and is part of a larger ethnic community that lives along the East African coast from southern Somalia to southern Tanzania and on many off-shore islands. The Swahili trace kinship bilaterally and although they inherit according to Koranic laws, there is a matrilateral bias in residence patterns and in association (Swartz 1978). The people of this group were once affluent, but their wealth has been declining since early in the present century as a consequence, in large part, of their loss of control of imports and of the trade with the interior. Currently, clerical, teaching, and civil service occupations form the main basis for their economy. The data examined in this article were all derived from work with the Mombasa Swahili, but there are suggestions that other Swahili groups elsewhere on the coast are similar to the Mombasa people (Bakari 1981, Caplan 1975).

The Swahili language distinguishes three different types of verbal abuse. There are supernaturally based curses (**maapiso**), obscenity and formalized insult (**matukano**), and personalized teasing (**matokozo**). In the first class are expressions such as the one that is the title of this article, in the second class are the standard insults and obscenity based in sexual reference, and in the third class are references to behaviors or characteristics that are known to annoy the target without regard to the nature of these behaviors or characteristics.

TEASING AND CURSING

The main cursers in this society are elderly men and women who differ from most others of their age in that they have neither money nor relatives to care for and protect them. The elderly are respected among the Swahili, and members of this group with pensions or property can be quite influential as can those, even if they have little money, who occupy honored places in the homes of their children. The rather unusual old person who has neither wealth nor surviving kin, however, is in an unenviable position both economically and socially. Not only are such people hard put to find food and lodging, but they are also defenseless since few will exert themselves on behalf of their insignificant non-relatives.

These defenseless old people are particularly attractive prey for the boys of the Swahili community who are, themselves, without either material wealth or social prestige and influence. These boys seem to be mainly between the ages of ten and fifteen (older boys turn to other pursuits) and wander about the Swahili section of the city playing soccer and generally amusing themselves when they are not in school or eating and sleeping in their homes. The segregation of the sexes entails all male members of a household being out of their houses save at meal times and at night.

Currently, Swahili children attend both religious and secular schools. This makes a fairly heavy work load for the youngsters, especially in comparison with the children of the city's Christian majority who attend only a secular school. As recently as twenty or so years ago, the teachers in the religious schools were extremely vigorous in their use of a heavy, braided whip made from banana leaf fiber (called **kikoto**), and a number of now middle-aged men have told me that it was not unusual in their day for mothers to have to soak their sons' garments off their backs because of the blood from the beatings the boys received at the hands of the religious teachers. In those days of frequent and serious beatings, the boys were said to be more abandoned in their activity once out of school than they are now, but even now the boys are very active in their games after school and show what has to be characterized as an active willingness to engage in hostile behavior.

Their preferred targets are the physically weak and the socially isolated. Most members of this group, as we saw, are destitute old people whose families and spouses are not available to support them. The boys persecute these elderly men and women with the kind of verbal abuse called **matazakozo** in Swahili and "teasing" here.

This teasing need not be obscene and may refer to common, accepted characteristics of its target. One old man abused by the Swahili boys was a Baluchi, a member of a group from what is now Pakistan that came to Mombasa centuries ago as soldiers for the Portuguese and that has lived among and intermarried with the Swahili for many generations. The boys taunted the man by calling him *Jamadar*, a Hindi-based word meaning anyone of Baluchi descent (and not necessarily insulting even as a term of address) and *Jamadar kijongo*, "Jamadar the hunchback."

Less obviously insulting, the boys would follow another elderly man, calling him *mwalimu*, "teacher." They did this, I was told, because it always made the target angry to be addressed by that title even though he was, in fact, a former teacher. Somewhat similarly, an old woman was teased by being repeatedly called *mama shere, shere* meaning nothing more ominous than "mother teased" and, as with the teacher, the seemingly harmless words always angered her.

The children's teasing was not always concerned with apparently harmless taunts. An elderly man whose forebears included some members of another African group, the Giriama, from whom the Swahili traditionally felt quite separate, was teased with the following poem:

Kombo, mwana wa Majimbo	Kombo, son of Majimbo
Nikampata nikpiga fimbo	I got him and hit him with a stick.
Mbili tatu, moja ya maungo	Two three [times], once on the back.

This poem probably refers to the slave status Kombo's ancestors may have had as indicated by its reference to beating. Ethnicity is not uncommonly a part of teasing. A poem used on defenseless people who have had any sort of connection with India makes derisive reference to the religious beliefs attributed to Indians and to the regard they have for cleanliness.

Baniani ganga	Hindu witchcraft
Pilipili manga	Black pepper
Kula wali chooni	Eats rice in the toilet.

These poems are used by boys against people who are even weaker than they are, but there is an occasion when the teasing can be turned against the most powerful figure in the boy's life: their religious school teacher. The Swahili New Year celebration, based on their own calendar, involves a certain amount of license for school boys. The boys take their school slates to the sea to wash them and, as they return to their religious school, they beat each other with the banana fiber whip normally used by their teacher on them and sing this song:

Si zetu n' za mwalimu wetu	Not ours but our teacher's
Mbao na kalamu zetu	Our slates and our chalk
Mwalimu wetu ni baa	Our teacher is naughty
Hutufunza nasi ubba	And he teaches us to be naughty
Aliuka nyote sabaa	He jumped seven walls
Chumba cha Mbwana, Kimefunga kiza	Our master's room, Has become dark
Na kiza	And actually it is not darkness
N' t'opa la nyiza	But a bunch of coconut fiber threads.

This poem refers to the teacher's pubic hair in its mention of "a bunch of coconut fiber threads" which it says are sufficient to be mistaken for darkness. It is insulting to refer to his pubic hair since honored Swahili custom calls for members of both sexes to keep their pubic (and axillary) hair shaved off. The fact that the socially weak pupils hurl such insult at their immensely powerful teacher might seem to indicate that the relationship between powerlessness and the use of badtalk hypothesized here is incorrect, but it must be remembered that the New Year celebration is a time of license for the boys, and the teacher can use his undoubted power against them only at the cost of being thought a fool.

Non-poetic references to a target's physical characteristics are used by boys against targets who are less powerful than teachers are. Weak elderly people are tormented with reference to any physical qualities which can be made to seem distinctive. **Tumbo tita** (big abdomen), **jitwa** (overly large head), and **domo** (huge mouth or lip) are commonly-heard phrases used to tease those without power.

The powerlessness of the boys is not hard to see given

their dependency on their parents for the necessities of life, and the elderly people they most often abuse with their teasing are hardly more able to get what they want on their own. The isolated elders are too weak to defend themselves against the boys with physical responses, and mobilizing social resources is hardly more practical for them, given that only those without kin or friends are attacked. The only responses available to the victims are ignoring their tormentors, which is difficult given the boys' persistence and vigor, or responding with words. The latter is the course taken, but there are strict limits on the kind of verbal defense the elderly can use effectively.

It is not at all common for the elderly victims of the boys' groups to respond to attacks with obscenities. In part this may be because of the fruitlessness of their use of obscenity. Adults who use obscenity, especially in public, are likely to be thought rather dull-witted, and this may have some effect in checking the employment of this type of badtalk by the elderly. It seems likely, however, that sheer ineffectiveness is the likeliest reason for old people's not using this type of language. The boys are expert and unabashed in the use of obscenity, and a grown person is more likely to find himself in a worse situation than before if he enters into an exchange of obscenities with them.

There is an area in life, however, where the elderly have clear immunity from counter attack in kind: this is through invoking God as their ally. The Swahili are an extremely and genuinely pious Muslim people. One of their proverbs says, "He who is without allies has God." Other proverbs assert that "God does not desert his servant" and "The abused person who keeps silent (i.e., does not return the abuse) is judged by God" (see Scheven 1981: 245-259). The old people are well within the limits of proper behavior in asking for divine assistance in dealing with their tormentors, while the tormentors, themselves quite religious in belief and many observances, have no basis for invoking the supernatural against their prey.

The understanding that God can be influenced to harm one's enemies is well established among members of Swahili society. There is, for example, a Swahili practice called **halbadiri** in which a religious teacher and his students are hired to read the names of the companions of prophet Mohammed and chant **Rathi alahu an** ("May God be pleased with him") following each name. This practice is understood to bring down God's wrath on whoever has won the enmity of the holder of this ritual; this is, in a sense, a cursing. However, this cursing is unlike the badtalk curse of particular interest here in that it does not offer immediate defense against direct attack. However, the existence of the understanding that **halbadiri** can be effective suggests that other forms of invoking God's help with enemies may also be viewed this way.

The curses used by the old people can be viewed as prayers calling on God to protect them against their enemies, to punish those enemies, or both. The first curse listed is one that prays both for protection and for revenge. The following are "pure" curses (we will see "mixed" curses below) that I have been able to collect in a total of 30 months of field experience among the Mombasa Swahili.

"God curse you!"
Mungu mbwakulani! or Mwana lana!

The word *lana* which is the heart of the curse and the general noun used for curses generally refers to "affliction." Thus, to use the example an informant gave me to explain this word, a man who is totally preoccupied with a woman and who gives her everything but still does not win her is said to have a **lana**, which I am rendering as "curse."

"God give you enough to occupy you!"
Mbwa kupa wa kutosha!

Informants explain that this curse calls on God to afflict the curser's target with enough trouble and pain that he has neither the time nor the energy to continue bothering the curser.

"God give you cholera!" **Mbwa akupe taunil!**
"God will defeat you!" **Mungu atakushinda!**

The last curse nicely summarizes the aim of the otherwise defenseless old people who employ this type of badtalk. Unlike the English badtalk phrase *God damn you*, which seems to have retained little of its theological meaning, these curses are fully meant and understood as such by both the elderly cursers and their young targets. The cursers do not seem to be very effective in stopping the persecution of their users, but at least they do not result in an exchange of badtalk in which the adult is likely to emerge looking worse than before, as happens when adults use obscene badtalk in exchanges with hostile boys.

MIXED CURSES
"God Make You As You Are!"

Curses as means of defense are used mainly by the elderly, but there is a sort of curse that is used by other kinds of people. This is a curse, like the one in the title of this article, that combines abuse with a call for divine intervention. This sort of curse seems to be used less frivolously than the obscene badtalk to be discussed below.

Let us now turn to curses used by people well integrated in the community. A woman struck another's child for no apparent reason. The mother heard the noise and came out asking why the child had been struck. The attacker offered no reason, and the mother said, "You are crazy to hit a child like this for nothing." At this the attacker hit the child again and said, "There, you see." The mother, enraged, said to the attacker: "God curse you, and the curse is that you be what you already are!" This is intended, informants say, both to wish something bad on its target and to make clear that the pronouncer of the curse considers the cursed as already in a condition that shows the results of divine disfavor.

A type of expression that is fairly often found in angry exchanges between women is closely related to this type of curse. If one woman accuses the other of something the first does not think she deserves, the accused can say **waleo**, which is based on an archaic form of the verb "to write" and means that God has written for the accuser that she is as she is: i.e., angry, unreasonable, and badly behaved. There is some elaboration of this semi-curse with two other common forms (**shauri yako,** "your affair"; **utaono mwenyewe,** "you will see for yourself") both referring to the view that God has set a bad fate for the object of the expressions. All of these call attention to the badness of their targets and underline God's role in that condition, much as the more active curses such as "God make you as you are" do.

OBSCENE BADTALK
"Your Mother's Cunt!"

The *mixed curses* include references to undesirable characteristics and qualities of the target along with their prayer for divine intervention. *Obscene badtalk* refers directly to undesirable qualities of the target and involves no appeal to the supernatural. The most common obscene badtalk phrases used in Swahili by those who use such phrases at all can be translated as "Your mother's cunt."

Obviously, the "mother's cunt" badtalk concerns sex

and suggests something improper about the target's mother: that her genitals are the most significant thing about her, that the target or the abuser has some special relationship with the mentioned organ, or that the mother can be insulted by having her private parts mentioned and the target can do nothing to prevent it. All of these meanings are probably involved in the use of the phrase, but an important meaning—I suspect it is *the* important meaning – is that the mother has a vulva. Similarly, the phrase "Your mother is fucked," to be considered below, has a number of meanings, but a crucial and related one is simply to call attention to the fact that this has actually happened and is being publicly stated.

The reference to the abused person's mother's genitals is the commonest insult in Swahili culture, and the same phrase is used by some Swahili—mainly women and children or young men—as an all-purpose exclamation of surprise, annoyance, and pain. The phrase comes in three forms (**kuma nyoko, kuma nina, kuma mayo**), all of which use the same word **kuma**, referring to the *cunt*, but which differ according to the words used for "mother," with two of them using obscure or archaic words for that parent, and the third and strongest (**kuma mayo**) using an ordinary word. One of the archaic words for "mother," **nyoko**, itself is a very mild exclamation when used in the isolation from the unusual gynecological companion word, **kuma**.

The fact that the mother's genitals receive a favored place in Swahili badtalk is itself interesting, and that it is the most common phrase in badtalk is even more so. After all, there need be no badtalk reference to the anatomy of kin. English language badtalk is almost free of such references. The only one I can think of is the briefly used "your father's mustache," and attempts to produce badtalk in this area—imagine "your sister's instep," "your brother's ear lobe," or "your grandfather's navel"—result in unimpressive insults or exclamations. It is not obvious, then, why the mother's genitals should receive so much verbal attention; an examination of why they do may result in some illumination of Swahili culture as the basis for the reference being widely used as well as some understanding of why, in fact, it is used.

The first part of the examination concerns the place the mother is understood to have in Swahili life. Since it is the mother whose genitals are verbally displayed, it seems important that something be known about how she is understood to act—and how group members think she should act—in society. Previous work showed that more than 35% of Swahili sons and daughters interviewed reported that children *should* love their mothers more than their fathers, while only about 9% of daughters and no sons said that children should love their fathers more than their mothers (Swartz 1982: 33). This is in accord with interviews and observations that show that Swahili mothers are understood to be (and most frequently actually are) far more nurturant, supportive, and warm (as well as more actively involved with their children) than are Swahili fathers. The positive emotion focused on the mother and the relative lack of it for the father is noteworthy.

Secondly, there is no standard badtalk referring to penises in general, to father's penis, or to anything traceably connected to father's sexuality. The possible incestuous implications of shouting, muttering, snarling, and announcing the words "your mother's cunt" are not hard to see, but it is noteworthy that explicit reference is to the locus of female sexuality in general rather than to incestuous activity. This is demonstrably connected, I believe, to Swahili understandings about female sexuality in general and about the roles of men and women in Swahili society.

In Swahili society, parents and others devote a great deal of attention to controlling the sexual activities of girls and women. One of the fairly common insults mothers use on their daughters (and that relationship seems to be the premiere venue for badtalk, with the mother doing all the abusing) is to call them **mkware** which can be glossed as something like "female with strong and constant sexual appetite." There is no corresponding term for boys and men,[3] but there is considerable elaboration of the idea for women. So, for example, the only "pure" curse I recorded not mainly used by the destitute elderly is one that women use on one another: **Mwana kizaya ya paka!** ("May you get the great shame of the cat!"). This refers to the fact that cats express pleasure—or at least the Swahili see them as doing this—by wiggling their bottoms. This is called **kucheza kiuno,** and a woman who does this, who wiggles her bottom, is expressing sexual pleasure; such expression is understood as an indication of a hopelessly abandoned (i.e., uncontrolled as a cat is) woman. Even in sexual relations with a husband of many years it is better for a woman, Swahili male informants say, not to indicate that she enjoyed the encounter.

Additional evidence focusing around the extreme concern for the chastity of daughters and sisters and the fidelity of wives (see Strobel 1979: 48-49, 88-89) could be adduced, but not enough has been presented to suggest that sexuality for women entails cultural understandings involving the possibility of uncontrolled and dangerous behavior. Mentioning the mother's vulva may include—I suspect it does—the idea that the mother enjoys sex and is, therefore, likely to seek it. If, after all, her vulva is her most salient feature, she is likely to go around seeking opportunities to use it, and this is more than likely to lead to activities contrary to culturally established goodness. This idea receives some support from a badtalk greeting exchange that was reported to me. This greeting can be understood only if its social context is provided.

Swahili society is divided into two castes, and the upper caste is divided into a number of classes. One caste is made up of the descendants of slaves, and the other caste is composed of **waungwana**, "nobles," those whose slave-free ancestry is socially accepted. As Swahili understand it, women of all classes are constitutionally far less committed to honor and standards than men are. This is why women are believed (and observed) to be the main ones to engage in emotional badtalk. Also, the lower classes within the noble caste are far less committed to honor and standards than the higher classes are, so their members of either sex are expected to behave with less decorum. The greeting exchange I am about to report is said to occur as a somewhat common joke among the more uninhibited women of the slave caste and of the lower noble class.

One of the simplest greetings in the Swahili language is to say **Hujambo**. **Jambo** can be glossed as "event," "occurrence," or "news" with the clear and constant implication of something bad or worrisome occurring. **Hujambo** means "Nothing worrisome has happened to you or concerns you?" The polite and usual answer is **Si jambo**, meaning "There is nothing unwanted, bad, or untoward that needs to be reported." The women of the lower noble classes or the slave caste are said jokingly to respond to the greeting **Hujambo** from another woman with **Ninalo nawe si hilo?** meaning, literally, "I have it and you, isn't that it?" with "it" referring to the vulva. That is, the joke in transforming the innocuous greeting hinges on the fact that women all have a bad or worrisome thing (a **jambo**), i.e., their vulvas.

Despite the fact that "your mother's cunt" is the commonest badtalk phrase heard, actual reference to mother's sexual activity—as opposed to reference to the equipment for that activity—does occur. It is most frequently, but not solely, children, who abuse one another by saying **Mamako atombwa**, which can be literally rendered as "Your mother is fucked."[4] It is noteworthy that no incestuous reference is explicit in this but rather, as with the anatomical references considered so far, the point is that the mother engages in sexual activity. Not that that activity is necessarily outside accepted relationships, but like the more common reference to the mother's genitals, "Your mother is fucked!" is a powerful and effective exclamation and insult in part because it calls attention to the danger of female sexuality. It focuses attention on the target of abuse by emphasizing the fact that the target's mother is a sexual female.

Some further support for this hypothesis comes from a use of "mother's cunt" as a triumphal exclamation, expecially as a notation that one has surpassed a fellow. An example of this can be seen in the following incidents. Two Swahili girls of the lower caste were in Nairobi walking down the street on a dull afternoon. Some boys in a car stopped to offer them a ride and some amusement. They were delighted at the prospect and, seeing a girlfriend across the street who had no prospect of sharing their good fortune or having any comparable diversion on her own, shouted to her: **Fatuma, kuma mayo, kuma mayo!** ("Fatuma, your mother's cunt, your mother's cunt!")

As this little account suggests, reference to the vulva of another's mother is a way of underlining the superiority of the one who makes the reference. This superiority derives from the fact that it is the vulva of the target's mother that is being called to attention, not that of the one who makes the reference.

Further support for the view that calling attention to a vulva is a way of asserting the superiority of the person who does the calling is indicated by the following incident. A Swahili woman was arguing with an Arab food salesman and angrily said **Kuma mayo!** ("Your mother's cunt!") to him. The Arab, long resident among the Swahili, replied: "Why do you mention that distant cunt when there is another right here?"

Another aspect of why the focusing of attention on a person's mother's vulva demeans the person has been left implicit. This is that the female organs, and probably the male organs as well, are looked upon as defiling and unclean. Members of the opposite sex should not touch one another—even the most innocent touching of hands—when one or both are about to pray. Should touching occur, both those involved must bathe and purify themselves before praying. Members of both sexes are enjoined by the requirements of decency to shave off their body hair, especially their pubic hair, and anyone who is thought not to do this is viewed as a disgusting and hopelessly dirty person.[5] This may not be rooted in the view that the genitalia are unclean and defiling (but see Leach 1958 for a discussion of hair as a symbol of the genitals), but it surely indicates a concern with that part of the body and an interest in its cleanliness.

A colorful insult, used exclusively by women as far as I could determine, aimed at the target's mother and delivered in rhyming form, is quite graphic in portraying the disgusting possibilities inherent in female parts:

Kuma mayo mbovu	Your mother's rotten cunt
Tini maji	Below it water
Juu povu	Above it foam
Iliyokuzaa, mziavu.	That which bore you, useless one.

This badtalk doggerel is quite explicit in associating the mother's vulva of the target of abuse with rottenness, with urine, and with vaginal fluids and, thus, given Swahili views of these things as polluting, clearly states the contaminating and disgusting possibilities inherent in the female genitalia.

Continuing with the doggerel insult for a moment, its reference to urine gives weight to the contaminating nature of the vulva as being in the area of its origin. Swahili, like many Muslims, are intensely concerned with cleansing the body of any residue of excreta. How seriously this is taken can be seen in the belief that when the three angels come to the grave of a newly dead person (as Islamic belief holds they do), they punish him or her right there in the grave for any failure in cleaning the self after elimination, whereas all other transgressions are punished later after the deceased has moved to the next world.

MORE OBSCENE BADTALK
"Bastard of a Bastard, Grandchild of Satan"

Swahili obscene badtalk is not limited to direct reference to female genitalia. The second most common focus of abuse is the target's legitimacy, and the phrase **mwana haramu** (literally, "child of forbidden," or "bastard") is rather frequently used, especially by women and young males. Being a **mwana haramu** is not only an indication of having been conceived in sin, but also of being a person who, as the Swahili understand it, is unable to behave properly. A Swahili proverb holds that "Even if you put a bastard in a basket, he will hold up his thumb." This means that however vigorous the attempt to conceal the fact of illegitimacy, it will surely fail because of the distinctive behavior of bastards.

An alternative to the phrase **mwana haramu** is **chisi** which also means "bastard" but which rarely occurs alone. I have heard the word **chisi** only in the phrase **Mwana haramu wa chisi, mjuku wa Ibilisi**. This redundant badtalk phrase is mainly used by children. It can be literally rendered as "Bastard of [a] bastard, grandchild of Satan." It is of some interest here in indicating the answer to a puzzling question: why mothers abuse their own children by calling them bastards and by saying "Your mother's cunt" to them.

A full explanation of the basis for this maternal use of badtalk is beyond the scope of this article but can be found elsewhere (Swartz 1990). In brief, a mother's abuse of her child with badtalk concerning its parentage as well as its mother's privates is most fully understood as a denial of the child's relationship to the mother, and even to the father (although fathers less commonly use badtalk at all and even more rarely use it on their children). In saying "Your mother's cunt" the mother is denying her own connection to the child; this is also the case when she calls her own offspring a bastard. Some support for this can be seen in two further badtalk phrases used by mothers (and, rarely but occasionally, by fathers) on their children:

Matumbo yangu huzaa maradhi
"My womb has born a disease."

Matumbo yangu haikuzaa "My womb has not born."

Both of these phrases explicitly deny the child's connection to the mother who is abusing him, or more often, her. Like the reference to the child's legitimacy and to the child's mother's privates, these badtalk phrases assert that the child does not have the status of a true offspring since, it is implied, the child's own mother would not refer to her own adultery or to her own genitalia.

Women do not limit their badtalk to their offspring. They abuse one another with it as well. Also, women are not the only ones who use this badtalk. Boys and young men use it very frequently and, in addition to the phrases so far considered, they use several others that women do not use.

THE BADTALK OF BOYS AND YOUNG MEN
"Your Free...!"

Much of the abuse boys and young men direct at one another focuses around the target's alleged involvement in homosexuality as the passive participant. Some of the more common phrases are the following:

> **Bure yako!** "Your free [anus]!" or "Your [anus is] without cost!"
> **Tu yako!** "Your anus!"
> **Shoga** or **hanithi** or **rambuza**: "catamite"
> **Wafirwa!** "You are a fucked man!"

In Swahili society it is generally understood that being the *active* participant in homosexual relations is a normal, male activity that carries no implication of homosexuality for that participant. Normally-sexed males, it is believed, are quite willing to sodomize any other male who is available, and it is only the *passive* partner who is perverted and subnormal. When a boy says "Your free [anus]!" to another boy, he means that the target allows himself to be sodomized without even the excuse of being paid for the act. The same insult is sometimes directed to girls and women from the lower caste or from other ethnic groups, where it means that they are more despicable than prostitutes. It is noteworthy that these last insults are never used within the family; also, I have no evidence that "noble" Swahili women use them at all.

It is worth noting that the boys and young men who use the mainly sodomy-related badtalk as well as those phrases also used by women are in a very weak position in their own society. As in other urban societies, money is essential for most of the material things members desire, and there are only two usual ways money can be obtained: through earning and through support from others. The most commonly cited "turning point" in a boy's life, Swahili youths tell me, is getting a job, but this is not an easy thing to do in an economy where unemployment is high and persistent as it is in Kenya. When a young man does get a job, he is liberated from his father's unwelcome supervision. Employed young men, like urban youths elsewhere, often use their new-found wealth to take a room of their own and escape parental restriction at the same time that they use their resources to obviate the need to ask their fathers for the money to buy entertainment, clothing, and other things they want. Employed youths are also in a position to think of marriage since, as in many African societies, this calls for considerable cash outlay at the beginning to meet the bridewealth payment to their intended's parents. The youth's own parents may help him with this payment, just as, in most cases, they will supply him with shelter, food, and some funds for entertainment. But he is at their—especially the father's—mercy to the extent that he seeks that assistance.

Boys and young men, then, are virtually powerless with regard to some of the main things that concern them, such as how they spend their leisure time (i.e., at home where they are under parental scrutiny), what they can buy, and even how and when they marry. Once they get a job they are freer than they were, and once they marry and establish a household of their own, they become full-fledged adult men. Vitally for the central hypothesis of this article, most males begin to use badtalk less as they become more established and, therefore, more in control of their own affairs. Boys and young men with no jobs are the only members of the group who rival women in the frequency of their use of badtalk. Employed but unmarried young men use badtalk a good deal, but notably less than their unemployed cohort; employed and married young men use badtalk less than their bachelor fellows; and married men with children of their own use it even less. In short, as the males move from being completely in the control of their parents to being more nearly in control of their own affairs, they use badtalk less and less. This is in accord with the hypothesis that holds that badtalk is mainly a device used by the powerless.

NOTES

1. A related paper, Swartz 1990, takes up some of the same data considered here, but it addresses itself to issues concerned with the distribution of Swahili culture not considered here, while this article considers data not dealt with in the other and approaches these data from a different perspective. F.G. Bailey, D.K. Jordan, F.J.P. Poole, and D.F. Tuzin were kind enough to read earlier forms of this article and to provide me with the benefit of their comments. Yahya Ali Omar generously tried to prevent mistakes in the usage of the Swahili language and helped me avoid errors of interpretation. None of these colleagues, however, shares responsibility for what is written here.

2. One of the sections of Old Town is renowned for the roughness, forcefulness, and shocking behavior of its residents. Men from this section of town—although undoubtedly of the noble caste and some of them reasonably well to do and well educated—are said to use badtalk more than others of comparable status, but I have not myself seen them do it.

3. Until they have had numerous opportunities to satisfy themselves, men who have been deprived of sexual activity for long periods—especially sailors and fishermen in this coastal society—are called **mshahawa** ("full of semen"), which is viewed as a dangerous but temporary state.

4. I was told that when mothers hear this being said to their children the mothers reply: "Is it as though your mother is not fucked? You were born in what way?"

5. Traditionally, but not commonly now, men also shaved their head hair.

REFERENCES

Bakari, Mtoro Bin Mwinyi. 1981. *The Customs of the Swahili People.* Berkeley: University of California Press.

Caplan, Patricia Ann. 1975. *Choice and Constraint in a Swahili Community: Property Hierarchy, and Cognatic Descent on the East African Coast*. London and New York: Oxford University Press.

Leach, Edmond R. 1958. "Magical Hair." *Journal of the Royal Anthropological Institute* 88: 147-165.

Salim, A. I. 1973. *Swahili-Speaking Peoples of Kenya's Coast*. Nairobi: East African Publishing House.

Scheven, Albert. 1981. *Swahili Proverbs: Nia Zikiwa Moja, Kilicho Mbali Huja*. Washington, D.C.: University Press of America.

Strobel, Margaret. 1979. *Muslim Women in Mombasa, 1890-1975*. New Haven: Yale University Press.

Swartz, Marc J.
- 1969. "The Cultural Dynamics of Blows and Abuse among the Bena of Tanzania." In Spenser, R. (ed.) *Forms of Symbolic Action*. Seattle: Washington University Press.
- 1978. "Religious Courts, Community, and Ethnicity among the Swahili of Mombasa: An Historical Study of Social Boundaries." *Africa* 49: 29-41.
- 1982a. "Cultural Theory and Cultural Sharing: Some Results of a Study of the Nuclear Family in Five Societies." *American Anthropologist* 84: 314-338.
- 1982b. "The Isolation of Men and the Power of Women: Sources of Power among the Swahili of Mombasa." *Journal of Anthropological Research* 38: 26-44.
- 1983. "Culture and Implicit Power: Maneuvers and Understandings in Swahili Family Relations." In Aronoff, M. (ed.) *Culture and Politics. Political Anthropology*, vol. II. New Brunswick, NJ, and London: Transaction Books.
- 1990. "Aggressive Speech, Status, and Cultural Distribution among the Swahili of Mombasa." In Jordan, D. and Swartz, M. (eds.): *Personality and the Cultural Constitution of Society: Essays in Honor of Melford E. Spiro*. Tuscaloosa: University of Alabama Press.

THE *PORTAGEE* IN SPEECH AND JOKE

George Monteiro

> Q: I know they call Spanish-speaking people "Spicks." But what do they call the Portuguese?
> A: Why, they call them "Pricks," of course. — *Anon.*, 1968

> Now that Catholics are allowed to eat meat on Friday, there goes the Portuguese economy. — *Anon.*, 1975
> *(from the 1960s)*

I

"I read that novel—*The Portygee*—and there wasn't one Portuguese native or Portuguese descendant in the whole book," a colleague once complained. The novel was the work of Joseph C. Lincoln, a prolific writer of fiction with a Cape Cod setting. It was published in 1920. What my colleague did not know then (and that I would learn only later) was that Lincoln's choice of title was based on the then common usage among Cape Cod sea captains of the term **Portygees** to refer to *all* foreigners. Since for Lincoln the term was generic, as he pointed out in the dusk-jacket blurb, he could use it precisely without worrying about its ultimate derivation. As a generic term for "foreigner," moreover, **Portygee** was even broader in coverage than the term **Dago**, which several decades ago referred commonly not only to the Italians but to the other southern Europeans as well, particularly the Spanish and Portuguese.[1] It was in its enlarged meaning, probably, that Mark Twain employed the term in naming his two characters in minor works "Portugee Joe" ("American Claimant") and "The Portygee" ("My Debut as a Literary Person"). Indeed, it was probably with this broader reference that the servant Abel Stebbins employs the term, when in Oliver Wendell Holmes's novel *Elsie Venner* (1861) he voices suspicion, "I can't help mistrustin' them Portagee-lookin' fellahs."[2] When Henry James employs a variant of the term in his novel *The Ambassadors* (1903), however, there can be no mistake. "I think I make out a 'Portagee,'" one of his characters says referring clearly to a native of Portugal.[3] For some time usage has so narrowed the term's meaning that it now refers only to the Portuguese and their descendants. In Valley Falls, Rhode Island, for example, there lives a man, now in his mid-fifties, who has been known since childhood as "Eddie the Portagee," or, simply, "Portagee." He was so nicknamed because when his taunters called him a "Portagee," he answered that he was proud of it. There is as well **Portugoose**, a bit of military slang.[4] I have also heard **Porkacheese**.

The term **Portagee**, to refer to the Portuguese, is also used, customarily in some orthographic version of **Portugee**, as the derisive part of an adjectival combination. The universally known, dictionary-sanctioned **Portuguese-man-of-war** refers to "any of several large marine organisms, having long, stinging-tentacles hanging down from a bladderlike float." A **Portuguese parliament**, according to sailors, is a gathering where everyone talks but nobody listens.[5] When someone is confused and doesn't know where to begin telling his story, he is in a **Portuguese pigknot**.[6] Of more recent vintage is **Portuguese time** (sometimes **Brazilian time**), which refers to any chronological time later than the appointed or prescribed time for an engagement. Translated from Portuguese and widely used by the Portuguese themselves, this adjectival combination calls attention to the national propensity, it is believed, for arriving late for work, appointments, solemn occasions, etc. Word combinations beginning, not with *Portuguese* but

Portagee (in any of its spellings) are, as one might anticipate, more pejorative. **Portagee colonial** (or **Immigrant Chic**), for instance, refers to that cheaply made "modern" furniture, the chief buyer of which is the unsuspecting recent immigrant; while a **Portagee lawnmower** is a goat used to keep down growth. Such **lawnmowers** are used by **South County Indians**. South County is in Rhode Island. From California come **Portagee overdrive**, the "gear" used by a trucker (or other driver) to coast downhill with gears disengaged, and **Portugee lift**, a combination used by longshorement to criticize one another when someone carries less than his share of the load.[7] In nineteenth-century America there was even a patent medicine, "sure to produce a miscarriage," called *Dr. Melveau's Portuguese Female Pills*.[8]

The full sociological import of such combinations has not been measured. If "in itself, the derisive adjective, either as a term or pattern is not important," writes one student of the phenomenon, "placed within a cultural context...it may indicate qualitatively, long-held prejudices and cultural antagonisms."[9] It's probable. Let us return, for example, to the case of the **Portagee lift**. The term was not only used on the docks in San Francisco years ago, it was employed and defined as recently as 1977 by the well-known writer Eric Hoffer, with no sensitivity to its prejudicial nature, in a P.B.S.-TV film entitled "Eric Hoffer: The Crowded Life." That prejudice against the Portuguese longshoreman continues to be rather widespread is suggested by Johnny Carson's "insulting" a person in his audience, by describing him as having seen "his mother in a stag movie with five Portuguese longshoremen" ("Tonight Show," May 22, 1979). The television comedian Dick Martin tells a similar joke, one involving an Aunt Martha who with great delight finds herself the only female shipwrecked with a boatload of Portuguese sailors ("Tim Conway Show," April 19, 1980). Both Carson and Martin work out of California, but since so much of television emanates from Southern California, perhaps little or nothing should be made of their anti-Portuguese jokes and the Portuguese presence in the state. Still, that the existence of such a connection is plausible is supported by still more jokes about the Portuguese emanating from California. In listing things to be thankful for on the eve of Thanksgiving Day in 1981, Steve Martin began: "I'm thankful for the Atlantic Ocean because without it a lot of Portuguese would be walking into my living room" ("My Best Show Ever," November 25, 1981). Here the joke is not at the expense of the libidinous nature of the Portuguese. Rather it appeals to xenophobic feelings about Portuguese immigration. Legislation doesn't keep them out. Only the cost of the plane fare keeps the hordes out. On another television special Martin presents as one of the "Bizarre Oddities of the World" a bit about Portuguese dentistry. Standing before two persons jumping up and down on a trampoline and speaking into a hand mike the trenchcoat-clad Martin says: "If you are thinking of going to Portugal this year, be sure to have your cavities filled because here in Portugal they still practice the art of trampoline dentistry" ("Comedy is Not Pretty," January 23, 1982).

II

The Brazilian's analogue for the American's Polish joke is the Portuguese joke. Told at the expense of those people who discovered, colonized, and until the nineteenth century, ruled Brazil, the Portuguese *piada* (joke) is recreated daily, it would seem, dozens of times. Such jokes are as often atopical as they are topical, and as such they not only correspond to the American Polish jokes in form but are often nothing more than variants adapted to the local scapegoat population.[10]

There is nothing comparable about the Portuguese in the United States. Polish jokes do reappear as Portuguese jokes, often with great alacrity, but they are first and foremost Polish jokes. Here are a few examples:

(1) There is a five-dollar bill on the ground. Three people come along—Santa Claus, the Easter Bunny, and a smart Portagee. Who, of the three, will get to it first? — Nobody. There is no Santa Claus, there is no Easter Bunny, and there is no such thing as a smart Portagee.

(2) A young unmarried Portuguese girl tells her mother that she has discovered that she is pregnant. Her mother, concerned, has a bright idea. She asks her daughter, "But are you sure the baby's yours?"

(3) How do you sink a Portuguese ship? – You put it in water.

(4) Portugal is the only country in the world where a man's mistress is uglier than his wife.

(5) Hear about the new Portuguese bank? You give them a toaster and they give you $500.

The makeup of the audience on any given occasion dictates whether these jokes are told at the expense of the Portuguese, the Polish or the Irish. And this is true for virtually all American jokes that are told at the expense of the Portuguese. Indeed, I know only a few Portuguese jokes that are not told as readily about other ethnics, and in some cases I am not entirely convinced of their Portuguese integrity. First, a sure thing. Question: "What is the longest bridge in the world?" Answer: "The Braga Bridge, because it links Portugal to the U.S.A." Since the bridge, a rather modest span, runs between Fall River and Somerset, both of which are in Massachusetts, it is necessary to know that Fall River with a total population (in 1983) of some 92,000 is over sixty percent Portuguese and Portuguese-American. In that sense it *is* Portugal. It is difficult to see how this joke could be adapted to any other ethnic group. Incidentally, long-haul truckers call the sometimes dangerously slippery bridge "the Portuguese slide." "Put two Portagees out alone in a rowboat in the middle of the ocean and they'll both get rich. You know how? They'll steal from each other." My doubt anent the Portuguese integrity of this anecdote arises from the fact that the same basic anecdote was told in the nineteenth century at the expense of Yankee big talkers who, though alone, would inevitably succeed in outtalking one another.[11]

A few years ago the Portuguese were made the butt of a joke post card inserted in *Hustler* magazine. It depicts a naked woman on a pool table and reads, *Greetings from New Bedford, Mass. The Portuguese gang-rape capital of America.*[12] It refers to an incident that culminated in a widely publicized trial. The movie *The Accused*, starring Jody Foster, was based on this incident, but it makes no mention of the Portuguese. A second movie, *Mystic Pizza*, however, centers on "Portagees" (as they are called and as they call themselves) in Mystic, Connecticut.

Let me conclude with a single example of riddles that are decidedly aimed at the Portuguese, for their solution involves punning on a Portuguese surname.

> *Question*: What do you call a guy who sleeps in a car?
> *Answer*: A car-dozer (*Cardosa*).

The *siesta* prevails, no matter what.

NOTES

1. According to A.A. Roback (p. 26), *Dago* was originally a nickname for Spaniards only, deriving from *Diego* (James). *A Dictionary of International Slurs* (Cambridge, Mass: Sci-Art Publishers, 1944); reissued in facsimile by Maledicta Press, Waukesha, Wisconsin, in 1979.

2. Oliver Wendell Holmes, *Elsie Venner—A Romance of Destiny* (Boston: Houghton Mifflin, 1889), p. 424.

3. Henry James, *The Ambassadors*, ed. Leon Edel (Boston: Houghton Mifflin, 1960), p. 127.

4. Roback, p. 59.

5. Roback, p. 59; Frank Shay, *A Sailor's Treasury* (New York: Norton, 1951), p. 178.

6. Roback, p. 59. He also lists *Portuguese pumping*, but does not define it, saying only "a phrase of uncertain but unquestionably questionable meaning, in the opinion of both Ware and Partridge" (p. 59).

7. These last two terms are listed respectively, by Roberta Hanley, "Truck Drivers' Language in the Northwest," *American Speech* 36 (1961): 273, and Archie Green, "John Newhaus: Wobbly Folklorist," *Journal of American Folklore* 73 (July-Sept. 1960): 211.

8. Ely van der Warkle, "The Detection of Criminal Abortion," *Journal of the Boston Historical Society* 4-5 (1870); quoted in Malcolm Potts, "History of Contraception," *Gynecology and Obstetrics*, ed. John W. Sciarra (Philadelphia: Harper & Row, 1982), p. 7.

9. Ed Cray, "Ethnic and Place Names as Derisive Adjectives," *Western Folklore* 21 (Jan. 1962): 34.

10. See Nelson H. Vieira, "The Luso-Brazilian Joke," *Western Folklore* 39 (Jan. 1980): 51-56.

11. See, for example, Irving Bacheller's novel, *Eben Holden: A Tale of the North Country* (Boston: Lothrop, 1900), p. 139.

12. "Magazine Assailed for Slur against Portuguese," *Providence Journal-Bulletin* (2 July 1983), p. A-8.

Copyright © 1989 by Jeffrey Weber
(From a comic strip about an Illinois Linguistics professor)

WORD FINDER & SPELLING CHECKER
OR, SOME OF MY BEST FRIENDS ARE KNITTERS

Reinhold Aman

Word Finder™ is an excellent electronic thesaurus for the Macintosh computer. It contains of 220,000 synonyms for 15,000 key words. While checking some "offensive" words, I found that the inclusion of such words is idiosyncratic. It contains such words as **asshole, prick, schmuck, shit, tit,** and **turd,** but neither **balls, broad** (female), **cock, cunt, dick, fart, fuck, piss** (yet **pissed, piss off,** and **pissed off** showed up as synonyms for *aggravate/d*), **pussy** (sexual), **putz,** and **twat,** nor any racial, religious or ethnic slurs, as far as I could see.

However, the thesaurus contains four synonyms for the noun *homosexual*: **bisexual, gay, lesbian,** and **queer.** Further, when I requested synonyms for *fairy*, the screen displayed **fag** (but not **faggot**), **pansy,** and **sissy.** Godnose, I am not known to be a pushy gay activist, but I believe that the inclusion of derogatory terms for homosexuals only is unfair to that group. It appears that the supervisor of the thesaurus project, Dr. Roger Schlobin, Professor of English Literature at Purdue University, is not socially "sensitive," to use an obnoxious term flung about by bleeding-heart social engineers and other busybody do-gooders.

In order to amuse myself—we lonely editors are easily amused—I ran the preceding text through the spelling checker program built into Microsoft's *Word* (versions 3.02 and 4.0) word-processing application. The program was unable to suggest any alternative spellings for **fuck** and **schmuck,** but it did suggest the alternatives shown in parentheses for the following words in boldface: **asshole** (ashore, asphodel), **cunt** (cant, cent, chunk, churn, chute, chutney, count, cut, kung, sun, sung), **fag** (fig, fog, fug, phage; the "word is already spelled correctly" in version 4.0), **fart** (Fahr, fair, far, fard, fat, fath, fear, fears, feast, fort), **putz** (but, butt, buzz, poult, pout, pouts, put, putt), **shit** (chit, shift, shipt, shirt, shot, shpt, shtg, shut, swift), **turd** (tour, toured, tours, thru, thrum, Thurs), and **twat** (dwt, thwart, thwarts, twit).

Continuing my amusement, I requested from the spelling checker more verbal nasties and got the following suggestions shown in parentheses for the words in boldface: **kike** (chide, chief, chile, chime, chine, chink, chinked, kiosk), **nigger** (knitter, nagger, Niger, Nigeria, niggler, nigglers, nudger, nudgers), and **spic** (skip, skips, spec, spice, spicy). The words **chink, kraut, Polack,** and **wop,** as well as **faggot, fairy, pansy, queer,** and **sissy** are "already spelled correctly," according to version 4.0, thus no alternatives were suggested.

ENGLISH

Peter Kunzke

I like your language
well enough.
It's well bred
of Anglo-Saxon stock
and well seasoned
with Latin and Greek.
It's the goddamned
fucked-up spellings
that annoy me.

THE TAXONOMY OF BENEDICTION AND MALEDICTION

Rudi Schmid

Maledictologists are well aware that malediction covers the gamut from banter and self-deprecation to the intentionally malicious. The former are the basis for much good humor and a psychological necessity for many persons. The latter may be humorous only in context and does not have universal justification. Because most people and most, if not all, dictionaries define *malediction* and its variants strictly in terms totally negative, I feel that we should make a distinction for positive malediction, for the bantering and self-deprecatory malediction. I refer to this as *benemalediction*, which I consider more euphonious and hence preferable to *malebenediction*. **Benediction, malediction,** and **benemalediction** can be directed both towards oneself and towards others, for which, respectively, the prefixes **auto-** and **allo-** are handy. The following table distinguishes among these variants and is a refinement of related terminology presented by James Matisoff (see *Maledicta* 1: 31).

(1) **BENEDICTION**: the conventional definition, that is, "an expression of good wishes" (*Webster's Ninth New Collegiate Dictionary*, 1983).

　(a) **Autobenediction**: benediction directed toward oneself, a frequent phenomenon, especially characteristic of the psychologically insecure. Example: "I'm the greatest!"

　(b) **Allobenediction**: benediction directed toward others, the usual phenomenon. Example: "May you go in peace!"

(2) **MALEDICTION**: the conventional definition, that is, "to speak evil of."

 (a) **Automalediction**: malediction directed toward oneself, an occasional phenomenon, especially characteristic of the psychologically unstable. Example: "Why, what an ass am I!" (Hamlet in *Hamlet*, Act II, Scene ii)

 (b) **Allomalediction**: malediction directed toward others, the usual phenomenon. Example: "You fucking asshole!"

(3) **BENEMALEDICTION**: a good-humored, bantering, mildly self-deprecatory malediction, the basis of much good humor. The subtypes noted probably occur with equal frequency. They are very often meaningful only in context, and occasionally the same expression is usable for each subtype (as some expressions in 3a).

 (a) **Autobenemalediction**: benemalediction directed toward oneself. Examples: "I'm a culinary opportunist" (to refer to one's laziness at cooking for oneself), "botanical tourist" (to refer to a botanist doing initial fieldwork in a country—this and preceding expression my coinage), "subversive country music" or "outlaw country music" (expressions heard on former KFAT radio, Gilroy, California—see *Maledicta* 4: 291).

 (b) **Allobenemalediction**: benemalediction directed toward others. Examples: "You motherfucker!" and in retort "*Your* mother!" and other examples of ritual insults or verbal dueling (see *Maledicta* 6: 199 and 7: 189), or "Stay fat!" (from KFAT radio).

Intonation and other circumstances, of course, can make the difference between one category and the other. Compare, for instance, the similar examples in 2b and 3b. Murray (*Maledicta* 7: 189) details well the distinctions between ritual and personal insults.

Webster's Dictionary, incidentally, dates *malediction* from the 14th century but *benediction* from the 15th, which perhaps suggests that it has always been easier to be a maledictor than a benedictor. The same notion is conveyed by Ambrose Bierce (*The Devil's Dictionary*, 1911, reprinted in 1958 by Dover Publications) in his sardonic definition of *malefactor* as "the chief factor in the progress of the human race."

> Pay attention, goddamn it, I said the *Schmidt* house!

Cigarette smoke is the residue of your pleasure. It permeates the air and putrifies my hair and clothes, not to mention my lungs.

THIS TAKES PLACE WITHOUT MY CONSENT!

I have a pleasure also: I like a beer now and again. The residue from my pleasure is urine. Would you be annoyed if I stood on a chair and pissed on your head and clothes without your consent?

Not at all, so long as I can put my fag out on your knob.

Poster seen by Neil Crawford in a London design studio, in August 1988. The word *fag* in the handwritten addition by a smoker is British slang for "cigarette." *Knob* is a slang word for glans penis.

AN OPEN LETTER TO MIKE ROYKO

Reinhold Aman

Mike Royko is a widely-syndicated columnist for *The Chicago Tribune* who writes snide comments about almost everything and everyone. His column containing the *Kraut* slur below appeared 15 Nov. 1988, when he sarcastically rejected the invitation by an auto dealer to test-drive a Porsche. Needless to say, some of my smartest and best friends are Slavs.

Mike Royko
The Chicago Tribune
435 N. Michigan Ave.
Chicago, IL 60611   21 November 1988

Hey, Mike, you Nasty Old Goat-Fucker!

Usually you are hilarious and witty. Sometimes you are boring. Sometimes you are a smartass jerk. And occasionally you are a really narrow-minded, ignorant, nasty son-of-a-bitch.

Which is why I am writing. Your recent article about the Porsche dealer generally was quite amusing, but you let your Slavic prejudices and ignorance tarnish a good column.

First, don't you know that ethnic and so-called sexist slurs are *the big taboos* these days? Your remark about "a couple of gorgeous blonde **Kraut dollies**" has no place in a newspaper, unless—in the spirit of American democracy and equality—you balance such slurs with similar ones. If you had received an invitation to test-drive an Italian Lamborghini (twice as expensive as the Porsche, about whose price you bitched), would you have wished that **Wop tomatoes** or **Dago dollies** would be thrown in as accessories? Or, if you had received an invitation from a Polish, Israeli or African car maker, would you have fantasized about — God forbid — **Polack broads, Kike chicks** or **Nigger mommas**?

You are a prejudiced jerk, and you know it. But I understand: it's the old Slavic inferiority complex which causes a normally level-headed fellow like you to dump on the Krauts. It's the old East European revenge mentality to snap at the allegedly racially superior Krauts who rightly believe that anyone with a name like "Royko" is at best fit to clean their latrines. Listen, chump, if your Slavic folks had not been allowed into this country—God knows where they crawled out under—you would now be squatting in some damp cave in Eastern Europe and buggering every goat that wanders by.

Second, your ignorance shows in your remark that you would not buy cars made in Germany or Japan, because of World War II. Hey, Mikhail, that war took place over four decades ago. More importantly, if those Krauts and Nips would not buy American goods worth billions of dollars in return for being able to sell us their superior products, millions of Americans would be out of work. That's *Economics 101* but apparently too complex for your Slavic brainlet. Further, those millions of unemployed Yanks wouldn't have the money to buy newspapers. Which means you'd be out of a job at *The Trib* and lucky to get a copy boy's job at the *Kankakee Weekly Shopper,* driving a crappy Yugo built by your compatriots. So, lighten up, you baldheaded jerkface. They buy our stuff; we buy theirs. Simple.

Picking on swinish politicians, crooked lawyers and similar scum is fine. But being nasty to ethnic, racial or religious groups is not the mark of an educated man. Of course, the *real* cause for your attacks on such easy ethnic targets to drain off your anger is your young, anti-smoking, bitchy wife who gives you a hard time for having a soft little dick.

Up Yours,

R. Aman

P.S.: Nasty letter to follow.

A FIRST LOOK AT ARMENIAN MALEDICTA

Vladimir Ilyich Želvys

When an Armenian hits his finger with a hammer, he probably shouts **Satanan tani!** or **Grokhe tani!** (The devil take it!). While these exclamations are not very offensive, there are many truly offensive terms and exclamations in Armenian, of which I shall present a sampling below. Several English equivalents are grammatical approximations.

Armenians are fond of damnations wishing death on their opponents: **Satkes bali!** (I wish you died!), **Takhem kez!** (I wish you were buried!), **Arnatatakh!** (I wish you bled to death!), or **Boyet takhem!** (I wish you were buried full-size!). A somewhat poetic "burying curse" is **Arevt takhem!** (I wish your sun were buried!), "I wish you'd never see daylight again!" or "I hope you'll die before sunrise!"

Names of animals appear frequently in very widely used abusive terms: **Shan pes mi nacha!** (Don't bark like a dog!), "Don't shout!", "Don't be so rude!" or "Stop your name-calling!" **Ezi glukh!** (Ox's head!) and **Eshi glukh!** (Donkey's head!) are vocatives meaning "fool, dunce."

But most of the dirty words and expressions are connected with sex and, less often, with filth. Among the latter are **kak** (shit), **sher** (piss), **vor** (arse, ass), **kakem beranet** (approximately: I'm shitting in your mouth), **kakem glhit** (appr.: I'm shitting on your head), or just **kekhtot** (filthy). One vulgar expression is impressively obscene: **Klri kekht** (Filth of my prick!), meaning roughly, "You smegma!"

Names of sexual organs include **klir** (prick), **klri glukh** (glans penis, lit. "head of prick"), **dzver** (balls, lit. "eggs"), **plorner** (balls), and **puts** (cunt).

Very strong insults are formed with terms involving copulation and other sexual activities: **kunem putsed** (approx.: I'm fucking a cunt), **Kunem meret!** and **Mairiket kunem!** (appr.: I'm fucking your mother!). Others are **Klires tstses!** (Suck my prick!) **kunem beranet** (appr.: I'm fucking you in the mouth), **kunem voret** (appr.: I'm fucking you in the ass), **bernumet dnem** (appr.: I'm putting [a prick] in your mouth), and the—for us—exotic **hokum kunem** (appr.: I'm fucking you in the soul). The last one is like the Russian *Yeb tvoju v dushu mat'!* (Fucked your mother in the soul! *or* Fucked your mother's soul!).

Some of the expressions are comparatively rare, for example, those referring to **tokhum**, "sperm": **Zhazh tam beranet!** (appr.: I shall pour [my sperm] in your mouth!) and **Zhazh tam vret!** (appr.: I shall pour [my sperm] in your ass!).

As one can see, Armenians are quite expressive when the situation requires it.

In summer 1989, a long-time reader and friend, Dr. John Solt, put one of our THANK YOU FOR NOT FARTING cards (see MAL 7: 154) on the advertising sign of the Gas Museum in Tokyo, Japan. Some 250,000 people pass by this sign daily; it is located at the Seibu Shinjuku train station. Our thanks to John and the photographer, Masafumi Suzuki.

KAKOLOGIA
A Chronicle of Ribald Riddles
and Wicked Wordplays

Reinhold Aman

I. INTRODUCTION

Hypocrites & Ignoramuses

It used to be the conservatives who had no sense of humor. Now it's the so-called liberals who have turned into humorless, "sensitive" Thought Police jumping at anyone who dares tell or write "sexist," "racist," "ageist" and other new-taboo "-ist" material. Those hypocrites are outraged at "insensitive" jokes told in public and write blistering columns condemning the perpetrator while snickering in private about such jokes or alleged slurs. They—including *The Milwaukee Journal*'s book reviewer—lament Khomeini's censoring of Rushdie's *Satanic Verses*; yet those bloody hypocrites and small-time Khomeinis suppress all information about *Maledicta*.

Regardless, I will continue to chronicle humanity's inhumanity by preserving the jokes and riddles and offensive glossaries in these pages, spicing "Kakologia" with double-entendre and downright-dirty stuff to add a chuckle to these dreary pages.

When it comes to "Kakologia," one also encounters double standards and much hypocrisy. If such material is published by a university professor (such as Alan Dundes), it's okay; if it's published by a *former* university professor (such as R. Aman), it's *verboten*. If it's presented on a Public Television program, it's okay; if it's presented in *Maledicta*, it's not. Hypocrites! Bloody hypocrites! When PBS presented "Ethnic Notions: Portraits of Prejudice," *The Milwaukee Journal*'s TV-Radio critic Mike "Drool" Drew called it "gripping, important, commendable, must viewing," giving four stars to that program showing "subservient Toms, happy-go-lucky Sambos, and nurturing Mammies" (MJ, 12 Febr. 1988: 8D). When I discussed similar material on a PBS special on language or on the NBC "Today Show," Drooling Drew suppressed all information about it. Hypocrite! Bloody hypocrite!

The editors at *The Milwaukee Journal* (hereafter known as *The Urinal*) have for some 15 years suppressed almost all national and international news stories about *Maledicta* from the AP, UPI, Reuters, and dozens more. It's no big loss, as publicity in Milwaukee is worthless. For example, when *Milwaukee Magazine* (50,000 readers) ran a good story about *Maledicta*, only five readers inquired; two ordered. When *The Urinal* (some 480,000 readers on Sundays) published a short report about our publications, I received two requests for gratis copies; one from a University of Wisconsin professor, the other from an optometrist in Oshkosh. *Gevalt!*

I am **not** seeking publicity. On the contrary; for many years I have refused most interviews nationwide and all interviews with the monopolistic *The Urinal*'s affiliated radio and television stations. It's just a matter of **principle**: if news stories about *Maledicta* are published in some 900 newspapers nationwide and internationally, the local readers, too, are entitled to read about it, regardless of what the bloody hypocritical mousebrains at *The Urinal* think of our journal. News is news.

Repressed mousebrains and bloody hypocrites suppress information about *Maledicta* not only in low journalism but also in high cacademia. Those fields that profit most from our material have ignored good old MAL for over a decade: our publications do not exist for most editors of journals and newsletters in anthropology, communication, English, folklore, foreign languages, journalism, law, linguistics, onomastics, philology, psychology, and sociology.

To be ignored by the cacas is also no big loss. Large display advertisements in the *LSA Bulletin* (Linguistic Society of America) and *PMLA* (Publications of the Modern Language Association of America) brought fewer than a dozen inquiries from their readers. The few newsletters and journals in academia that do mention *Maledicta*, such as *American Name Society Bulletin, American Speech, Dictionary Society of North America Newsletter, Mid-America Folklore, Names, Newsletter of the American Dialect Society*, and *Western Folklore*, also result in only three or fewer inquiries (not orders) from their readers allegedly interested in language. Why? Are those folks too cheap? Too repressed? Too humorless? Too "sensitive"? Too dull? All of the above?

Anyway, word gets around and our topic is on many people's mind. Suddenly, there are cacademic Johnnies-come-lately in the "Kakologia" business. I don't mean such experts as Professor Alan Dundes (Anthropology, University of California in Berkeley), a widely-known scholar of this topic who has researched jokes and riddles for decades. He has published many articles and several books on kakological folklore and jokes. When not twisted with anti-German prejudice and Freudian *shtik*, his interpretations are valid and insightful.

But there are newcomers to this field who act as if they had discovered this ancient field of interhuman nastiness. They include pop psychologist Dr. Joyce Brothers who glibly quotes stuff first published in MAL without mentioning her source. They are professors of education, English, psychology or speech who either steal material from *Maledicta* without giving credit or who are ignorant of the nearly 3,000 pages we have published in this journal. *The Urinal* (22 Sept. 1988: 19A) ran a long, three-column news story about a University of Wisconsin communications prof who is working on a project entitled "The Power of Midwestern Ethnic Humor to Hurt and Heal" with the headline: "Jokes found to be racist, sexist." *No shit!* That prof and that rag's education reporter obviously are ignorant of the years of research by you-know-whom and his colleagues as well as of Dr. James Leary, an outstanding Madison scholar of folklore and ethnic studies.

To quote the mind-boggling discoveries of that communications prof about anti-gay and anti-black jokes:

> I think there's a connection between who [sic] we joke about and who [sic] we're afraid of. There's a lot of fear, anger, aggressivity [sic] that is released towards people who make up less than 10% of the population in Madison.

Do these novel findings blow your mind, or what?

Much has been written about whether kakological jokes should be told and published, and several intelligent articles have advocated such jokes. I don't have the time to elaborate on the many news stories and magazine articles about banning AIDS and JAP jokes, ethnic slurs, why "sick jokes" are told, and the like.

Informants Needed

In most cases, our contributors of kakological material are acknowledged semi-anonymously or not at all, for several reasons, but they know who they are. I want to thank all of you who have sent material for "Kakologia" and other departments, who have taken the time to jot down the latest riddle and whip it out to me, who faithfully clip and mail envelopes stuffed with items about verbal aggression, jokes and Xeroxlore. Without your help, "Kakologia" could not exist. Waukesha, where men are still men (and sheep are nervous), is not an intellectual hotbed. Thus your cards and letters keep me abreast of what's happening outside Metro Milwaukee. As far as I know, *Maledicta* is the only journal in the world that presents uncensored riddles and similar material from English-speaking countries worldwide. If you readers in Australia, Canada, Great Britain, South Africa and wherever English is spoken send me the latest jokes (riddles) you have heard, your fellow readers in other parts of the world can be informed; and you, in turn, will be able to read material circulating elsewhere in the world. Thus it is in your best interest to keep me informed of your local celebrity or disaster "jokes." So, please keep stuffing my mailbox, and if I ever catch up with work, I'll stuff yours. Please don't forget to write legibly and to put different items on *separate* sheets, each with your name and postal code, so that I don't have to cut up your letters or copy the items onto separate sheets for filing.

Types of Riddles

After several years of chronicling "Current Events" and "Celebrity" jokes (or *riddles,* as they should be called) in "Kakologia," I have noticed several patterns.

A. As to **GEOGRAPHY**, there are three types of jokes:

(1) **international:** told on several continents (about AIDS, *Challenger,* Chernobyl, Ethiopian famine);

(2) **national**: circulating mainly in the nation where the event occurred or the person lives (South Africa's "necklace," West Germany's General Kießling, America's gerbils and minor politicians, Canada's Ben Johnson, England's Hillsborough stampede);

(3) **regional** or **local**: (New York's Hasidim, Ontario's shopping-mall homosexuals, Pennsylvania's Budd Dwyer).

B. As to TARGET, there are *generic* and *specific* jokes.

(1) **generic** ones are interchangeable, frequently recycled, and, when not involving wordplay, can be translated into most languages: jokes about *stupidity* are told here and abroad about Poles, Italians, the Irish, Frisians, Austrians, Portuguese; jokes about *homosexuality* circulate about Rock Hudson, Liberace, any gay.

A related subtype also uses the **same punch line**: *wash up on shore* (drowning victims Klinghoffer, *Challenger* crew, Natalie Wood); *head and shoulders* (decapitated Vic Morrow, Christa McAuliffe); *last thing through his/her/its mind* (crash victims Commander Scobee, McAuliffe, a bug on the windshield); *not wash between hymns/hims* (any male homosexual). Most of these cannot be translated into other languages, as wordplay is often involved.

(2) In contrast, **specific** jokes cannot be recycled or applied to anyone else, and most cannot be translated into other languages, if (a) the wordplay is derived from multiple meanings of a name or word (*crack, dike, blow, Bias-bias, Rock-rock, Hudson* [man, river]) or sounds like another word (*profit-prophet, neighbors-Nabors; drier-Dwyer*); (b) if the event or object is unique (Klinghoffer's wheelchair, Egyptian commandos' rescue, Rafael Septien's scoring, Green Bay Packers' convictions, Oral Roberts's check, Tammy Bakker's make-up); and (c) if the characteristic "shortcoming" of the ridiculed target exists in that specific group only: "kinky" hair and big lips, blacks only; self-centered sex and lack of humor, lesbians only; or the pronunciation of *l* for *r*, Chinese only (reverse for Japanese).

This is just a tentative classification. What an interesting, useful topic for theses and dissertations for graduate students starving for something *new*, thinking about something other than the same old boring shit suggested by their boring, unimaginative, brain-dead professors.

Another topic begging for research is why certain events produce jokes, while others do not. The British ferry disaster produced a few in Europe, but not here, even though we read and saw much about the accident. The sinking of a boat in the Congo where about one hundred victims were eaten by crocodiles did not; neither did the scores of Haitians killed by sharks, or the hundreds of Asians drowned in the Bay of Bengal. Why not? Why were there no jokes about the unique toxic gas bubbles from Lake Nyos that left over 2,000 dead in Cameroon (21 June 1986)? It has nothing to do with the color or race of the victims; my guess is that we don't identify with the victims and that such disasters happen so often that we hardly bat an eye when yet another hundred drown in Bangladesh, or when yet another bus with dozens of passengers tumbles down a mountain road in Nepal or Mexico. Ho-Hum. What's for supper, dear?

Why were there no jokes about the attack on the USS Stark, where 37 Americans were killed by an Iraqi war plane? Is the loss of 37 American sailors less shocking than the loss of "only" seven astronauts? Was the unique explosion of a space shuttle more devastating than the murder of 37 "run-of-the-mill" sailors? Or was it saturation by endless repeats of the explosion on television and the excessive, obnoxious pre-launch media hype about the bloody Teacher-in-Space that caused so many jokes? Why was there only one oblique joke about the fire catastrophe in Philadelphia, where the police miscalculated, burning down the MOVE members' house and accidentally a city block with it, killing eleven children and radical blacks? Or, how about the Philadelphia doctor, Martin Spector, who in July 1986 shipped human head by UPS to Colorado? Or the guest who drowned in the swimming pool at a New

Orleans lifeguard party a few years ago? Planning to publish *Weird World* some day (already copyrighted), I have been clipping many hundreds of such shocking or weird news stories since 1985, wondering why these truly bizarre events don't result in a flood of jokes nationwide.

Why are there no jokes or riddles about abortion, abortion clinics, and demonstrations against clinics, topics we read about and hear and see on the news almost daily? The only language-oriented development is the euphemizing of both positions: anti-abortionists call themselves now *pro-life*, while abortionists call themselves *pro-choice*. Neat trick. The ugly word *abortion* is not mentioned, and nobody is *anti* anything—both are *pro* something.

What are the criteria for unusual events to become joking matters? Uniqueness? Amount of saturation by the media? Identification with the victims? Height of rung on the Celebrity Ladder? Obnoxiousness of the Star? Notoriety of the person? Flagrancy of the crime? Gruesomeness of the death? Students of English, Folklore, Linguistics, Philology, Psychology, Sociology: start thinking!

Joseph Goodwin's "Unprintable Reactions to All the News That's Fit to Print" (*Southern Folklore* 46 [Jan. 1989]: 15-39) contains two very important appendixes dealing with kakological matters. One treats Events, the other Rock Hudson and AIDS, with dates of occurrence and jokes resulting from the events. General Events are chronicled from 1963 (J.F. Kennedy assassination) to 1986, and Hudson-AIDS jokes from 1984 to 1987. He lists worldwide disasters, accidents, deaths, etc., whether they produced jokes or not. Just analyzing these lists would be a good start.

Jokes Not Understood by Outsiders

There are some current event jokes circulating in other regions of the world that make no sense to the listener unfamiliar with the events. For example,

> What's the difference between a Smartie and a Cockney?
> — *Smarties don't melt in the tube.*

This joke, sent by Neil Crawford, appeared in the British *The Guardian*, 10 May 1989, "Young Guardian" page. Readers and listeners unfamiliar with the event and situation don't understand this riddle. What's a *Smartie*? What's the *tube*? Why *Cockneys*? Why *melt*? If you are a newshound you may remember the disastrous fire in one of London's busiest subway stations, King's Cross, in Nov. 1987, where 31 or 34 people were burned to death and 80 more were injured. But the joke is not yet clear.

Now comes the detective work: *Smarties* must be candy-coated chocolate drops like the American M&Ms (that "melt in your mouth, not in your hand"). *Tube* must be a colloquial term for the London subway. *Cockneys* probably is a generic term for "Londoners." Now that joke makes more sense. To see whether my guesses were right, I wrote to Neil, who confirmed that what I had figured out was correct, with two useful additions: actually, the candy—that according to the advertising slogan doesn't melt in one's hand—is not *Smarties* but *Treats*, chocolate-coated peanuts, and, more importantly, that *Smarties* are sold in cardboard *tubes*. Ahá! Now the joke makes perfect sense, as the "melting in the tube" double-meaning is explained. The original joke actually is flawed by taking the *non-melting* slogan from *Treats* and combining it with the *tube*-shaped container of the *Smarties* to come up with the analogy.

II. JOKES AND RIDDLES

Jokes with two or more topics (e.g., AIDS, South Africa,) are not repeated in other categories. They are normally listed in the category dealing with their *major* topic. Thus, to find all jokes about a certain topic, it will be necessary to read all sections.

Also, I have added information to many riddles, not only because you may have forgotten or never known the details needed to understand the jokes, but also because *Maledicta* is read in at least 71 countries. Still, many readers abroad will not be able to understand all jokes, especially those based on television and other aspects of general American culture.

A. USA

POLITICIANS

Dan Quayle

What do you get when you cross a chicken and a hawk?
— *A Quayle.*

Why did the chicken cross the road?
— *To join the National Guard.*

Why didn't Quayle go to Vietnam?
— *Because his father couldn't reach all the Vietcong by phone.*

What's the new Dan Quayle game show?
— *"Dialing for Deferments."*

Why do Mexicans want to breed with Dan Quayle?
— *Because it's easy to pick lettuce with no spine.*

What would you get if you crossed Quayle with a Greek?
— *A waiter who won't serve.*

What ball team does Dan play for?
— *The Draft Dodgers.*

Why does Dan Quayle never catch a cold?
— *Because he's good at avoiding drafts.*

What did Quayle and Pat Robertson do on election eve?
— *They swapped war stories.*

What's 14 inches long and dangles in front of an asshole?
— *Dan Quayle's necktie.*

What's the seven most frightening words President Bush could utter?
— *"Dan, I am not feeling very well."*

Who would be the perfect pilot for the Stealth bomber?
— *Dan Quayle. Nobody ever sees him.*

What's the latest Secret Service directive?
— *If George Bush gets shot, shoot Dan Quayle.* [Massachusetts Senator John Kerry told this joke at a business man's breakfast in Boston and was reprimanded for it. MJ, 17 Nov. 1988: 7A]

What was Quayle's favorite opening line at college?
— *"Hey, baby, can my dad buy you a drink?"*

What's the title of the new movie about Quayle's Vietnam war experience?
— *Full Dinner Jacket.*
— *Full Metal Filing Cabinet.* [Both are references to Stanley Kubrick's superior Vietnam film, *Full Metal Jacket* which, by the way, is a goldmine of verbal abuse]

What's Quayle's favorite war song?
— *"Over Here...."*

What's the difference between Jane Fonda and Dan Quayle?
— *Jane Fonda did go to Vietnam.*

What's the title of the TV documentary on Quayle's military career?
— *"Thirty Seconds over Indianapolis."*

What do Dan Quayle and Yoko Ono have in common?
— *They both are yellow and live off large inheritances.*

What does Mickey Mouse get for Christmas?
— *A Dan Quayle watch.*

How many Indiana National Guardsmen does it take to screw in a lightbulb?
— *One hundred. One to put in the lightbulb, and the rest to keep an eye out for the Viet Cong.*

What is a Quayle?
— *A bird that ducks.*

What advantages does Dan Quayle have over Lloyd Bentsen?
— *A blow-dryer and a pulse.*

What's the difference between Vietnam and Paula Parkinson?
— *Dan Quayle was never in Vietnam.*

Have you heard of the new Quayle Bonds?
— *They have no principal, they have no interest, and they never mature.*

What did George Bush answer when asked if he wanted to ride in the limousine with the bubble top?
— *"No, let Dan Quayle take another car."*

Why doesn't Dan Quayle read the *Congressional Record*?
— *Because there are no pictures in it.*

What does Dan Quayle think *Roe vs. Wade* refers to?
— *Different ways of crossing the Potomac.*

What do John F. Kennedy and Dan Quayle have in common?
— *Both have been brain-dead for 25 years.*

What did Marilyn Quayle say to her husband after making love on their wedding night?
— *"Dan, you're no Jack Kennedy!"*

What are the dogs in the White House doing these days?
— *Chasing Quayles and pissing on Bushes.*

Who is the offspring of Mr. Ed and Carly Simon?
— *Marilyn Quayle.* [Mr. Ed is a talking horse on a TV show. Simon is a singer. Both have long slim faces and prominent teeth.]

A comedian suggested that Mrs. Quayle has a hairdo like a 1940s librarian.

Poster seen in Washington, D.C., Winter 1988-89

Michael Dukakis

According to our reader Alkis Doucakis, *Dukakis* means "little duke" in Greek. From δουξ *douks* "duke" + diminutive *-akis*.

What's Michael Dukakis's idea of foreign policy experience?
— *To eat breakfast at the International House of Pancakes.*

Why does Dukakis kiss the women while campaigning?
— *Because he's too short to kiss the men.*

What's two feet long and hangs between Dukakis's legs?
— *His necktie.*

Why did the homosexuals vote for Dukakis?
— *Because they are more into kaka than into bush.*

What's the exit for a JAP and an entrance for a Greek?
— *Kitty Dukakis's asshole.* [Mrs. Dukakis is Jewish]

What do you call an empty six-pack?
— *Kitty Litter.* [Circulated after her alcoholism was revealed. Latest version, Dec. '89: syringes in Boston harbor]

What did Lloyd Bentsen say to Kitty Dukakis?
— *"Kitty, you're no Joan Kennedy!"*

"Duke and *Kitty* are wonderful names. They sound like a pimp and his top hooker." Robert Anton Wilson, *The Realist* (No. 108, Winter 1989, p. 6).

Bush and Dukakis

The Oregonian cartoonist Jack Ohman (WF, 22 July 1988: 4) introduces Dukakis's favorites: His favorite color: Olive drab. Movie: *The Invisible Man*. Flavor: Vanilla. Book: *The Miracle Worker*. Drink: Water. Music: Elevator, waiting room. Brand: Generic. TV Show: Test pattern. Joke: "A budget analyst and an econometric specialist are in a bar. The budget analyst says, 'That's no outyear projection, that's my fiscal paradigm curve!!!'"

Lapel buttons seen in 1988: **LICK BUSH IN 88** and **DON'T STEP IN DUKAKIS**.

"The Great Debate of 1988" cartoon is based on the currently very popular expression SHIT HAPPENS. Preppy Bush uses the euphemism *doo-doo,* while Dukakis, who during his campaign stressed that he speaks Spanish, uses the Spanish equivalent. The expression now seen on T-shirts, bumper stickers, etc., became popular after 1985, when I first heard it from a surgical nurse in Wisconsin. A contemporary equivalent of *That's the way the cookie crumbles* or *C'est la vie,* SHIT HAPPENS neatly sums up one's fatalistic philosophy. Several journalists have interviewed me about the expression; the most extensive feature on this expression was Ellen Bartlett's "A Scatological Debate" in *The Boston Globe*, 7 Nov. 1988: 20-22.

The vice-presidential candidates Bentsen and Quayle were called **The Codger and The Dodger,** while Bush and Dukakis were referred to as **The Wimp and The Shrimp,** also in a comic strip by Griffith's "Zippy" (MJ, 3 Oct. 1988: 4G). Dukakis and Bentsen were called **The Duke and The Fluke** as well as **The Greek and the Geek.** Bush and Quayle were **A Yankee and a Dodger.**

What's the difference between George Bush and Michael Dukakis?
— *Bush gets up on the soapbox to be heard, Dukakis to be seen.*

This clever cartoon was adapted from an older general cartoon shown below, based on the wordplay *fucking thing* = sex organ.

The names of the candidates inspired the specific presidential version. I received 13 copies of the cartoon, most of which are stylistic variants, of which three are shown below. The first copy was sent by Roscoe S., Oklahoma, in early Sept. 1988, followed by a different version from Harvey F., New York. In October, seven new variants arrived from California (Michel J. and Reno

"It's just one fuckin' thing after another."

T.), Florida (Gordon S.), Illinois (Michael F.), Kansas (Thomas M.), Maryland (*Rosetta S.), and Wisconsin (Dennis D.). Further variants arrived in November from New York (Len A.), in December from Connecticut (George K.) and Wisconsin (Jackie Y.). The final one came in January 1989, from Texas (Gordon W.).

Variants of "The True 1988 Presidential Race"

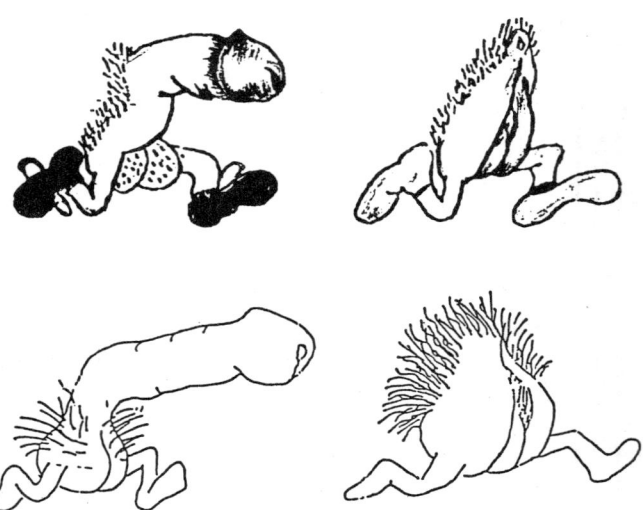

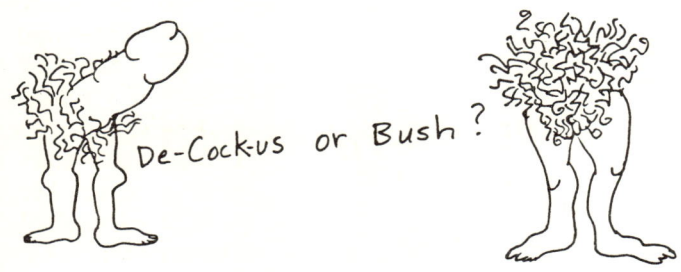

Ron and Nancy Reagan

What size dress does Nancy wear now?
— *Seven and a half. She used to wear size eight.* [After her breast surgery]

What has four legs and one tit?
— *Ron and Nancy.*

Why did Ronald visit Nancy every day in the hospital?
— *He wanted to keep abreast of things.*

When does Nancy Reagan converse with a disembodied spirit?
— *Every time she talks with Ron.* [After her interest in astrology was revealed]

Why does Reagan call Nancy "Mummy" when *he's* the one with all the wrinkles?

In June 1989, Queen Elizabeth bestowed honorary knighthood on Ronald Reagan. What's his new name?
— *Sir Napalot.*

    Reagan to Gorbachev: "Say, Mike, what's that red mark on your head?" – "Well, Ronnie, that's a birthmark." – "Gee, Mike, how long have you had that?"

Jesse Jackson

Have you heard of the Jesse Jackson bumper sticker?
— *It says*, RUN, JESSE, RUN! *You put it on the* front *bumper.*

What's the name of Jesse Jackson's new Mexican restaurant?
— *NACHO MAMMA.*

What four new holidays will Jackson create, if he gets elected President?
— *The birthdays of Jesse Jackson, Michael Jackson, Reggie Jackson, and Sept. 4.*
Why September 4?
— *That's when the new Cadillacs come out.*

What changes will Jesse Jackson make if he's appointed head of the Defense Department?
— *He'll change the name to "Department of Dé-fence."*

What did Jesse Jackson's wife ask Nancy Reagan?
— *She wanted to measure the White House windows for boarding up with plywood.*

What team did the Rev. Jesse Jackson and Col. Ollie North form?
— *Sambo and Rambo.*

John Tower

The attempted nomination of Senator John Tower to Secretary of Defense produced many jokes about Tower's drinking problems and womanizing. I heard no riddles, but there were many jokes and cartoons. One such cartoon by the *Arizona Republic*'s Steve Benson, run in the *San José Mercury News* on 6 March 1989: 6B (sent by Bruce R.) shows two large billboards. On the left is George Bush's slogan, READ MY LIPS. On the right is that of John Tower: SMELL MY BREATH. *Newsweek* (20 Febr. 1989: 15, sent by Greg W.) ran two jokes. Comedian Jay Leno: "This is a ladies' man? He looks like Yoda with a bad haircut." TV's

Pat Sajak also quipped about Tower's news conference where the senator would deny everything. Tower's invitation: Ladies get in free; BYOB [= Bring Your Own Booze].

Other Politicians

What's the title of Hart's new cookbook?
— *69 Ways to Eat Rice.*

How did Gary Hart prepare himself for the Presidency?
— *He made a plaque for his desk:* THE BABES STOP HERE.

If Gary Hart got Donna Rice pregnant, what would she be called?
— *Puffed rice.*

What's between Gary Hart and Donna Rice?
— *Not even a sheet.*

What did Gary Hart answer when reporters asked him if he had committed adultery?
— *"Do blowjobs count?"*

What was Donna's favorite song?
— *"You've gotta have Hart, inches and inches and inches of Hart..."*

What's Ed Meese doing these days?
— *Oh, eight to ten* [years in prison].

Why was the Ed Meese postage stamp pulled from circulation?
— *Because it kept falling off— people were spitting on the wrong side of the stamp.* [Recycled. Also circulated some 20 years ago about a stamp honoring former Czechoslovak president Novotný. See *Hammer and Tickle: Clandestine Laughter in the Soviet Empire.* Boulder, CO: Golem Press, 1969, 1980, p. 79. $4 (foreign=$4.50), Box 1342, ZIP 80306]

What's so special about Mikhail Gorbachev?
— *He's the first Russian Premier who weighs more than his wife.*

How do you get François Mittérrand to laugh in church?
— *Tell him a joke on Wednesday.* [M. is not a swift thinker]

What's the name of the Chinese student who stood in front of the tank on Tiananmen Square?
— *Sum Dum Fuk.*

Why doesn't Margaret Thatcher wear mini-skirts?
— *Because her balls would show.*

If a land ruled by a king is called a *kingdom*, and a land ruled by an emperor is an *empire*, what do you call England?
— *A country.*

Budd Dwyer

Pennsylvania State Treasurer R. Budd Dwyer, 47, killed himself in Harrisburg on 22 Jan. 1987 during a press conference, after a long, rambling statement denouncing his bribery conviction. He pulled a powerful .357-caliber Magnum revolver from a manila envelope, stuck it in his mouth, and pulled the trigger. This gruesome suicide was shown on a Pennsylvania TV station in full, but most newscasts stopped the show when Dwyer put the gun in his mouth. Jokes circulated mainly in Pennsylvania, of which Bill B. sent most of the following.

What do you do with a wet gun?
— *Put it in the Dwyer.*

What did Budd's wife tell him just before he left for the press conference?
— *"Now don't go shooting your mouth off again."*

What did Budd think as he pulled the gun out of the envelope?
— *"I'll give these guys a piece of my mind."*

Did you hear that Dwyer had a drink named after him?
— *It's called "A Bud and a Shot."*

Who are Budd Dwyer's dentist and barber?
— *Smith and Wesson.*

What was the last thing that went through Budd Dwyer's mind?
— *A .357 Magnum.*

What did Dwyer's press secretary tell the ambulance crew?
— *"This Budd's for you."* [Budweiser beer commercial]

What brand of toothpaste did Budd Dwyer use?
— *AIM.*

What was Budd Dwyer's favorite drink?
— *Beer with no head.*

What was Budd Dwyer's favorite song?
— *"I think I'm going outta my head."*

What's the name of the new beer without a head?
— *Budwyer.*

What do Tom Selleck's girlfriend and Budd Dwyer have in common?
— *They've each had a Magnum go off in their mouths.*

Bill also mentioned, "I've heard of head-jobs, but this is ridiculous," and that Dwyer was not a nationally known figure, thus the jokes were mainly regional (Carlisle and Mifflintown) and died out quickly—like Budd.

I am often asked where such jokes come from. In most cases, they appear independent from one another throughout the country, made up by quipsters. But now I have proof that such jokes also are the creation of a specific individual, and then are spread nationwide (if they are good enough): Long Island's (NY) "tasteless" comedian Jackie ("The Joke Man") Martling wrote 32 jokes on this topic. In a night club with drunk listeners and delivered in the infectious Martling style, most of his jokes are funny, but without that ambiance, just printed on paper, many are not that funny, showing forced humor and marginal wordplays, thus not recorded below. (Sorry, Jackie!)

How are Budd Dwyer's brains like Lionel Richie?
— *They're dancing on the ceiling.*

Why did Budd Dwyer put money on the ceiling of the press conference?
— *He wanted to get his face on a dollar bill.*

Did Budd Dwyer enjoy his suicide?
— *Sure. He got a bang out of it.*

What did Ralph Cramden [Jackie Gleason] say when he saw the tape of Budd Dwyer killing himself?
— *"Pow!! Right in the kisser!!"*

How was Budd Dwyer like a virgin?
— *One bang and it was all over.*

Why did Budd Dwyer shoot himself in the head?
— *Because his gun had a hair trigger!!*

Was Budd Dwyer Jewish?
— *Maybe. But he wasn't shot in the temple.*

What was Budd Dwyer's favorite Beatles song?
— *"Happiness Is a Warm Gun."*

Why did Budd Dwyer shoot himself?
— *Because he'd recently had a blood transfusion from Liberace.*

What did Budd Dwyer announce at his last press conference?
— *"I've got a mind-blowing idea."*

What did Budd Dwyer say to the devil before he pulled the trigger?
— *"This Bud's for you!"*

What did the witnesses at the press conference chant?
— *"Ready! Aim! Dwyer!!"*

Why didn't Budd Dwyer jump into a woodchipper?
— *Because a woodchipper wouldn't fit into a manila envelope.*
[See "Stewardess" jokes, p. 278]

Harold Washington

The heart-attack death of Chicago's mayor Harold Washington in his office, in 1987, produced several jokes, sent by Steve W. (Chicago) and William R. (D.C.). Washington's successor was Eugene Sawyer.

How did Harold Washington make history?
— *He's the first black man to die on the job.*

What's engraved on Sawyer's gold-plated plaque on his desk?
— *Harold Washington slumped here.*

What would Harold Washington be doing if he were alive today?
— *Scratching on the lid of his coffin.*

What did God yell at St. Peter?
— *"I said the Mayor of Washington, not Mayor Washington!"*

Evan Mecham

In 1986-87, Arizonans laughed about their governor, Evan Mecham, whom they considered dimwitted and racist. Professor Alleen Pace Nilsen wrote an excellent article about Mecham and the jokes about him: "Evan Mecham: Humor in Arizona Politics," published in *Dialogue: A Journal of Mormon Thought* 22/3 (Fall 1989): 81-89. Some samples:

What's the difference between George Wallace and Evan Mecham?
— *George Wallace is paralyzed from the waist down.*

What's a pity about Mecham?
— *Wasting a $400 toupee on a two-bit head.*

What's Mecham's idea of integration?
— *Eating breakfast with a Baptist.*

Why did Mecham cancel Easter?
— *Because he heard the eggs were going to be colored.*
[Reference to his cancellation of Martin Luther King's birthday as an official holiday]

Professor Nilsen sent me additional jokes that apparently were unsuited for the above publication:

When Evan and Flo have sex, why is Flo always on top?
— *Because Ev can only screw up.* [Also told earlier about presidents Richard Nixon, Gerald Ford, Jimmy Carter, Ronald Reagan and others who can only *fuck up*]

What are three things you can't give a black?
—*A fat lip, a black eye, and a Mecham Pontiac.* [The governor also had a car dealership]

Restroom graffito above toilet paper dispensers:
PORTRAIT OF THE GOVERNOR
WIPE TO DEVELOP

Barney Frank

Massachusetts congressman Barney Frank, like his colleague Rep. Gerry Studds (see jokes, MAL 7: 293), openly admits that he is a homosexual. In late summer 1989 it was revealed that Frank had paid for a male prostitute and then hired the man, who allegedly ran a homosexual prostitution business while living in Frank's Washington apartment. Judge S. sent me the following jokes circulating in Massachusetts in Oct. 1989:

What's the difference between a Massachusetts senator and a Massachusetts congressman?
— *The senator chases women.* [Teddy Kennedy]

What's the name of the new hot dogs sold at Fenway Park?
— *"Barney Franks." If you don't like them, you can stick them up your ass!*

Why will Barney Frank move to Cape Cod?
— *Because he saw a roadside sign* ENTERING DENNIS.

What will Barney Frank do after resigning from his congressional seat?
— *Move to Cape Cod to become a carpenter and bang Studds.*
— *Manage the Red Sox. He may blow a few but he won't choke on the big ones.*
— *Coach the Patriots, because he likes tight ends and wide receivers.*

SPORTS

Len Bias

On 19 June 1986, University of Maryland basketball superstar Len Bias, 22, became the Boston Celtics' No. 1 draft pick. Two days later he died of cocaine intoxication causing seizures and cardiac arrest. Eight days later, Cleveland Browns' safety Don Rogers, 23, also died of a cocaine-induced heart attack, on the day before he was to be married (*Time*, 7 July 1986: 52 and 25 Aug. 1986: 53). The first tragic death produced many jokes; the second none. Bias's senseless death was shocking; Rogers's identical death was apparently less so; just "another stupid nigger killing himself with crack"?

What do Len Bias and wildflowers have in common?
— *Two days after you pick them, they die.*

Why are the Boston Celtics so disappointed with their selection of Len Bias?
— *Because they drafted a stiff who wasn't all he was cracked up to be.*

Why are so many blacks and other minorities enrolling at the University of Maryland?
— *Because they heard there is no bias there.*

Are the Celtics still as prejudiced against blacks as they used to be?
— No. Now they are the most unbiased team in the NBA.
— No, they have no bias any more.

What's black on the outside and white on the inside?
— Len Bias's nose. [Actually, he didn't sniff the cocaine]

How did Len Bias make history?
— He was the only NBA first-round draft choice under six feet. [*Six feet under*=buried, dead. Actually, another player, Calvin Murphy, was five foot eight. Info from Merritt Clifton]

Where is Len Bias now playing?
— In the Under-Six-Foot league.

What do Len Bias, Liberace, and Rock Hudson have in common?
— They all got hold of some bad crack.

What's the difference between Len Bias and Rock Hudson?
— One died taking it up the nose.

Dallas Cowboys

Former Dallas Cowboys placekicker Rafael Septien in 1987 pleaded guilty to indecency with a ten-year-old girl.

Why was Rafael Septien elected to the NFL Hall of Fame?
— Because he's the first player in NFL history to score before the first period.

Why did the Dallas Cowboys hire two nuns and a prostitute for their team?
— Because they needed two Tight Ends and a Wide Receiver.

Green Bay Packers

On 18 Dec. 1986, Green Bay Packers wide receiver James Lofton [black] was charged with one count of second-degree sexual assault of a 30-year-old [white] woman. He allegedly forced her to engage in fellatio in a nightclub stairwell (MJ, 23 May 1987: 1A+6A). Also, on 4 Nov. 1985, Packer defensive back Tommories (Mossy) Cade [black] was charged with three counts of second-degree sexual assault involving his 44-year-old aunt from Houston who had come to visit him in Wisconsin (MJ, 23 May 1987: 1A+12A; WF, 6 Nov. 1987: 9). Wisconsin Attorney General Don Hanaway told a popular joke at a speech and was severely criticized by the Green Bay Packers' president, the players' defense attorneys, and in Milwaukee newspaper editorials by the usual hypocrites who told the jokes themselves but made a big deal out of it because Hanaway told it in public.

Why should they build a new prison in Green Bay?
— *So that the Green Bay Packers can walk to work.*

Why is James Lofton quitting the Packers?
— *Because he wants to enroll at Morehead University.*

How do you know that Mossy Cade has just a tiny pecker?
— *Because he fucks ants.*

What new game show will Mossy be hosting?
— *"Up Your Auntie."*

Last year's bumper sticker said: THE PACK IS BACK. What does it say now?
— *COVER YOUR CRACK—THE PACK IS BACK!*

Pete Lindbergh

In 1985, drunk Pete Lindbergh, goalie for the Philadelphia Flyers hockey team, died by crashing at a high rate of speed his bright red Porsche into a brick wall. A *face-off* starts or resumes the hockey game.

What do Charles and Pete Lindbergh have in common?
— *They are both dead flyers.*

How did they know a hockey player was killed in the crash?
— *They found a face off in the back seat.*

Jim O'Brien

Jim O'Brien was the weatherman at WPVI television in Philadelphia. An enthusiastic skydiver, he was killed on a Sunday in 1986 (or 1987?) when during a jump his parachute got caught in another diver's chute. He freed himself, but his reserve parachute didn't open.

What was the last thing to go through Jim O'Brien's mind?
— *His feet.*

What do Jim O'Brien's parachute and the Pennsylvania liquor stores have in common?
— *They don't open on Sundays.*

OTHERS EVENTS

Salman Rushdie

What's the title of Salman Rushdie's new book?
— *Buddha is a Fat Fuck.*
— *Buddha: Just Another Fat Gook.* [Canadian version, sent by John M.]

What's the heaviest-armored vehicle in the world?
— *An Iranian Bookmobile.*

What's bad luck in Iran?
— *Being the winner in a Salman Rushdie look-alike contest.*

What's the newest insult in Iran?
— *"May you win first prize in a Salman Rushdie look-alike contest!"*

1989 Fruit Scares

In the summer of 1989, there were two news stories about poisoned fruit from Chile and American apples treated with the chemical Alar. These two events were combined by a quipster with the plight of long-striking airline pilots:

What's the definition of a three-time loser?
— *An Eastern Airlines pilot who owns apple orchards in Chile.*

This joke about three-time losers uses the same formula as the one found in the "Negroes" section, p. 295, and the following one:

— *A pregnant whore driving an Edsel with a "Nixon for President" bumper sticker.*

The Drought, Summer 1988

How dry was it in the summer of 1988?
— *The cows were giving powdered milk.*
— *The trees were chasing the dogs.*
— *The farmers told their kids what rain was, so they wouldn't be frightened if they ever saw any.*
— *The creek was squeaking as it rounded the corners.*
— *The river was running only every other day.*
— *The baby frogs were four months old and didn't know how to swim.*
— *No water spaniels were born in summer.*
— *The morticians stopped cremation and let the sun turn the bodies into dust in one day.*

How deep went the roots of sweet corn to find water?
— *They were trimmed by an Australian farmer.*

Bronx Zoo

Several years ago, two boys went into the Bronx Zoo (New York) after closing hours to swim in the moat surrounding the polar bears' lair. The bears tore one boy apart.

How much does it cost to get into the Prospect Park Zoo?
— *An arm and a leg!*

Larry Singleton

Rapist-mutilator Lawrence Singleton, 59, is a Contra Costa, California, man convicted in 1979 for raping Mary Vincent, a 15-year-old runaway girl, then hacking off her forearms with an ax and dumping her in a canyon to die. In May 1987, he was paroled for good behavior, but several California cities have sought court action to prevent him from being paroled in their community. He's now living in San Quentin (*Time*, 1 June 1987: 31).

What is the new charge filed against Larry Singleton?
— *Selling arms to the Iranians* (or the *Contras*).

Larry Singleton went to a car dealership and wanted to buy a BMW. The salesman said, "But mister, you just got out of jail. This car will cost you an arm and a leg." Larry replied, "I'll be back in ten minutes!"

McMartin Preschool Molestations

Seven administrators and teachers at the McMartin Preschool in Los Angeles were accused in 1985 of having had (homo)sexual relations with young children. The trial involving over 200 charges of child molestation is still underways.

What's the new sandwich at McDonald's?
— *The McMartin. It's a great big weenie in two little buns.*

Dan White's Suicide

Dan White, a former San Francisco supervisor, in Oct. 1985 committed suicide by inhaling carbon monoxide from his car's exhaust. On 28 Nov. 1978, he shot to death the city's mayor, George Moscone, and San Francisco's first openly homosexual supervisor, Harvey Milk. At that time, I received no jokes about these murders, but when White committed suicide, I received the following:

Why did Dan White commit suicide?
— *Because his AIDS test came back positive.*

Is Dan White dead?
— *No, he's just exhausted.*

Whom did Dan White kill this time?
— *Someone I didn't like.*

What did Dan White's wife say after he shot the two city officials?
— *"I told him to get milk and baloney, not Milk and Moscone!"*

Lost Whale

"Humphrey" the humpback whale, who in October 1985 made a left turn at the Golden Gate Bridge and swam for a couple of weeks aimlessly in the Sacramento River delta northeast of San Francisco until he was guided back to the Pacific Ocean, gave rise to one joke:

How did Humphrey the Whale get AIDS?
— *He got rear-ended by a San Francisco ferry.*

Texas Oil-Bust

The drop in oil prices caused hardships for many Texans. Similar jokes were told about the Yuppies and Stockbrokers, which see below.

What do you call it when a West Texas oilman gives his sons ten stripper wells?
— *Child abuse.*

How do you get a Texan down from a tree?
— *Cut the rope.*

Why do they sell Mercedes cars without seats in Odessa, Texas?
— *Because they all lost their ass.*

What do you call a Texas petroleum geologist?
— *"Hey, waiter!"*

What's better than being deep in the heart of Texas?
— *Being six inches into Dixie.*

Woodchipped Stewardess

Comedian Jackie Martling also wrote 48 jokes about Helle Craft, 39, an airline stewardess allegedly murdered by her husband Richard, 48, an airline pilot in Newtown, Connecticut. In Nov. 1986, he allegedly disposed of her body by putting it through a woodchipper (grinding and chopping it up) and dumping the bits into a lake or the Hoosetonic river. Again, many of the jokes are not funny enough to tickle my fancy, thus only the better ones will be reported, cruel as they may be. I have not received any other riddles on this topic from anywhere else.

How do you collect a woodchipped stewardess?
— *You just pick up the big pieces, and the rest is gravy.*

Why is the stewardess worried about her career?
— *Because she can no longer fly united.*

What did the pilot sing to his wife after he put her through the woodchipper?
— *"Love me tinder."*

What's the new airline food made from woodchipped stewardesses?
— *Pan Spam.*

How did the pilot feel when he got up that fateful morning?
— *Chipper.*

What are the fish calling the stewardess?
— *Breakfast.*

What did the pilot say to his wife on that fateful morning?
— *"You rent the woodchipper, and I'll feed the fish."*

In what order did the woodchip murder take place?
— *He came, he conked her, he sawed.*

How do we know the stewardess is in trouble with her airline?
— *Because now she's a ground stewardess.*

What does the Hoosetonic river have in common with London?
— *Plenty of fish and chips.*

What did the homocidal pilot have for his rotten marriage?
— *Grounds for divorce.*

What does the pilot have in common with Ollie North?
— *They both shredded the evidence.*

How do you make a stewardess float?
— *Two scoops of icecream, one scoop of stewardess.*

What do you call a woodchipped stewardess sitting on the lawn?
— *Fertilizer.*

What do you get when you join the Stewardess Chopping Club?
— *A dismembership card.*

What's red and blue and goes "tha-thump, tha-thump"?
— *A stewardess in a woodchipper.*

Exxon Oil Spill

The catastrophic spilling of some 11 million gallons of oil into the pristine waters off Alaska by the *Exxon Valdez* supertanker, 24 March 1989, resulted in many longer jokes and some riddles. You may have noticed, by the way, that Exxon officials and spokespersons never talked about "11 million gallons" but tried to minimize the amount by calling it "240,000 barrels."

What's the name of the new TV show about Alaskan yuppies?
— *"10-W-thirtysomething."*

How many captains does it take to run an Exxon supertanker aground?
— *One and one fifth.* [In Canada, a metric version is told; the answer is *1.2*]

What do you do with a drunken sailor...? [Sing melody]
— *Make him the skipper of an Exxon tanker.*

What's an Exxon cocktail?
— *Ten million gallons on the rocks.*

What did the Exxon captain run?
— *A really tight ship.*

What's the new name of Exxon after the oil spill?
— *"Accidental Petroleum."*

What did the Exxon captain shout to his mate?
— *I said I want a* Tanqueray *on the rocks!*

Ted Bundy Execution

When serial killer Ted Bundy was killed in Florida in the electric chair in Febr. 1989, there were a few jokes:

Did you hear who finally stopped smoking?
— *Ted Bundy.*

What was Ted Bundy's last meal?
— *Juice.*

Prison guard to Ted Bundy the night before electrocution: "Ted, I've got good news and bad news. The bad news is that you'll be in the electric chair tomorrow morning. The good news is that Boeing will do the wiring."

Newsweek (6 Febr. 1989: 66, sent by Bruce R.) also reported about the carnival-like reveling at Bundy's electrocution. Placards carried by some of the 300 people celebrating his death bore such slogans as: **Thank God it's Fryday, This Buzz is for You,** and **Roast in Peace.**

California Earthquake

On 17 Oct. 1989 an earthquake devastated parts of San Francisco, collapsed almost a mile of a concrete double-decker freeway (I-880) in Oakland, killing some 60 people, and interrupted the baseball World Series between the San Francisco Giants and the Oakland Athletics. A few days later, I received three jokes from Jeanne B. and Richard B., who live near San Francisco:

What's the best place for safe sex in San Francisco?
— *Under a doorway.*

What were the newspaper headlines after the interrupted game?
— *Oakland A's Win by Default.*

How many were killed by the freeway collapse?
— *No accurate body count is possible until they turn up some concrete evidence.*

AIDS

Because the AIDS hysteria has made me paranoid, too, before starting to type this article, I've slipped condoms over my index fingers. So, now I'm ready to whip out another chapter on AIDS and jokes about it....

> **AVIS**
>
> Due à la croissance du taux de SIDA, il est formellement interdit à tous les employés de baiser le cul du boss.
>
> **La Direction**

French-Canadian version of the American AIDS poster shown in *Maledicta* 9: 292.

Sent by W.D., Ontario

Even though AIDS is publicized worldwide through newspapers, television, and other media, I have received only a few AIDS jokes from Canada, England, Australia, and South Africa. Except for the Netherlands and West Germany, no AIDS jokes have been sent from other non-English-speaking countries, including France and Spain, where this disease is known as SIDA. *Somebody* must be telling such jokes in other countries—so, come on, guys, mail 'em! Incidentally, French SIDA is the acronym for *syndrome d'immuno-déficience acquise* (information from friendly Fanny). Spanish SIDA is from *sindrome de inmunodeficiencia adquirida*. In South Africa, the Afrikaans acronym is VIGS, from *Verworwe Immuniteitsgebreksindroom* (also *Immuungebreksindroom*), as informed by Dr. Casper S.

What other acronyms and terms besides AIDS, SIDA and VIGS are used in other countries? What is it called in Tanzania, where AIDS is also known as "the Ugandan disease," while the Ugandans blame the Tanzanians for it? (Information from Lisa S., *Chicago Tribune*, 20 Nov. 1986, "Commentary.") This reminds one of the good old days when syphilis was blamed on the French, the English, or the Neapolitans.

I believe that the abundance of AIDS and other kakological jokes in Germany is caused by the heavy dosage of news from the USA, by the widespread knowledge of English, and by the German (and European) habit of importing everything from *Amerika*, be it heavy-metal music, aluminum Christmas trees, shrill & castration-happy feminists, fanatical ecologists, and buzz words.

"We are afraid of AIDS"

German Xeroxlore, June 1989. Sent by folklorist Uli K.

In West Germany, I have observed old people in retirement homes fearfully discussing AIDS, worried about catching it, including the oldest resident, a 104-year-old lady with whom I often walked around the halls.

Where will it all lead to? I predict that humanity, to

continue enjoying non-lethal sexual fun, will enter The Golden Age of Masturbation: "Friends, Romans, Countrypersons—lend me your hand...."

A Good Name for a Bad Disease

The deadly disease AIDS unfortunately has a harmless, if not favorably-sounding name. It should have a deadly-sounding name. As to a new name, we cannot do much, because the name is too deeply entrenched and because the letters A, I, and D must be used. Still, I propose to replace AIDS, the acronym for *Acquired Immune Deficiency Syndrome*, with DAID, the acronym for *Deadly Acquired Immune Deficiency*. This new name sounds like a southern pronunciation of *dead*. If the name could be changed, it would be a blessing for various businesses and groups that now have losses or are embarrassed because their names sound too much like AIDS. For example, **AID** Insurance and **Ayds**, the candy-like hunger suppressant (sales down by some 50%), have changed or are planning to change their names. Also, many school and other aides don't want to be called "aides" any longer: a group of Oregon teachers' aides are asking to be called "instructional assistants" (WF, 25 June 1987: 1 and MJ, 6 March 1988: 3J).

AIDS UPDATE REPORT
FLASH! NEW STRAINS OF AIDS TO CREATE FURTHER MISCONCEPTIONS AND HYSTERIA

- If you catch it from a cocktail waitress: BARMAIDS
- If you get it from a virgin: FIRST AIDS
- If you've been infected by Jack Lemmon: LEMONAIDS
- If you catch it at school: GRAIDS
- If you contact it from a follower of Jim Jones: KOOL-AIDS
- If you get it in Florida: GATORAIDS
- If it's spread by cockroaches: RAIDS
- If you're lucky enough to have gotten it from Bo Derek: BRAIDS
- If you catch it while marching: PARAIDS

- If you get it from touching an air freshener: GLAIDS
- If you give it back to someone who infected you: TRAIDS
- If you caught it in France: PARLEZ-VOUS FRANÇAIDS
- If you've been diddling with a gang member: SWITCHBLAIDS
- If you get it from a Black: ZIPPITY DO DA DAIDS
- If you're infected by Ronald Reagan: PRESIDENTIAL AIDS
- If you catch it from Anthony Perkins dressed like an old lady: NORMAN BAIDS
- If you've touched a pair of sunglasses: SHAIDS
- If you get ill during the end of a work week: T.G.I.FRIDAIDS
- If you get it playing party games: CHARAIDS
- If you get it on Halloween: MASQUERAIDS
- If you're sleeping with Gumby: GREEN CLAIDS
- If you get it from leather jackets: SUAIDS
- If you've been using an infected dishwasher: CASCAIDS
- If you've been screwing a Jamaican: REGGAIDS
- If you eat an infected chocolate bar: MILKY WAIDS
- If you catch it from an orchestra: BANDAIDS
- If you get it from a pest control person: ORCAIDS
- If you get it from the swamps of Florida: EVERGLAIDS
- And now the worst! Did you know that you can catch it all by yourself? That's called MASTURBAIDS.

Sent by David B., Arizona, March 1988. A somewhat shorter version sent by Tom M., Tiburon, Calif., April 1988. *The Spartan Review*, a conservative student newspaper at San José State University, Calif., also published the above "Report," causing a storm of outrage by the campus Gay and Lesbian Alliance (*San José Mercury News*, 10 Nov. 1987: B1, sent by Bruce R.).

AIDS Riddles

What do you call AIDS if you get it in a horror movie?
— *AFRAIDS*

What do you call Rock Hudson in a wheelchair?
— *Roll-AIDS*.

Why are all the alligators in Florida dying?
— *Because they have gator-AIDS*. [After a *fruit* drink called *Gatorade*]

Why do Polacks wear condoms over their ears? [Also told about *Newfies* in Canada]
— *So they don't get hearing AIDS.*

What cure did they finally find for AIDS?
— *Extra-Strength Tylenol.*

How did Liberace catch AIDS?
— *He ate someone who didn't agree with him.*

Why can't kaffirs get AIDS?
— *Because you can't get them off their asses.* [Told in South Africa. Kaffirs, black Africans, are the equivalent of "niggers" in the USA. See following version told here]

Why don't government employees get AIDS?
— *Because all they do is sit on their asses.*

What do you call a guy with herpes and AIDS?
— *An incurable romantic.*

What's the first symptom of AIDS?
— *A pounding in the asshole.*

What does AIDS stand for?
— *Anal Intercourse Deserves Sympathy.*

What does AIDS stand for?
— *Another Iowan Discovers Sex.* [Told in Minnesota]

Why do they have to come up with a new name for AIDS?
— *Because too many blacks are applying for it.*

How can you get AIDS from a toilet seat?
— *If you sit down before the other guy gets up.*

What would you get if the IRS screwed you out of house and home for back taxes?
— *Government AIDS.*

What would California [or San Francisco] get if it had an earthquake measuring 7 on the Richter scale?
— *Federal AIDS.* [Told in 1987!]

What's the new CPR kit for AIDS victims?
— *A straw and Plumber's Helper.* [A sink drain cleaner]

How did the current AIDS victims get this disease?
— *70% were backed into it, 30% were sucked into it.*

What's the biggest health risk for bartenders?
— *Catching hearing AIDS from listening to too many assholes.*

What is sickle-cell anemia?
— *AIDS for spades.*

How come women get AIDS far less frequently than men?
— *Because they don't fuck assholes—they just marry them.*

Why can't you get lost in San Francisco?
— *Because there are aides on every street corner.*

What's the phone number of the AIDS hotline?
— *OIC-U812.*

How did Mary Lou Retton get AIDS?
— *Because she's been eating what the big boys eat.* [The former Olympics winner advertised with this slogan for a cereal]

What did the doctor tell John Holmes?
— *"Well, John, it won't be long now."* [Porno superstar John Holmes, who reportedly had a 14-inch penis, last year died of AIDS]

How do you give artificial respiration to an AIDS victim?
— *Blow towards the victim lying on the ground.*

What's the worst part of having AIDS?
— *You have to leave your friend's behind.*

Wim van den G. sent the following AIDS joke circulating in the Netherlands, here translated and condensed:

> A man goes to a doctor complaining about his face all covered with little brown spots. The physician tells him that he has AIDS. "Jesus," says the man, "I'm only 30 years old! What can I do?" - "Take a daily mudbath, but add less water every day," advises the doctor. "Do you think it will help?" - "No,

not really. But you can already get used to the earth." (*Nee, dat niet, maar dan kun je vast aan de aarde wennen.*)

A cartoon in the Louisville (Kentucky) *Courier-Journal*, 20 July 1987: A6 (sent by Frank N.) shows President Reagan in a triple body cast, surrounded by the symptoms that have caused his malady: Meese, Poindexter, Casey, Deaver and other "Terminal AIDES."

"Urban Legends" about AIDS circulate widely, as reported in many newspapers by folklorist Jan Harold Brunvand; the most common one is discussed by Gary Alan Fine in *Western Folklore* 46/3 (1987): 192-197, "Welcome to the World of AIDS: Fantasies of Female Revenge."

Above advertisement in *National Lampoon*, Oct. 1988: 113

Gays, Rock Hudson, Liberace

Harvey Fierstein, an outspoken homosexual playwright, denounced "gay jokes" in *Playboy* (August 1988: 43):

> If gay people had enough self-respect to stand up when somebody made a gay joke and say, "Fuck you in the heart, you little asshole, I'm gay and I resent that"— that would make all the difference.

How are Rock Hudson's designer jeans different from regular jeans?
— *They have kneepads and a zipper in the back.*

How did Jim Nabors die?
— *They found him bobbing up and down on the Hudson.*

What do Rock Hudson's buttocks and a basketball court have in common?
— *They've both had a lot of balls bounced off them.*

What do you call a woman with AIDS?
— *A rockette.*

What do Rock Hudson, King Henry VIII and Donald Manes have in common?
— *They all died while screwing queens.* [Manes was Borough President of Queens, N.Y., who killed himself with a butcher knife when it was discovered that he had been part of a financial scandal]

What was Liberace's favorite Chinese food?
— *Cream of Sum Yung Gai.*

What happened when Liberace and Johnnie Ray were golfing together?
— *Johnnie Ray beat Liberace on the drives, but Liberace licked him on the putts.*

Why do sailors prefer liquid soap?
— *Because it takes longer to pick up.*

Why did the homo tattoo a **W** on each of his buttocks?
— *So every time he bends over, his friend would see* **WoW**.

What do you call a queer from Tulsa?
— *An Oklahomo.*

What's the difference between a microwave oven and anal sex?
— *A microwave doesn't brown your meat.*

What's the difference between a refrigerator and anal sex?
— *A refrigerator doesn't fart when you pull your meat out of it.*

What do you call a gay who's on fire?
— *A flaming homo.*

What's special about the new, all-lesbian construction company in San Francisco?
— *They use no studs—everything is strictly tongue-in-groove.*

For what do they use rubbers in San Francisco?
— *Seal-A-Meal.* [A plastic bag]

Why do homos have mustaches?
— *To hide their stretch marks.*

How can you tell that you've entered a gay church?
— *Only half the people are on their knees.*

How do you get rid of crabs?
— *Find a gay that likes sea food.*

What's the name of the new gay sitcom?
— *"Leave it – It's Beaver!"*

Graffiti seen by Greg W. at the University of Toronto (University College, East Wing washroom, 12 April 1988), written in three different hands:

To think straight...be gay!
— Go piss up a rope you Jism-Swallowing Bum-Blaster!
— *Such language!*

Individuals

In Nov. 1987, Douglas Ginsburg was nominated as a Supreme Court judge, but he withdrew after it became known that he had smoked marijuana in his younger days.

What happened to Ginsburg's nomination?
— *It went up in smoke.*

What did the Senate Judiciary Committee think of Ginsburg?
— *They thought he was serious about the **High** Court.*

What did Ginsburg make of his nomination?
— *A hash.*

Why did Reagan choose Ginsburg for the Supreme Court?
— *Because he was a tokin' Jew.* [From *token* and *to toke* "to take a puff on a marijuana cigaret"]

What do Ginsburg and Donna Rice have in common?
— *They both blew a little dope.*

What did Sammy Davis Jr. say to Vanna White?
— *"Give me an I."*

Why did Maria Shriver marry Arnold Schwarzenegger?
— *To breed bullet-proof Kennedys.*

What is this? 10, 9, 8, 7, 6, 5, 4, 3, 2, 1?
— *Bo Derek getting older.*

What did Joan Collins say to King Kong?
— *"Is it in yet?"*

Why did Rep. Patricia Schroeder's husband watch *Deep Throat* 69 times?
— *Because he wanted to get it down pat.* [Recycled Nixon joke]

What is Ollie North's favorite cereal?
— *Shredded wheat.*

Why did Jackie Kennedy marry Aristotle Onassis?
— *She wanted to find out what it was like to have old age creeping up on her.*

What's green, dead, sings, and plays the guitar?
— *Elvis Parsley.*

What's green and slimy and does pirouettes on ice skates?
— *Peggy Phlegm.*

What's special about the new beer named after Morton Downey Jr.?
— *It has no head.*

What did Cary Grant have that Natalie Wood could have used?
— *A good stroke.*

How does Oprah Winfrey's boyfriend ask her during sex to change positions?
— "How now, brown cow?"

What do you call a black civil rights leader who is into S&M?
— Martin Luther Kink.

What do you call a rabbi who is into S&M?
— A kinkajou.

Women and Men

What do you call lesbian twins?
— Lick-alikes.

What's the difference between a *dog* and a *fox*?
— About six beers.

What is the musical definition of a woman?
— Three quarters jazz and one quarter ragtime.

Why do women have four lips?
— So they can piss and moan at the same time.

What do older women and dried dog turds have in common?
— They both are easy to pick up.

How are women like a piano?
— When they're not upright, they're grand.

What do you call a woman with PMS and ESP?
— A bitchy know-it-all.

What's the difference between a terrorist and a woman with PMS?
— You <u>can</u> negotiate with a terrorist.

What's the difference between a *slut* and a *bitch*?
— A slut sleeps with everyone; a bitch sleeps with everyone but you.

What do you get when you inseminate a hooker with fish eggs?
— *A gal who does it for the halibut.*

Artwork courtesy Trici Venola, Santa Monica

Statistics: Happily married women gain an average of 18.4 pounds in the first 13 years of marriage, while unhappy wives gain 42.6 pounds in the same period. (From: Nutri/System Information Bureau. MJ, 6 Sept 1989: 2A)

What is six inches long, has a head on it and drives women wild?
— *A $100 bill.*

What is on a man that is round, hard and sticks so far out of his pajamas that you can hang a hat on it?
— *His head.*

What's the difference between young men and old men?
— *Old men have dry dreams and wet farts.*

How does the new birth control pill for men work?
— *You put it in your sock—it makes you limp.*

Why are men so much better at reading road maps?
— *Because only the male mind can picture one inch being 100 miles.*

Who is the most popular man in a nudist colony?
— *The fellow who can carry two cups of coffee and twelve donuts.*

Who is the most popular woman in a nudist colony?
— *The woman who can eat the last two donuts.*

Negroes

What's the name of the sequel to the movie *Cocoon*?
— *Ninigger.*

What did the black man say why he wore a tuxedo when he went to get a vasectomy?
— *"If Ah's gonna <u>be</u> impótent, Ah's gonna <u>look</u> impótent!"*

What's different about the new card game they play in Howard Beach?
— *In this game, 3 clubs beat 4 spades.*

Why do the blacks have such big nostrils?
— *Because that's where they were held when they were spray-painted.*

Why are the blacks' palms and soles so much lighter in color?
— *That's where they were set down to dry.*

What's the difference between a white fairy tale and a black fairy tale?
— *The white fairy tale starts out: "Once upon a time..." and the black one: "Motherfucker, you ain't gonna b'leeve dis shit...."*

What's the name of the new French-Black restaurant in Oakland?
— *CHEZ WHAT?*

What do you get when you cross a Negro with an octopus?
— *A great shoeshine!*

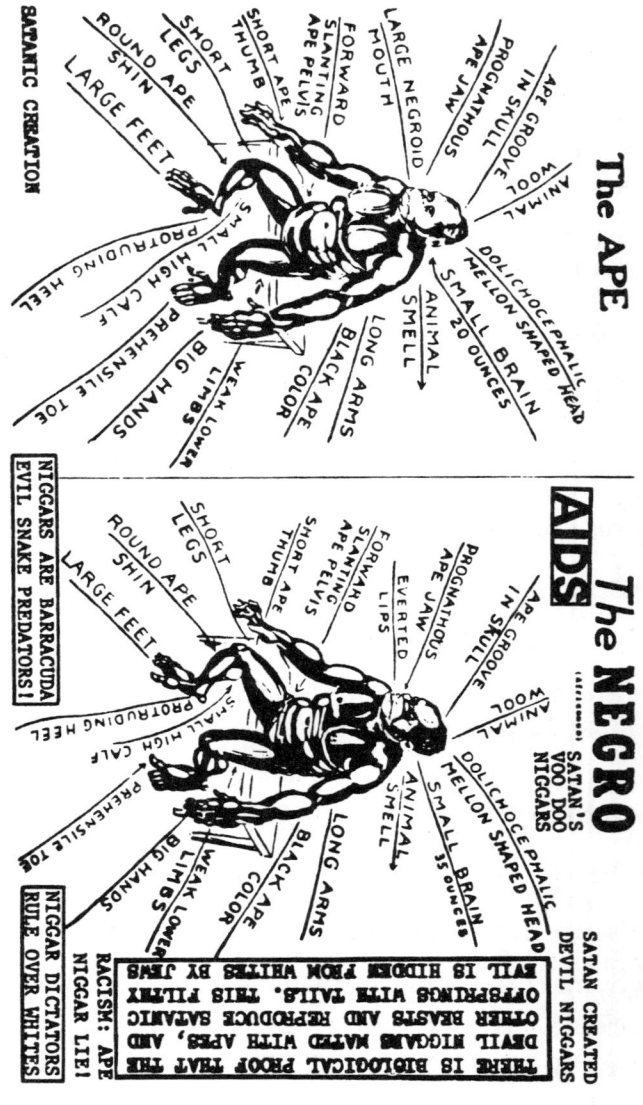

This vicious illustration combines anti-Negro poison with AIDS scare and a dash of anti-Semitism. It is circulated by Mark Margoian (Illinois) who calls himself "God's True Prophet." The illustration comparing apes with Negroes also was circulated on the University of Wisconsin campus in Milwaukee in 1988. To my knowledge, it first appeared in 1970, distributed by the American Eugenics Party, as shown in Sam Keen's excellent *Faces of the Enemy: Reflections of the Hostile Imagination* (Harper & Row, 1986), p. 62, a richly illustrated chronicle of international (wartime) propaganda and hatred.

What's the definition of a three-time loser?
— *A nigger with a small dick who can't play basketball.*

Why did Michael Jackson have two nose jobs?
— *Because the exotic animals in his private zoo smell pretty bad.*

What's black and blue and floats down the river?
— *A honky who tells "nigger" jokes.*

Fan to Stevie Wonder: "Stevie, I've always enjoyed your work. But it must be terrible being blind." - "Oh, it's not that bad. It could be worse... I could be black!"

Poles

What do you get when you cross an Iranian with a Polack?
— *A guy who takes himself hostage.*

What do Polish girls and hockey teams have in common?
— *They both shower after four periods.*

What did the Polack complain about at the police station when he saw a poster of a black guy WANTED FOR RAPE?
— *"They get all the good jobs!"*

Why don't Polacks hunt elephants?
— *Because the decoys are too heavy.*

What is this?

```
 IN ⇒        ⇐ OUT
REPEAT IF NECESSARY
```

— *A Polish Sex Manual.*

When the doctor asked for a urine and stool sample, what did the Polack give him?
— *His underwear.*

How can you tell when a Polack has been using your word processor?
— *There's White-Out on the screen.* [A liquid to cover mistakes on a typed page]

What did the Polack do who didn't like the movie in the drive-in?
— *He slashed his own car seat.*

Jewish-American Princesses

What do the Pope and a Jewish-American princess have in common?
— *They both spend millions on travel and fancy gowns and won't let you have sex.*

Why don't JAPs go to orgies?
— *Because they would have to write too many* THANK YOU *notes.*

What's the difference between a JAP bride and a WASP bride?
— *The WASP bride has fake jewelry and real orgasms.*

What do you get when you cross a JAP with an apple?
— *A computer that doesn't go down.*

What's the difference between a JAP and a toilet?
— *A toilet doesn't follow you around after you're done using it.*

Jews

What do rabbis do with the foreskins after circumcision?
— *They sell them to faggots for chewing gum.*

Why do Jewish husbands die so young?
— *Because they want to.*

What did the Jewish father answer when his son asked him for $50?
— *"Forty dollars? What do you need thirty dollars for?"*

Various Groups

Why did the stupid Siberian freeze to death outside the whorehouse?
— *Because he was waiting for the red light to change.*

Why did the Japanese call girl go broke?
— *Because no one had a yen for her.*

How do you make an Oriental go blind?
— *Put a windshield in front of him.*

How can you tell that Orientals have moved into the neighborhood?
— *When the Mexicans get car insurance.*

What did the Puerto Rican name his two penises?
— *Hose A and Hose B.* [José...]

Why don't Puerto Ricans have checking accounts?
— *Because it's too hard to sign your name with a spray can.*

What's redneck foreplay?
— *"Get in the truck, bitch!"*

What's Irish foreplay?
— *"Brace yourself, Bridget!"*

Why do Scots wear kilts?
— *Because sheep can hear a zipper a mile away.* [Also told about the Arabs' *flowing robes and camels.*]

What do Ethiopians use Venetian blinds for?
— *Bunkbeds.*

What do you get when you cross a Mormon and a Mexican?
— *A basement full of stolen canned goods.*

How many teamsters does it take to screw in a lightbulb?
— *Fifteen. You got a problem wid dat, buddy?*

How many New Yorkers does it take to screw in a lightbulb?
— *What the fuck is it to you?*

What is the difference between a bachelor party and a bulimics party?
— *At a bachelor party, the girl jumps out of the cake.*

How can a Kentucky man tell if his daughter has a yeast infection?
— *When his son's dick tastes like bread.*

What's the battle cry of the Dyslexics?
— *Dyslexics, Untie!*

What's the acronym for the new parents' group, "Mother's Against Dyslexia"?
— *D.A.M.*

What did the dyslexic atheist shout?
— *"There is no dog!"*

How does a WASP woman indicate she's ready for sex?
— *When she comes to bed wearing only rubber gloves.*

In the USA they say on TV: "It's 11 o'clock. Do you know where your children are?" What do they say in France?
— *"It's 11 o'clock. Do you know where your wife is?"*
What do they say in Poland?
— *"It's 11 o'clock. Do you know what time it is?"*

Yuppies and Stockbrokers

After the stock market crash in Oct. 1987, many jokes about Texans and farmers were recycled:

How do you get the attention of a Yuppie whiz-kid stockbroker?
— *"Hey, waiter!"*

What's the difference between a stockbroker and a pigeon?
— *A pigeon can still make a deposit on a new Mercedes.*

How do you get a stockbroker out of a tree?
— *Cut the rope.*

What are the chances of precipitation today?
— *30% rain, 70% stockbrokers.*

What do you call mutual oral sex by Yuppies?
— *sixtysomething.*

Other Professions

How can you tell if you're making love to an actress?
— *When she comes, she calls out her own name.*

What happens when you dial 911?
— *You make a cop come.*

Can you get pregnant from anal sex?
— *Sure. Where do you think all those lawyers come from?*

Why should lawyers be buried 12 feet deep?
— *Because deep down they're not bad.*

Why does the state of New Jersey have 10,000 hazardous waste dumps and the city of Washington 50,000 lawyers?
— *New Jersey was given first choice.*

What did the constipated mathematician do?
— *He worked it out with a pencil.*

Religion

What was Jimmy Swaggart doing in the motel room?
— *Waiting for the Second Coming.*

What's different about the "McSwaggart" hamburger?
— *You buy it and watch someone else eat it.*

What magazines will Jimmy Swaggart and Jim Bakker publish?
— *Repenthouse and* Prayboy.

What was Jim Bakker's last request before beginning his 45-year prison sentence?
— *To be strip-searched by Jessica Hahn while Jimmy Swaggart watches.*

What's the name of Tammy Faye Bakker's new makeup line?
— *Sherwin-Williams.* [Paint company]

For what did Tammy Bakker donate her eyelashes?
— *For minesweeping in the Persian Gulf.*

With what did God threaten Jerry Falwell if he didn't raise $10 million in two weeks?
— *Jerry would have to marry Tammy Bakker.*

What's the name of the pope's fax machine?
— *Fax Vobiscum.*

What did the rabbi trapped in a priest's body contemplate?
— *A sects change.*

What happened when Jesus went to Mount Olive?
— *Popeye beat the shit out of him.*

What did the Roman soldier say to Jesus?
— *"Okay, buddy, drop that cross one more time and you're out of the parade!"*

What did the Roman soldier tell Jesus as he was about to be crucified?
— *"Do you mind crossing your legs? We've got only one nail left."*

Animals

What do you call a deer with no eyes?
— *No idea.*

What do you call a deer with no eyes and no legs?
— *Still no idea.*

What do you call a deer with no legs and no dick?
— *Still no fucking idea.*

Why is the Siberian husky the fastest dog in the world?
— *Because the trees are so far apart.*

What did the elephant say to the naked man?
— *"That's cute. But does it pick up peanuts?"*

Have you heard about the Rambo Gerbil?
— *He goes in and comes out with two of his buddies.*

How do you circumcize a whale?
— *With four skin divers.*

Why do Canadian geese fly upside down over Wisconsin?
— *Because it ain't worth shitting on.*

What's the worst part about fucking a cow?
— *You have to walk so far to kiss her.*

What do you get when you put 50 pigs and 50 deers in a pen?
— *A hundred sows and bucks.*

What did the asp say to Cleopatra as it bit her?
— *"Fangs for the mammaries."*

How many animals can fit into one pair of pantyhose?
— *One ass, one pussy, two calves, ten little piggies, a batch of hares, a mess of crabs, and a dead fish you can't find.*

What do you get when you cross a redneck with a pit bull?
— *An all-white neighborhood.*

What do you get when you cross a donkey with an onion?
— *A piece of ass that puts tears in your eyes.*

What do you get when you cross a rooster and a telephone pole?
— *A 24-foot cock that wants to reach out and touch someone.*

What do you get when you cross a WASP with an orangutan?
— *I don't know, but he won't let you into his tree.*

What do you get when you cross a WASP with a gorilla?
— *An athletic scholarship to Harvard.*

What do you get when you cross a pit bull with Lassie?
— *A dog that rips your arm off, then runs for help.*

Why did the pervert cross the road?
— *Because his dick got stuck in the chicken.*

Miscellany

Why is *sixty-nine* now called *seventy*?
— *Because the price of eating out has gone up.*

What's the difference between *brown-nosing* and *ass-kissing*?
— *Depth perception.*

What's the cause of the population explosion?
— *Too many fucking people.*

Do you know why the logtruck stopped?
— *To let the lumberjack off.*

What's the difference between *pussy* and *parsley*?
— *Nobody eats parsley.*

What's the difference between *broccoli* and a *booger*?
— *A kid won't eat broccoli.*

What's a mustache?
— *A womb-broom.*

What's a grasshopper?
— *A fellow who can't afford to screw in a motel.*

What's better than to meet your woman in a park?
— *To park your meat in a woman.*

What's 69 + 69?
— *Dinner for four.*

What part of one's anatomy does cocaine make bigger?
— *One's asshole. It just gets bigger and bigger until you're a complete asshole.*

What are the dirtiest words ever spoken on a family TV show?
— "Ward, weren't you a little too hard on the Beaver tonight?"

If TGIF means "Thank God It's Friday," what does OSIM mean?
— Oh, Shit, It's Monday.

Why does the new restaurant print its bills on a condom?
— So you can stick your date with the tab.

What's the difference between a eunuch and an Eskimo?
— The eunuch is a massive vassal with a passive tassel; the Eskimo is a frigid midget with a rigid digit. [In MAL 9: 313, we had only the Eskimo definition]

What's a definition of *trouble*?
— To be stuck at a toll booth with a Pinto in front of you and an Audi 5000 behind you.

What's special about the new douche made with marijuana, talcum powder and chicken fat?
— It keeps you high, dry and is finger-lickin' good.

What do you get when a cement truck collides with a paddy wagon?
— Hardened criminals.

Who is the world's only surviving kamikaze pilot?
— Chicken Teriyaki.

Why did the guy marry Siamese twins?
— So he could have a girlfriend on the side.

What's the difference between an oral thermometer and an anal thermometer?
— The taste.

What's a four-letter word ending in -*k* that means "intercourse"?
— Talk.

How do you make Manischewitz wine?
— You just squeeze his balls.

How far is it from the Gaza Strip to Tel-Aviv?
— *About a stone's throw.*

In February 1988, the Israeli National Tourist Bureau cancelled an advertisement that had run in Dutch newspapers and TV program guides, emphasizing the short distances between Israeli cities and other tourist attractions. The ad (written in August 1987, before the Palestinian youths started to hurl rocks at the Israeli troops): "**The distance between Tel Aviv and Jerusalem? About a stone's throw.**" (The actual distance is 37 miles. Boston Globe, 18 Febr. 1988, sent by Phil M.)

B. FOREIGN

Achille Lauro and Leon Klinghoffer

On 8 Oct. 1985, during the hijacking of the cruise ship *Achille Lauro* by PLO terrorists, Leon Klinghoffer, 69, a wheelchair-bound Jew from New Jersey, was killed by the terrorists when he argued with them. The murderers shot him twice, then pushed him overboard in his wheelchair. Later, his body washed up on a shore.

How do you make the "Leon Klinghoffer" cocktail?
— *Two shots and a splash of water.*

What does PLO stand for?
— *Push Leon Overboard.*

What's the difference between Arab terrorists and Israeli terrorists?
— *Israeli terrorists would have kept the wheelchair.*

What do the fish in the Mediterranean call Leon Klinghoffer?
— *Meals on Wheels.*

Why didn't Leon Klinghoffer take a shower on the ship?
— *Because he wanted to wash up on shore.*

Why is Leon Klinghoffer so famous?
— *Because he's the only Jew to be found in a wake.*

Armenian Earthquake 1989

What do you call a pile of rubble with 500 Armenians in it?
— *A hotel.*

To which religion did the Armenians convert after the earthquake?
— *They are all Quakers now.*

What's the new unit of currency in Armenia?
— *The rubble.*

What is this? [Knock on ground]
— *An Armenian door-to-door salesman.*

What does an Armenian barman say at closing time?
— *"Have you no homes to go to?"* [The usual call at closing time in Ireland. All riddles from Feargal, Ireland]

Australia

In March 1986, a car bomb exploded outside the Russell Street Police Headquarters in Melbourne, Australia, injuring 22 policemen and civilians. A common shuttle joke was immediately adapted, as reported by Dr. M. S. of Footscray Institute of Technology in Victoria:

What colour were the policemen's hats?
— *Blue. Some blew **this** way, and some blew **that** way.*

How do you circumcise a Tasmanian?
— *Punch his sister in the jaw.* [Australians portray the Tasmanians as inbred, similar to Kentucky hillbillies in the USA]

Austria's Waldheim

What's the newest disease in Austria?
— *Waldheimer's Disease. You can't remember if you were a Nazi.*

Have you heard about the new disease called Waldheimer's Disease?
— *You get so old you forget you were a Nazi.*

Why were the majority of Austrians diagnosed as having Waldheim's Disease?
— *Because of their convenient selective amnesia concerning the years between 1938 and 1945.*

Canada

Ben Johnson

Jamaican-Canadian runner Ben Johnson was stripped of his gold medal after it was discovered that he had used steroids at the Seoul Olympics to improve his performance. This produced no jokes in the USA, but *Peter Ben-Wa, Ontario, sent me several circulating in Canada:

What do anabolic steroids and hurricans have in common?
— *They both make Jamaicans run fast.*

Did you know that Ben Johnson has AIDS?
— *Yes: Another Immigrant Does Steroids.*

How can you tell Ben Johnson's girlfriend?
— *Her lips look like starting blocks.*

Do you know why it's called the Canadian Track Team?
— *Because the runners have track marks up and down their bodies.*

What was faster than Ben Johnson at the Seoul Olympics?
— *Carl Lewis's accusations.*

Did you hear about the new Ben Johnson pantyhose?
— *It's guaranteed not to run for two years.*

Cartoonist Edwards (*The Whig Standard*, Ontario) published three identical illustrations of Ben Johnson with different captions: *Canadian Wins Gold Medal* • *Jamaican-Canadian Accused of Steroid Use* • *Jamaican Stripped of Gold Medal.*

Wayne Gretzky

Peter also sent a number of jokes circulating in Canada after ice hockey superstar Wayne Gretzky (No. 99 on his jersey) was traded by the Edmonton Oilers to the Los Angeles Kings. Canadians were very upset about losing Gretzky and his marriage to an American, Janet:

How cold will it be this winter in Edmonton?
— *Minus 99.*

What is Janet's favorite position?
— *99.*

Other Canadiana

What's the difference between Canada and the United States?
— *The U.S. has Ronald Reagan, Bob Hope, Johnny Cash, and Stevie Wonder. Canada has Brian Mulroney, no hope, no cash, no wonder.*

Susan I., Los Angeles, heard the same joke about Iran, with *Ayatollah* instead of *Brian Mulroney*. She also reports that in Iran "Polack" jokes are told about the inhabitants of Rasht, a town ridiculed for its ignorant and obtuse inhabitants.

How do you know that Brian Mulroney was a test-tube baby?
— *He wasn't worth a fuck back then either.*

Why should Toronto's new stadium be called the "Brian Mulroney Dome"?
— *Because its roof, like a Mulroney statement, is retractable.*

In May 1988, 155 illegal immigrants (mainly Tamils) were drifting for days in a lifeboat off the coast of Newfoundland, causing this joke, a wordplay on *Camel* cigarets:

What's the favorite cigaret of Newfoundland fishermen?
— *Tamils. They come in packs of 155, and even if you take them to sea for five days, they won't get wet.*

Why do Newfies keep ice cubes in their condoms?
— *To keep the swelling down.*

What did the Newfie waitress say when the Toronto businessman asked her if she had frogs' legs?
— *"No, sir. It's the high heels that make me walk this way."*

Why do Canadians like to fuck doggie-style?
— *So they can also watch "Hockey Night in Canada" at the same time.*

Why does a one-ounce letter cost 44 cents postage?
— *24 cents for delivery, and 20 cents for storage.* [Reference to slow mail delivery]

Egyptian Commandos

In December 1985, three Arab terrorists hijacked an Egyptian Boeing 737 to Malta. Egyptian commandos tried to free the hostages, but they bungled their operations, during which 58 of the 79 hostages were killed, over 40 alone from the fires ignited by the commandos (*Time*, 15 Sept. 1986: 35).

What's worse than being hijacked by Arab terrorists?
— *Being rescued by Egyptian Commandos.*

England

Hungerford Mass Murder

In Hungerford, England, 27-year-old Michael Ryan committed the worst mass murder in Britain in modern times. On 19 Aug. 1987, he shot and killed 16 people and wounded 14 more before shooting himself to death (*Time*, 31 Aug. 1987: 27). Even though this terrible event must have been more shocking to the British than the *Challenger* explosion, I did not receive any jokes from England. It does not surprise me that no jokes about this mass murder were told in the USA. We are used to mass murders here, almost a monthly occurrence. The sole riddle I received was from an Irishman:

Why should you go shopping in Hungerford in the morning?
— *Because in the afternoon it's murder.*

Pan Am Crash over Lockerbie

The airplane disaster of Pan Am 103 over Lockerbie, Scotland, on 21 Dec. 1988 produced three riddles:

What sale did they have in Lockerbie?
— *A half-price suitcase sale.*

What's the difference between a First-Class seat and a Tourist-Class seat on Pan Am?
— *About three miles.*

What song is number one in Lockerbie?
— *"Plane Drops Keep Falling on My Head."*

Midlands Airways Crash-landing

Soon after, on 8 Jan. 1989, a British Midlands airplane crash-landed on a motorway (expressway) near London:

What's the difference between British Midlands and Pan Am?
— *British Midlands bring you as far as the motorway, but Pan Am drop you at the house.*

Hillsborough Soccer Stampede

The stampede at the soccer match at Sheffield's Hillsborough Football stadium, 15 April 1989, where 95 people were squashed against a fence and trampled to death, produced a few riddles:

What do the Hillsborough disaster and a Skoda have in common?
— *They both go from 0 to 95 in six minutes.* [The *Skoda* is a Czech car with slow acceleration]

What was the bloke doing outside Hillsborough?
— *Waiting for his flat mate.*

What are the two most popular sports in Sheffield?
— *Fencing and Squash.*

Neil Crawford sent a clipping from *The Guardian* (17 Aug. 1989, p. 6) with a news story about the "Hillsborough Jokes" teacher: Alan Corkish, 43, a teacher in Liverpool, was dismissed for "telling his pupils sick jokes about the Hillsborough disaster." In his defense, Corkish said his first-year students "fabricated their claims in revenge after he admonished them for bad language and behaviour." Mr. Corkish is fighting his firing with the help of the NUT, his union.

British Ferry Sinking

On 6 March 1987, the British ferry *Herald of Free Enterprise* rolled over and sank shortly after leaving the Belgian port of Zeebrugge, killing 193 travelers. The bow doors, entrance for the autos loaded onto the ferry, were left open, and water rushed in, sinking the ferry quickly. This disaster received much more publicity than the "usual" drownings of hundreds in Asian and African waters (e.g., when in Aug. 1988 some 400 East Indians drowned after a ferry capsized in the monsoon-swollen Ganges river; or, the century's worst disaster at sea, when over 1,600 people drowned in the Philippines when the ferry *Doña Paz* sank in Dec. 1987—neither of which produced jokes), but to my knowledge, no jokes circulated in the USA. I received one French riddle from Marie, a Belgian lady in Paris, two from a Belgian in Bangladesh, and several from Feargal, an Irishman who was chased out of a Dublin bar for telling the following one:

What cocktails were they serving on the *Herald of Free Enterprise*?
— *Harbour-Wall-Banger.* [Reference to the drink called "Harvey Wallbanger"]

What do a condom and the *Herald* have in common?
— *They're both full of dead seamen.*

What is a RO-RO ferry?
— *A Roll On, Roll Over ferry.* [The actual meaning is "Roll on, roll off," referring to the ease of driving cars on and off the ferry]

What song were they playing in the *Herald*'s disco?
— *"Dancing on the Ceiling."*

What were the last words heard in the kitchen of the *Herald*?
— *"This fish is too fresh!"*

What were the last words heard on the *Herald*?
— *"Were you born in a barn?"* [Because the door was left open]

Why did the court decide not to indict any of the crew?
— *Because they were having an open door day.*

Why were the bows doors open?
— *Because a Jehovah's Witness had stuck his foot in them.*

Why did the Dutch passengers who were discovered in an air bubble refuse to leave?
— *Because they had paid for a round-trip ticket.*

How do you make a "Belgian" cocktail?
— *Take one car ferry and three quarts of water.* [The original French wordplays are: *un car* [also, *quart*] *ferry* [from *sherry*] *et trois quarts d'eau*]

Other Jokes Told in England

Here are some jokes circulating in England, sent by Tim H. in South Yorkshire. Note that our "Polacks" are usually replaced with Belgians, Norwegians, the Irish, and others.

How do you grow your own joke?
— *Plant a pom.* [Australian and New Zealand derogatory term for the English, short for *pommy*]

Why do Australian men keep their eyes closed when they make love?
— *Because they can't bear to see a woman having a good time.* [Same joke told about Jewish women (JAPS) in the USA]

Why are Aussie blokes such fast fuckers?
— *So they can get back to the pub and tell their mates all about it.*

Why don't Australian men eat quiche?
— *Because they can't pronounce it.*

How can you tell the bride at an Australian wedding?
— *She's the one with the new flip-flops.* [=rubber sandals, thongs. Similar jokes circulated years ago about other ethnic groups, e.g., the Polish bride wears a new bowling shirt, and the Frisian bride attracts all the flies.]

What happens when an Irishman emigrates to Australia?
— *It raises the average IQ in both countries.* [The same is told in the USA about a Texan moving to Oklahoma, etc.]

What's the difference between an Australian wedding and a funeral?
— *There's one less drunk at the funeral.* [Also told about the Irish]

What is Australian foreplay?
— *"You awake?"*
— *"Brace yourself, Marleen."*

How do you recognize a Belgian in a submarine?
— *He's the one wearing a parachute.*

Why are Norwegians not allowed to serve in submarines?
— *Because they like to sleep with the windows open.*

Why did the Irishman complain at the launderette?
— *Because he put £2 in the washing machine and <u>still</u> couldn't get a decent picture.*

How many Welshmen does it take to change a lightbulb?
— *Five million. One to get a government grant, and the rest to flatter him.*

Britain's Olympic swimmers were reprimanded for wearing T-shirts in Seoul with the imprint: Ar**seoul**ed. "It's an insult to Korea," complained an official. "I gather the word means getting drunk and it's not fair to use Seoul's good name this way." [From U.K. slang, *to be arseholed*, "very drunk." *Sun* (London), 26 Sept. 1988. Sent by Michael H., Hamburg]

Iran

A very clever joke with a triple wordplay from West Germany, sent by Ingrid B.:

> Khomeini and the Pope are strolling through Munich's red-light district. A whore invites them, "Komm eini! Komm eini!" (=Khomeini; also Pseudo-Bavarian "Come in!"). Khomeini sadly shakes his head, "Islam! Islam!" (=Islam; also *is' lahm*, "[my penis] is lame" [impotent]). But the Polish Pope smiles and shouts to the whore, "Vatikan! Vatikan!" (=Vatican; also *Vati kann*, "Daddy can [copulate].")

Libyan Bombing

After President Reagan had Libya bombed on 15 April 1986, the following jokes circulated:

Why doesn't Gadhafi go out drinking any more?
— *Because he can stay home and get bombed.*

Why was Gadhafi angry at his children?
— *Because they got bombed.*

What was the benefit of the Libyan raid by the US?
— *As Reagan's poll went up, Margaret Thatcher went down.*

Why has Gadhafi been so quiet lately?
— *Because Reagan threatened to send the Philadelphia police.*

[Reference to the MOVE disaster, where police trying to fire-bomb a black radical group's house burned down dozens of houses. See p. 253]

Why didn't the missing F-111 fighter plane return?
— Because the Puerto Rican pilot forgot his jumper cables.

What goes *plop-plop, fizz-fizz*?
— Libyan jets.

Did you hear about the Libyan whore?
— She likes to cream in her Gadhafi.

Mexican Earthquake

The devastating earthquake in Mexico on 19 Sept. 1985 killed some 7,000. This disaster produced one joke:

What's the new name of the Mexico City Hilton?
— The International House of Pancakes.

Poland

The following joke circulates in Poland. It could be told in any Communist country.

> Under what rules do the Poles live today? 1. Don't think. 2. If you think, don't speak. 3. If you speak, don't write. 4. If you write, don't sign. 5. If you sign, don't be surprised.

Rhine River Poisoning

The ecological disaster in November 1986 caused by letting at least 30 tons (French TV reports claimed 1,000 tons or more) of toxic chemicals wash into the Rhine, Europe's busiest river, resulted in more demonstrations than jokes. At least 500,000 fish were killed, and people living along the Rhine in Switzerland, France, Germany, and the Netherlands were without clean water for days. A chemical accident and an industrial fire in Basel, Switzerland, on 1 Nov. 1986, caused the catastrophic poisoning of the Rhine. This is the only joke I heard, combining the nuclear accident in Chernobyl with the French name for Basel, *Bâle* (*New York Times* and *Los Angeles Times*, reprinted in the MJ of 11 and 16 Nov. 1986):

What is the new name for Basel?
— *Chernobâle.*

South Africa

Radical South African blacks use the "necklace" to kill (moderate) fellow-blacks suspected of being police informers, collaborators, and sympathizers of the white régime. The "necklace" is an automobile tire, put around the neck and/or body and arms of the victim, doused with gasoline, then set afire. (NBC evening news, 26 Sept. 1986). Contrary to NBC's Tom Brockaw's statement, this method is indeed well known to the white South Africans who have circulated such jokes as the ones below. The "necklace" method was also reported in the *Montréal Gazette* of 5 July 1986: B1, sent by Merritt Clifton:

What is a combi [van] with six tires on top?
— *A circuit court.*

What is a "bicycle tire"?
— *A last warning.*

What is a "tractor tire"?
— *Family size.*

What does UDF stand for?
— *Uniroyal, Dunlop, Firestone.* [From United Democratic Front, an umbrella organization of anti-apartheid groups. *Newsweek*, 2 June 1986: 34]

Other Jokes Told in South Africa

Why do kaffirs have such big nostrils?
— *Because they change their mind too often.* [*Kaffirs* are the RSA equivalent of U.S. *niggers*]

What do a black's brain and anus have in common?
— *They both think of shit the whole time.*

How can you tell that an airplane is flying to Lesotho?
— *By its roof-carrier.* [In Africa and Asia, people often travel on the roof of busses, trains]

Why can't P.W. Botha scrap apartheid?
— *Because he's in a Catch Tutu situation.*

What did Botha say when he heard that Bishop Tutu was dead?
— *"I didn't even know he was arrested!"*

What's the definition of *speed*?
— *Fucking a girl through a fan.*

What do you call a lesbian?
— *A koeksister.* [A sugar-dumpling, cruller. From *koek* 'cake' + *suster* 'sister.' Also spelled *koeksuster*]

The Nov. 1987 crash of a South African Airlines plane near Mauritius, en route from Taiwan, produced some jokes:

Why were there no sharks in South African waters?
— *Because they all went for a Chinese takeaway.* [U.S. *takeout*]

What is South African Airlines [SAA] called these days?
— *Sub-Aquatic Airlines.*

What is SAA's new slogan?
— *"Come fly with us and do scuba diving for free."*

What new outfit did the SAA crews get?
— *Wet suits.*

Finally, Dr. Casper S. informed me that FREE MANDELA graffiti now are changed by pro-government vandals to FREEZE MANDELA.

After this volume had been typeset, Neil Crawford sent more riddles about several British disasters, to appear in the next volume. If *you* have any additions, please send them!

NOTES ON CONTRIBUTORS

REINHOLD AMAN, born in Bavaria in 1936, received his Ph.D. in Medieval Literature and Germanic Philology from the University of Texas in 1968. He taught at a University of Wisconsin campus from 1968 to 1974, then left that immoral cacademic dungheap in disgust and established Maledicta. Dr. Aman typesets, edits, publishes, and ships MAL to 71 countries. He has been featured on hundreds of radio and television shows here and abroad and has lectured on Verbal Aggression in the USA, Canada, Europe, and South America. He is listed in *Who's Who in America*. An intelligent journalist called him "The Noah Webster of Verbal Aggression," and his friends call him Rey, Uncle Mal, or Dr. Dildeaux. (More information earlier)

RICHARD O. BARTON, who sustained a degree in Political Science from the University of Michigan, works as a respiratory therapist in San Francisco. His book, *From Paper to Practice: Starting Pulmonary Rehabilitation/Homecare*, is scheduled for publication in December 1989.

MERRITT CLIFTON, an American in Québec, publishes *Samisdat*. He now lives in a former pig barn near the Vermont border, just down the hill from the sties of Canada's élite at Knowlton. (More info earlier)

AARON COHEN is a deadly earnest poet and writer who has, on occasions, been more earnest than deadly. Before he was consumed by AIDS, he danced to a variety of tunes. He was born on a Friday, the 13th, in 1936 in Brooklyn, fucked his way around Manhattan, and believes he'll die in Rochester, New York.

LOUIE CREW, 52, teaches writing at Rutgers University in Newark, New Jersey. Recently he taught for four years in Beijing and Hong Kong, and before that at the University of Wisconsin in Stevens Point. Publishers have issued more than 700 of his works, including "The Gay Academic" (*ETC*, 1978) and two poetry volumes, *Sunspots* (Lotus, 1976) and *Midnight Lessons* (Samisdat, 1987).

ALAN CROZIER, an Ulsterman from Trillick in Northern Ireland, took his doctorate in Germanic Philology from Cambridge University in 1980. He taught the History of English at the University of Iceland in 1979 and now lives in Lund, Sweden, where he works as a full-time translator and part-time researcher. Apart from taboo language, his publications concern philology, place-names, and dialect. A book about the English dialect of Southwest Ulster, *As The Man Says*, is to appear shortly. Dr. Crozier is married to Dr. Gunilla Byrman, whose equally profound interest in taboo language has led to a recent study of expressions for pregnancy in Swedish, *Graviditetsuttryck i svenskan* (Lund: Lund University Press, 1989).

RANDAL FORD graduated from the University of Denver's Creative Writing Program with a minor in Latin. He is currently finishing his M.A. degree in Theatre (emphasis in playwrighting) at the University of Colorado. He has published his own poems in several journals.

TABITHA KING has published four novels, the most recent of which is *Pearl*, published by New American Library in 1988 (paperback Nov. 1989). She is a native of Maine, where she lives with her husband Stephen and the one of three children still at home. Free speech prevails: everyone in the family uses the *f-word* whenever they feel like it, no one's been in jail lately, and they all still call on Mother's Day.

PETER KUNZKE, born in Nürnberg, Germany, in 1956, has worked as a lifeguard, paratrooper, technician, programmer, and research assistant. Currently he divides his time between Hughes Aircraft Co. and various libraries in Southern California.

MONICA MACAULAY received a Ph.D. in Linguistics from the University of California, Berkeley, in 1987, specializing in the syntax and morphology of Native American languages. While in graduate school, she did a weekly show on the alternative rock-and-reggae radio station KALX, 90.7 FM, Berkeley. She now teaches in the Department of English and in the Program in Linguistics at Purdue University.

SANFORD MARGALITH left Brooklyn at 15, when he grew too big for the bed he shared with two brothers in a bathless apartment behind a butcher shop. After serving in the U.S. Army and Navy, he finished four years of high school in 18 months, studied philosophy at New York University, and became an "archetypical beatnik." He now lives in Southern California, where he sometimes writes unpopular opinions for obscure publications and maintains that he has met only three people he really liked: Dylan Thomas, Joey Gallo and another guy.

GEORGE MONTEIRO holds dual appointments at Brown University as Professor of English and Professor of Portuguese and Brazilian Studies. He holds the A.B. and Ph.D. degrees from Brown University, and the M.A. from Columbia University. Within the past year he has published three books—*Robert Frost & the New England Renaissance* (criticism), *Self-Analysis and Thirty Other Poems by Fernando Pessoa* (translations), and *Double Weaver's Knot* (poems)—and has received the Order of Prince Henry the Navigator, a decoration awarded by the Portuguese government. (More information earlier)

FRANK H. NUESSEL, Ph.D., University of Illinois (1973), is Professor of Spanish and Director of the Program in Linguistics at the University of Louisville, Kentucky. (More information earlier)

DILWORTH B. PARKINSON received the Ph.D. degree in Arabic Linguistics from the University of Michigan in 1982. He has since taught

Arabic at Brigham Young University. He is also currently the Executive Director of the American Association of Teachers of Arabic, and is on leave in Cairo for one year to do research supported by the Fulbright Commission. His publications include *Constructing the Social Context of Communication: Terms of Address in Egyptian Arabic*, as well as several articles in the fields of Arabic sociolinguistics, Arabic language pedagogy, and Arabic computer-assisted instruction.

DENNIS R. PRESTON, Ph.D., University of Wisconsin, is Professor of Linguistics at Eastern Michigan State University in Ypsilanti. He is a sociolinguist, dialectologist, and ethnographer. His most recent books are *Sociolinguistics and Second Language Acquisition* (Blackwell, Oxford) and *Perceptual Dialectology* (Foris, Dordrecht). Dr. Preston currently is working on a book on the functions of malediction. (More info earlier)

*****BORIS SUKITCH RAZVRATNIKOV** is Professor of Russian and chairman of a Slavic Languages Department at a large American university. (More information earlier)

ALLEN WALKER READ, born in Minnesota in 1906, is Professor Emeritus of English at Columbia University, New York. In 1988 he was awarded the doctorate by Oxford University. Dr. Read's special interests are the development of American English, place-naming in America, graffiti, General Semantics, and lexicographical theory. His large collection of materials on Briticisms is now being edited for publication with the collaboration of Prof. John Algeo. His life and work was profiled in "At Play in the Language," *The New Yorker* 65/29 (Sept. 4, 1989), pp. 51-74. (More information earlier)

JOSEPH S. SALEMI holds a Ph.D. in Renaissance literature from New York University. He has published translations from Greek, Roman, and Provençal poets in journals throughout the country. His critical articles have appeared in *Chaucer Review, Allegorica, Blake Quarterly, Novel, Classical and Modern Literature, Victorian Newsletter,* and elsewhere. His most recent position was Assistant Professor of English at Fordham University in New York. (More information earlier)

JOE SALMONS received a Ph.D. in Germanic Linguistics from the University of Texas, Austin, in 1984. He now teaches in the Department of Foreign Languages and in the Program in Linguistics at Purdue University. In addition to writing on historical linguistics and sociolinguistics, he plays bass and guitar for Bored Records recording artists *Phrogs*.

SOL SAPORTA, Ph.D., University of Illinois, 1955, is Professor of Linguistics at the University of Washington in Seattle. His current interests include The Linguistic and Political Thought of Noam Chomsky. Dr. Saporta recently published "On Sports Illusions and Realities: Our Heroes as We See Them," in *Against the Current*.

RUDI SCHMID, Ph.D., University of Michigan, 1971, is Associate Professor of Integrative Biology at the University of California in Berkeley. Dr. Schmid does Victorian-type research on cloves, kiwis, and other higher plants and teaches plant anatomy and plant morphology for majors and non-majors. He relishes semantic and terminological fencing in botany and other areas.

*ROSETTA STONE was born and raised in rural Texas, from where she emigrated to study linguistics at Georgetown University. She graduated *summa cum laude* with an M.A.T. degree and is continuing her study at the doctoral level. Ms. Stone says she "sure as hell ain' goan be assimilatin' t' no gawd-damn bourgeois East-Coast sissy-ass culture."

JOSEPH TUNICK STRAUSS and his "Condom Couplets" collaborators are graduate students in materials engineering and powder metallurgy at Rensselaer Polytechnic Institute in Troy, New York.

MARC J. SWARTZ is Professor of Anthropology at the University of California in San Diego. His B.A. and M.A. are from Washington University in St. Louis (1952, 1953) and his Ph.D. is from Harvard (1958). He has done fieldwork with the Swahili in Mombasa since 1975 and has made eight visits totaling 30 months. Dr. Swartz has published a number of papers about them in anthropological journals. In the 1960s, he worked with the Bena in Tanzania and in the 1950s, with the people of Truk in Micronesia. His books include *Culture* (with David Jordan) and *Political Anthropology* (with V.W. Turner and A. Tuden). He has just completed *That's the Way the World Is, Sir: A Status-Centered Theory Applied to the Mombasa Swahili*.

*SUE TURE is a learnèd Surgical Head Nurse practicing in metropolitan Milwaukee, Wisconsin, hospitals. The sacred bond of confidentiality between author and editor prevents me from telling you *what* she is practicing.

ROBERT WIND, Ph.D. University of Iowa, is Professor of Classics at Muhlenberg College, Allentown, Pennsylvania.

VLADIMIR I. ŽELVYS, born in 1931 in Leningrad, is an Associate Professor of English Philology at the Pedagogical Institute in Yaroslavl, USSR. Dr. Želvys received his degree in Philological Sciences from the Thorez Ped. Inst. of Foreign Languages in Moscow. Among his publications are "Invektiva: opyt tematicheskoj i funktional'noj klassifikatsii," in *Etničeskije stereotipy povedenja*. Moscow: Nauka, 1985, pp. 296-322 ("Invective: An Attempt at Thematic and Functional Classifications"), and "Invective Strategy as a Specifically National Characteristics" (in Russian), in Y.A. Sorokin (ed.), *Etnopsikholinguistika*, Moscow, 1988. For the past 15 years, he has been studying the strategy and tactics of verbal abuse in some 50 languages in the Soviet Union and will from time to time share his findings with us.

• FINIS • DEO GRATIAS •